Family Treatment in Social Work Practice

Second Edition

Curtis Janzen and Oliver Harris

School of Social Work and Community Planning

University of Maryland at Baltimore

F. E. PEACOCK PUBLISHERS, INC.
ITASCA, ILLINOIS 60143

To our families . . .

from whom we have learned so much

Contents

Preface

The second edition of *Family Treatment in Social Work Practice* seeks the same objectives as the first: to address the needs of social workers in finding effective ways to deal with family problems encountered in practice. This effort continues to be generated by our perceptions of what is involved in treating families within the context of a social work agency and the need expressed by many students and practicing social workers for more direction in their work with families.

Much of the family treatment literature addresses families and family problems that are not frequently encountered in the day-to-day practice of social workers in agency settings. This book, therefore, extrapolates from existing theory and technique to provide an approach to treatment that more readily conforms to the specific constraints of social work agencies.

On the other hand, much of what is written about the kinds of families that social workers serve does not offer the family systems orientation that we seek to bring to our work with families. It is still possible to read much of the child abuse literature, for example, without gaining an understanding of the family as a whole. What one reads is about a victimized child and an abusing parent who is "the family" of the child. In many situations the problems of the family are seen as the result of personality deficits of the actors in the family system.

Families are often perceived as having a negative effect on the identified problem person, but helping professionals have less often been aware of the effects that families and identified problem persons produce in each other and their reactions to each other's reactions. Stilll less frequently are helping professionals aware of the mechanisms and rules which govern such transactions and of the effects of the presence and behavior of other family members on transactions within a dyad. Effective intervention may frequently have occurred without conscious knowledge of the family as an organized system. Systems knowledge however will aid the social worker both in understanding what has been done and in planning what is to be done in producing change in families.

In many situations agency constraints have a tremendous impact on the social worker's treatment activities. In some agencies contact with families is often of short duration, requiring immediate assessment of the problem and brief treatment to alter dysfunctions. Many times the tasks are specific, as in helping a family to make the shifts and realignments required by the loss of one of its members or to adapt to the return of a family member after a period of absence. The family struggling to regroup after separation and/or to form in remarriage, the family in which children are abused, the minority family, and the family of low socioeconomic background are typical of the practice encounters of the agency-based social worker. At issue in these situations is sufficient understanding by the social worker of the way family transactions relate to the problem in question and the impact intervention is likely to have on the family's pattern of operation.

Thus, our first objective is to introduce a family systems conceptualization which social workers can use in assessing family situations and in defining an overall approach to their work with the family. The emphasis on systems is more inclusive than on individuals as parts of a larger whole and on interaction more than on personality. Having given that base for assessment, our second objective is to outline a general approach to the family which follows from a family systems understanding.

Our third objective is to bring family systems understanding to work with specific kinds of families and family problems. In doing so, we have drawn heavily on existing literature and placed it within a family systems framework. We think that this offers a more complete understanding of these situations than has often been available and a better basis for defining the interventions needed. We have also made an effort to identify outcomes that have been achieved by understanding and working with the family as a whole.

This book is directed to undergraduate and graduate social work students who are beginning to study and familiarize themselves with theory and techniques relative to family functioning and family treatment. It is also directed to the practitioner who is beginning the transition from treating individuals to treating the family as a unit.

We would like to thank the many practitioners, students, client families, and colleagues who have reinforced our recognition of the need for this book and stimulated our thinking in many ways. We are grateful to all of them for helping us to become aware of some of the limitations of the first edition and hope that the insight and subject matter appearing here which was not in the first edition will be evident and helpful to all of our readers. We appreciate very much the supportiveness of the School of Social Work and Community Planning and of our dean, Dr. Ruth Young, in making the completion of this effort possible and timely. We are also very grateful to Virginia Peggs, whose patience and undying efforts in typing the manuscript will never be forgotten, and to the F. E. Peacock Publishers staff, who were extremely helpful to us in rewriting this book.

Curtis Janzen
Oliver Harris

Part I

Theoretical Framework

The purpose of Part I is to introduce the field of family treatment and some of the most widely accepted support for the study and treatment of the family. No single theoretical structure for treating families has yet been developed, and we draw on several approaches to family treatment. All these approaches, however, use systems concepts to understand how the family operates to achieve growth and resolve problems. It is in this context that this part of the book has been written. Each of the chapters contributes to building an understanding of family functioning and suggests ways to plan appropriate strategies for changing interactional patterns when families become dysfunctional.

The first chapter gives a brief overview of family treatment in social work practice and presents theory and concepts with emphasis on a systems view of family processes. This presentation is centered on the content of the communicative-interactive and structural approaches to work with families, though it also considers the work of individual clinicians who have contributed to the existing body of knowledge relative to family treatment. The family's struggle to maintain a balance in relationships and to cope with being close and being separate is discussed. Developmental cycles of the family and processes that contribute to growth and dysfunction are presented, in order to explore the interior of family transactions and provide in part a base upon which change strategies can be organized.

Chapter 2 continues the task of building a framework for the study and treatment of families by examining the impact of various problems on the organization and functioning of the family, making extensive use of crisis theory as a framework for understanding them as critical transitions in the life of the family. It also emphasizes the kinds of realignments and changes necessary to resolve problems when they occur. Meeting the material needs of the family, adapting to role changes, resolving conflict between family goals and individual goals, and communication and negotiation around changed circumstances are among the issues discussed in this chapter. The interrelatedness of a family's problems and its problem-solving efforts is demonstrated, with examples of the intimate relationship between the persistence of family problems and the effectiveness of problem-solving methods.

Chapter 3 completes our suggested framework for assessing family functioning and planning intervention. This chapter moves into the social worker's process of intervention with families. The ways in which the systems view of the family affects the beginning of treatment and engaging the family are delineated. The use of conjoint sessions with families, the task of actually engaging the family, procedures for beginning with the family, the social worker's role in treatment, and contracting with the family are among the topics discussed. A major emphasis is the worker's concurrent efforts in solving the problems presented by the family and changing the way in which the family goes about solving these problems.

Chapter 4, new in this edition, takes the reader beyond the beginnings of treatment by giving an extended overview of our general orientation and overall approach to treatment and its objectives. It focuses on here-and-now understanding, and on changes in feelings, thinking, and behavior. It draws attention to various dimensions of family functioning that may need to be changed, examining what may be wrong in each dimension and how it needs to be righted. Specific techniques are not described, but those proffered in the larger family treatment literature are clearly usable in the schema we describe.

CHAPTER 1

Introduction to Family Treatment

The idea of involving the entire family in resolving a problem expressed by one of its members is still relatively new when compared with other well-established modes of intervention. Prior to the advent of treating the family as a client system, most therapists, including social workers, approached problem solving from the viewpoint of changing the individual who by reason of his or her behavior was identified as the change target. It was believed that the cause of the maladaptive behavior was within the individual and it was necessary to deal with the psychic aspects of the personality if problem-solving efforts were to be effective. This was supported by psychoanalytic theory and the prevailing emphasis on individual treatment.

These beliefs were largely discontinued as therapists began to work with more than one member of the family. Social workers in public and private agencies were among those involved in this new movement which began in the early 1950s and was usually referred to in social work circles as *multiple-client interviewing*. At this time only limited knowledge was available regarding the process and outcome of this mode of problem solving; yet, many practitioners were engaged in exploring this dimension of practice. Interviews usually involved two members of the nuclear family,

3

most often the parents seen together. New information not previously fur-
nished by individuals when seen alone became available, and differences
in the way family members perceived the same problem situation were
revealed. This caused social workers and other professionals working with
more than one member of the family to seek better ways to understand these
observations, and they began to pay more attention to the way family
members were experiencing each other in their various encounters. This
signaled the beginning of a new way of thinking about problem configuration and the ways of intervening with those involved in family conflict. The
client was no longer identified as an individual with symptoms, but a family
with a problem.

FROM INDIVIDUAL TO FAMILY TREATMENT

The movement away from the traditional approach of treating an individual with a problem to treatment of the family as a unit has been a
gradual process. Though family treatment as a mode of practice was for-
mally introduced in the 1950s, some of the underlying ideas and observations that support this process appeared in social work literature as early as
the first quarter of the century. Mary Richmond addressed the components
of problem assessment in her book *Social Diagnosis* (1917), which in many
ways reflected the beginning of a family orientation in casework practice.
In discussing the caseworker's activity in diagnosing problem situations, she
noted the importance of knowing the main "drift" of the family's life as a
key to understanding what might be troubling the individual family member. In other words, she was emphasizing the importance of family history
in delivering casework services to individuals. Richmond also recognized
the importance of family unity and suggested that it would be useful to
learn of the difference between the power of cohesion in stable and unstable
families. She believed the caseworker should inquire about the family's
interest, its hopes and ambition, and the activities its members engaged in
together.

While Richmond stopped short of suggesting family interviews, she moved
closer to this a few years later. In commenting on the development of
casework, she suggested, "The next stage in development is to bring the
client and those to whom he is socially related together ... and then to
observe the relationship in being, instead of merely gathering a report of
it second hand" (Richmond, 1922, p. 138). This also hints at the importance

of family interaction which is accepted as the "center piece" of contemporary work with families.

It is fair to say that Richmond's perception of the caseworker's activity in providing services to clients is reflected in contemporary family treatment. Her vision of involving family members in change efforts takes on additional significance when we consider the fact that it occurred at a time when psychoanalytic theory and individual treatment formed the prevailing base of social work practice.

Further development of the observations set forth by Richmond and others continued over the years and culminated in a thrust toward working with families. This movement to family treatment was widely reflected in the literature through the writings of a number of social workers who viewed the interactions of family members as an appropriate area of attention. Scherz (1953) in writing about family-centered casework saw the individual as a part of the family constellation and suggested this individual "could not be adequately understood or helped in isolation from persons with whom he had close emotional ties" (p. 343). She also emphasized the value of seeing more than one family member when exploring family difficulties. By seeing more than one member, knowledge of family interaction and the role of each participant in this process could be obtained. The move toward treating the family was also supported by Siporin (1956), who recognized the importance of role theory and small group theory in the conceptualization of theory and practice relative to changing the behavior of the family group. He was among those who initially visualized the necessity of understanding family structure and viewing the family as a social system.

Gomberg (1958) pointed up the limitations implicit in relying solely on individual psychology for an understanding of human problems and stressed the need to include social factors and the family in order to encompass the larger whole. He cautioned that we should not choose between a concept of the family and a psychology of the individual, but should seek a balanced understanding of the interrelatedness between the two. Gomberg was aware of the growing importance of such phenomena as complementarity, role reciprocity, and the congruence of relationships in understanding the family. He further recognized the need to understand "the nature of family equilibrium, social roles, and role expectations characteristic between husband and wife, parent and child, siblings, and within the family group as a whole" (p. 75).

About the same time as Gomberg was reporting on the limitations of individual psychology as the single theoretical base for intervention, Sherman (1959) was writing about the growing trend of seeing two or more family members in an interview, which he defined as joint interviewing. This reflected a shift from viewing the distress of the individual as the problem to recognizing this distress as symptomatic of a family problem or as pathology in the whole family. Sherman also saw a connection between individual treatment and family treatment and suggested "sometimes the best treatment for the individual is treatment of his family" (p. 22).

Coyle (1962), like Siporin, advanced the idea of the applicability of small group theory in helping the family. She emphasized group structure and dynamics as relevant to family organization and the distribution of power and authority. Coyle also likened the emergence of subgroups within the group process to subsystems in the family, each with specific roles and responsibilities for achieving the goals of their respective organizations.

Pollak and Brieland (1961), reporting on the Midwest Seminars on Family Diagnosis and Treatment, recognized the importance of understanding breakdown in interpersonal relationships within the family. They found relationships became more complicated as family size increased and additional subsystems came into being. The interrelatedness of the subsystems was such that deterioration in one was likely to cause deterioration in others. Focusing on the whole family was strongly supported, including concern for the developmental stage of the problem family and viewing the family group in its natural habitat through home visits and partaking of a meal or other hospitality in the home as a way of better understanding family interactions. This was quite a departure from the traditional hour with an individual in the caseworker's office.

Scherz (1962), continuing the move from individual to family treatment, stressed the necessity of focusing on the whole family in order to gain sufficient understanding to diagnose and treat the problems expressed by individual family members. She recognized that this way of dealing with family interactional processes introduced more complications and placed more demands on the caseworker than would be experienced in working with an individual client. In spite of her acceptance of the contributions of multiple-client interviewing, she did not see this as something to be used exclusively, suggesting that both multiple-client and individual interviews should be used in some cases. She wrote, for example, "The emergence of strong dependency needs that cannot be sufficiently gratified in a group treatment process is an indication that individual treatment should supplement family group treatment" (p. 123).

Klein (1963), writing about the systemic aspects of the family, recognized the difference in treating the family as a system instead of treating the individual. He viewed the family group as a medium through which individual change is realized. In other words, he proposed that a change in family interactional patterns would produce change in the way the individual interacted with others within and outside of the family.

The late 1950s and early 1960s can therefore be seen as bringing a shift in emphasis from individual to family functioning and a shift from individual treatment to family group methods of treatment. We fully agree with Sherman that this is not just a shift in intensity but represents a basic shift in the way problems of individual and family functioning are conceptualized. While the field at the time was clearly trying to find a new way and many of the concepts were in early stages of definition, it is clear that core concepts were identified. These concepts have been developed over the last couple of decades and are currently in use, both by social workers and other family therapists.

To summarize the current status of family treatment, the social worker working with families cannot be solely concerned about what one person is doing, but must think in terms of two or more people interacting and influencing each other. For example, if a child is experiencing problems at school or is involved in negative peer group behavior outside the home, the problem should not be viewed solely as the child's. It must be remembered that the child is a member of a family system that includes others, such as parents and siblings, and experiences a relationship which is influenced by the behavior of those with whom he or she is interacting. Therefore, it becomes necessary to acquire a different perspective of problem formation and problem solution when treating the family as a unit than when working with an individual.

It might be helpful to remind social workers making the transition from work with individual clients to work with families that breaking old patterns of behavior is not always easy. It is not uncommon for the new family therapist to approach the task by interviewing individuals in the presence of other family members. This is to say that the social worker may carry on a dialogue with one family member at a time, which can result in an overemphasis on changing individual behavior rather than focusing on changing the way family members relate to each other. In this case the family's participation as a unit is limited, and the opportunity to assess family interactional patterns will be impaired. This is not to suggest that attention should never be focused on the individual in family treatment. It may indeed be necessary at times to focus on an individual in certain situations, such as when the family should listen to a member who is seldom heard or to give support to a family member who needs help in gaining or maintaining a sense of individuation.

To illustrate the change in therapeutic considerations between the traditional one-to-one approach and the family treatment perspective, consider an adolescent client who is truant and has difficulty in school. In the traditional approach, therapeutic efforts would likely focus on the client's fears, feelings of inadequacy, and so on. The objective would be to help the client develop insight into the cause of the problem, which would pave the way for a change in behavior. The involvement of parents and siblings would most likely be peripheral. The parents might be asked to provide some information about the problem; contacts with them would likely be separate from those with the child, and neither they nor other children would be given more than minimum responsibility for the problem.

Conceptualization of the problem is quite different in the family treatment method. The family member whose behavior is in question is thought of as the symptom bearer of a family problem. Among the objectives of the social worker is the shifting of attention from the symptom bearer to the family and involving other members in working toward necessary changes. Seeing family members together is useful because it provides an opportunity to observe various family patterns as members interact around the problem, and this reveals a more complete picture of the problem. The therapist who sees only one family member gets only that person's view of the problem, which represents the way it is experienced from the unique position held in the family by that individual.

Take the case of a child in treatment who reveals a reluctance to play with other children in the neighborhood. The mother responds to the child's remarks by saying she realizes this isn't good, but the playgrounds are unsafe and she is fearful that the child might get hurt if allowed outside to play. The mother's comment gives the social worker and the child a different idea about the problem. The child experiences a conflicting message with regard to the inappropriateness of staying in the house and the danger of going outside to play. And the worker now has a notion about the mother's role in the child's behavior. If they had not been seen together, the manner in which the mother impacts on the child's behavior might never have been connected in this way.

To understand the way people interact and perform as members of a family, it is necessary to be aware of conceptualizations about the family as a functioning unit. For example, some notion of family structure and the processes in which the family engages as it maintains its existence is necessary. In the remainder of this chapter we will present some of the essential concepts used in family treatment. These concepts are drawn largely from the structural and the communicative-interactive approaches to the treatment of families, but contributions from clinicians and theoreticians who do not necessarily adhere to these approaches will also be included. The presentation of these concepts will lay the groundwork for a theoretical framework for understanding the dynamics of the family as a complex interactive system and this will be developed further in Chapter 2.

THE STRUCTURAL APPROACH

The theory of structural family treatment as set forth by Salvador Minuchin (1974) emphasizes family structure, subsystems, and boundaries. Minuchin defines family structure as "The invisible set of functional demands that organizes the ways in which family members interact. Repeated transactions establish patterns of how, when, and to whom to relate and these patterns underpin the system" (p. 51). For example, a mother tells her child to stop playing and go to bed. The child refuses; the father is infuriated at the child's disobedience and yells at him after which he complies with the mother's wish and goes to bed. Repetition of this way of dealing with the child establishes a transactional pattern and creates a structure in which the mother is an incompetent disciplinarian and the father is competent.

Another aspect of family structure is the rules which govern family organization and transactions within the family. Such rules are often recognized in the way various family members protect each other. If the parents cannot handle intimacy and closeness in their relationship, the child behaves in such a way as to demand their attention and thereby prevent the necessity of the parents having to relate to each other on an intimate level.

Nichols (1984) suggests that family structure is also shaped by universal and idiosyncratic constraints. This involves a power hierarchy in which parents and children have different levels of authority. A complementarity of functions is also necessary with both husband and wife accepting an interdependency of functioning and supporting each other as a team.

The second component of structural family theory is *family subsystems.* Subsystems are created by family members joining together to carry out various functions. Coming together in this way may be centered around age (generation), gender function, or common interest. Among the natural groupings that form subsystems are husband and wife, siblings, parent and child. There are many roles to be filled in the family, and each member may play several roles in a number of subgroups. The husband may be at different times a father, son, or nephew, while the wife may be a mother, daughter, or niece depending on time, place, and circumstances.

The third component is *boundaries.* Boundaries are "invisible barriers which surround individuals and subsystems, regulating the amount of contact with others" (Nichols, 1984, p. 474). The function of boundaries is to safeguard the differentiation and autonomy of the family and its subsystems. For example, if a mother restricts her child's play to the immediate neighborhood and this is accepted, a boundary is established which protects the child from wandering far from home and perhaps becoming lost. On the other hand, if a wife always turns to her mother to settle disputes with her husband and the mother responds, the boundary around the husband and wife has been invaded and is no longer sufficiently established to protect the autonomy of the spouse subsystem.

Among the basic underpinnings of the structural approach to family treatment is the belief that the family is a system that functions through the support of subsystems. The major subsystems that develop over time within the nuclear family structure are the *spouse subsystem,* the *parental subsystem,* the *sibling subsystem,* and the *parent-child subsystem.*

Spouse Subsystem

The spouse subsystem is the first to emerge and comes into being with the joining of two adults of the opposite sex with the expressed purpose of forming a family (Minuchin, 1974). Complementarity and accommodation are the primary components of a successful spouse subsystem. This means that each spouse should develop patterns of behavior that lends support to effective functioning of the other. In carrying this out, a kind of joining and cooperating takes place. Yet the ability to be and act separately is also essential to effective functioning of the spouse subsystem. Therefore, the spouses must seek a balance between being close and supportive, and maintaining the individuality necessary for independent action.

Thus, the spouse subsystem, like all subsystems, is characterized by a boundary within a boundary structure. The inner boundary maintains the individuality of the participants, while the outer boundary defines the subsystem and protects it from the intrusion of outside forces. The outer boundary which surrounds the spouse subsystem differentiates it from other family systems and provides a turf over which these two participants are the rulers. When the boundary is appropriately in place, the spouse subsystem is clearly separated from the participants' families of origin, and it controls extended family interference. At the same time, the individual boundaries provide each spouse a turf over which he or she can rule within the subsystem boundary, as exemplified by the ability of each to act without complete support and validation of the other. A spouse with an individual boundary can identify a self and take responsibility for individual action.

When children are born into the family, the spouse subsystem boundary also protects against the children's intrusion into the husband and wife domain. This does not mean the spouse subsystem is isolated from other systems. However, it symbolizes the right of the spouse subsystem to engage in its own internal processes without interference from outside its boundary.

In spite of the boundary's objective of safeguarding the integrity of the system, boundary violations do occur. Take the case of a newly married couple who moves in with in-laws. The in-laws may insist on maintaining a parent-child relationship by invading the psychosocial space of the newlyweds, which is a serious threat to the boundary around this subsystem. If the newlyweds accept the in-laws' wishes to direct their lives, these two subsystems become diffuse, and the identity of two separate systems does not exist. And in the case of such encroachment, it is not uncommon to find a coalition existing between two principals who are of different generations. For example, the wife and her mother may enter into a coalition against the husband of the newly married couple. This is a generational boundary violation which reflects the lack of a clear boundary between the wife and her mother. It also contributes to dysfunctioning in both systems. While the mother is involved with the daughter against the daughter's husband, she is also likely to be neglecting the relationship with her own husband.

The Parental Subsystem

Until the arrival of the first child the marital pair is viewed as a spouse subsystem, with the members reflecting primary concern for their roles as husband and wife. When the first child is born, three new subsystems come into being which must be recognized in considering family functioning. The new family units are the parental subsystem, composed of mother and father; the sibling subsystem, which at this time is the only child; and the parent-child subsystem, which comes into existence as a functional unit when the mother and father individually or collectively interact with the child.

The parental subsystem is largely child-focused and has executive responsibility for the entire family system. This responsibility is rooted in the hierarchical position accorded the parents, who provide the leadership and authority necessary for family growth and development. If parents do not demonstrate leadership and authority, the family system, including wholesome development of their children, is placed at risk. Parents who do not direct and lead children leave them on their own to find appropriate role models and authority figures by trial and error, which can be devastating for a child. A problem is also presented in cases where one part of the hierarchical system, for example, the father, is absent. This creates a void into which a child may be elevated for a number of reasons. For example, a lonely and distraught mother may turn to a child to replace the affections of the absent husband and thereby create a closeness in their relationship that denies the child the opportunity to develop autonomy and ties the mother so closely to the child that she views the two as one. This can result in a symbiotic relationship which does not allow either participant to function without the other and seriously impairs the adjustment of mother and child.

In order to perform effectively as a parental subsystem, parents must be flexible and maintain a delicate balance between exercising control over their children and promoting their independence. Unlike the spouse subsystem, which is protected from the intrusion of children, the parental subsystem operates differently where children are concerned. The boundary of the parental subsystem permits free movement of children back and forth across the perimeters of the system. This new role of parent carries with it responsibility for the rearing of children. One of the first things parents must do is give up some of what they previously shared exclusively when occupying only the role of spouse.

In systems theory, a change in one part of the system requires change in other parts. With the birth of the first child, parents experience a demand for change in the family system; the addition of a third member automatically sets the change process in motion. The birth of the child has its first impact on the relationship between husband and wife. The previous balance they enjoyed in their relationship is disrupted, as a new boundary must be established around themselves and the child. The inclusion of the child means each parent must make room for an additional relationship. Because the child must be nurtured, the parents must restructure their own need-meeting activities to allow for meeting the physical and emotional needs of the child.

Sometimes changing to include a child is difficult for new parents. Before the birth of the child they are primarily concerned with their own and each other's needs and expectations, in an intimate and personal relationship. When they become parents, there is likely to be less time for enjoying each other. Leisure time may have to be spent differently, or recreational activities may be sharply curtailed in the interest of child care. If parents are unable to make these adjustments by redefining the manner in which they interact within their own life space, in such a way as to include the nurturing of the child, functioning as a family is likely to be problematic.

These role adjustments must be repeated with each additional child, and the older children also become involved in the sharing and need-meeting process as it relates to each new member. For example, the birth of the new baby who joins an existing sibling subsystem affects the next oldest child, who must give up the role of "baby" in the family and relinquish some of the closeness previously shared with the mother. The mother must extend her nurturing role to include the new member, and by so doing, she alters her relationship with the other children. Physical accommodations must also be made for the new baby which may affect the other children's play activities, sleeping arrangements, and so on. Sometimes these changes will impact negatively on the older children, who may react with such behavior as withdrawing, thumb sucking, or bed-wetting. Such behavior is usually temporary if parents are able to demonstrate caring for the older children.

The role of parents can become more difficult as the children grow and seek increased individuality. This places great demand on the control and permission functions of the parental subsystem. Maintaining a balance between these functions in a manner that supports autonomy, while exercising the necessary control at appropriate points in the developmental process, can be a difficult task for parents. The difficulty is enhanced by our changing society in which values are continuously tested and disagreements are evidenced in many areas

We believe conflict is inherent in the parenting role, and this should be kept in mind when working with families, especially around problems involving adolescents. Minuchin (1974) suggests, "Parents cannot protect and guide without at the same time controlling and restricting. Children cannot grow and become individuated without rejecting and attacking" (p. 58). This presents a difficult problem for parents and children and a challenging situation for social workers intervening with families unable to cope with these interlocking conflicts.

The Sibling Subsystem

In order to grow and develop individuality children need their own turf where experimentation and learning can take place without interference from adults. This makes the sibling subsystem a very important part of the family organization. It is in this subgroup that children learn how to relate to each other, including how to share, disagree, make friends, bargain, and protect themselves from the down position of a complementary relationship.

This experience serves as a shield of protection for the child in encounters with other systems. The first use of this experience may be seen as the child interacts with the parents and learns to adjust to a relationship of unequal power. Although the young child does not master the skill of negotiation and compromise from the sibling subgroup experience, alternative behaviors in personal encounters are likely to be learned and will be further tested with elders in the future. In this way the child establishes and broadens patterns of relating.

This is not to imply that the child learns only within the confines of the sibling subsystem experience. Much is also learned from interacting with parents and later with extrafamilial systems. However, experiences in this subsystem remain among the most important for the child, as they provide one of the earliest opportunities to test behavior and to learn from trial and error. And this type of learning is essential for the child's growth and development.

Like other subsystems, the sibling subsystem has a boundary which protects the system from intrusion by adults. Nevertheless, the boundary is permeable. This allows parents to move back and forth across it but gives children the right to privacy without parental interference when the need arises. For example, children need the opportunity to have their own special interests, try out their own thinking in specific areas, and offer their own kind of support to each other in times of stress, without direct guidance from parents. Some adjustment becomes necessary in this system as a result of the growth and development of children. With this growth and age differential come different interests, privileges, and responsibilities. At this point the subsystem is usually divided into two groups, along the lines of teenagers and subteenagers. Such a division ensures more effective functioning of the system, while at the same time it protects the integrity of the system as it relates to the life cycle of participants.

If a permeable boundary exists around the family, children should be able to interact freely with extrafamilial systems involving age-appropriate activities. The children will make inputs from these experiences into the family system, and if the substance of these inputs seriously threatens the way the family wishes to operate, the boundary around the family may become inappropriately rigid. For example, consider the teenage daughter who shares with her parents the desire to spend a weekend camping with her boyfriend, as others among her peer group are doing. The parents are very much opposed to such association between boys and girls and disapprove not only the weekend camping but also the daughter's association with the peer group. This reflects increasing rigidity in the family boundary and may well interfere with the daughter's separation from the family.

The Parent-Child Subsystem

In the parent-child subsystem, parent(s) and child or parent(s) and children interact as a functional unit within a boundary. It is different from the three subsystems previously discussed in that at least one of the persons composing it is of a different generation. While a subsystem composed of different generations can become dysfunctional, this is not an automatic outcome. For example, mothers and young children are usually closely involved in an interactional process which forms a subsystem of two different generations, but as long as the boundary around this system is not inappropriately rigid and permits crossing by other family members, it is not likely to become pathological. If, on the other hand, mother and child should become aligned in such a way as to exclude the father from entering the system, it would then be dysfunctional.

Minuchin (1974) suggests that the clarity of boundaries surrounding a subsystem is more important than who makes up the system. Take the case of a single-parent family; the mother is employed and depends on the oldest child to help with the care of younger children. This places them in a boundary together with shared responsibility. However, this boundary will remain functional as long as the limits of authority and responsibility placed with the child are clearly defined and the hierarchy is maintained. In other words, if the mother tells the child that overseeing the behavior of younger children is to be done only in the mother's absence, and when at home she will be in charge of the family, the system can function smoothly.

Difficulty will develop when the lines of authority are not clear and the child becomes locked in a rigid boundary with the mother. In this case the individual boundaries around mother and child become diffused, and the child's authority will not be limited by the mother's presence. The child then becomes a "parental-child" and may act indiscriminately as an extension of the mother where the younger children are concerned. This denies the other children free access to the mother and may result in problem behavior for these children.

SEPARATENESS AND CONNECTEDNESS

The importance of the family members to act both in concert with others and individually is implied by a number of authors who have discussed family functioning. Among the various approaches to family treatment, Minuchin (1974), with the structural aproach; Kempler (1973), with the Gestalt approach; and Satir (1967), with the communicative-interactive approach, to name a few, all emphasize the significance of separateness and connectedness in family relationships. Others, including Hess and Handel (1967), Friedman (1971), Bowen (1966), and Boszormenyi-Nagy and Sparks (1973), have also contributed significantly to the understanding of this process. Our view as presented here takes into consideration some of the conceptualizations of these authors.

Human relationships are characterized by a process of being together and being apart from one another. Two strong emotional forces are at work in this process: the need for emotional closeness, which brings people together; and the desire for the individuality and autonomy, which moves the individual away from the control of others.

The family is characterized by a connectedness between members and also a separateness of members from one another. Hess and Handel (1967) recognize this duality in their reference to the situation of the newborn infant. Although coming from the parents, the infant is physically a separate individual and must remain so. Returning to the womb is impossible, and the child's psychobiological individuality will exist despite experience with the socialization process. Hess and Handel likewise see the parents as maintaining their psychobiological individuality regardless of their emotional closeness. This type of separateness is always present.

The infant also exemplifies connectedness among family members. The newborn must depend on parents for nurturance in order to survive and therefore cannot sever this connection. And if the parents are to fulfill the infant's needs, they must come together and accommodate each other in the parenting role.

The other side of being separate and connected involves emotional issues. Friedman (1971, p. 171) sees fusion and differentiation behavior among family members as essential elements in their coming together and being able to separate. He defines fusion behavior as an adaptation of speech and actions designed to establish a system of feeling and responses that is in keeping with the family's preferred pattern of behavior. He sees differentiation behavior as the opposite of fusion behavior, in that the individual develops speech and actions that will disengage his own feelings and responses from a pattern of automatic compliance with what is preferred by others. This means that the individual seeks freedom from control by others, freedom to be different from others, and freedom to be apart from others.

Maintaining connectedness to others creates a sense of belonging, which satisfies the basic human need for closeness and identification. Yet, we must keep in mind that excessive closeness minimizes the opportunity for separateness; in that case enmeshment and loss of identity result. Separateness has a similar quality in that it contributes to individuality and autonomy, but when carried to the extreme, it can produce loneliness and isolation. Therefore, a balance must be sought which will allow family members to come together to share and support but also separate and follow individual pathways to fulfillment and satisfaction.

The ways in which family members want to be together and the ways they want to be apart is reflected in the family's patterns of behavior. Some families develop around an excessive need for emotional closeness, while other families place great emphasis on separateness as shown in autonomy of behavior. If the need for closeness is too great, fusion within family relationships is likely to result. And when fusion is attained, family members will not be able to express themselves in a manner other than what is preferred by the family. If the drive for individuality and self-determination exceeds all other interests, the ability of family members to be close and supportive in relationships with one another is lessened. Extremes in either case contribute to family dysfunction.

The pattern of relating within a family is not the result of an accidental process. It is influenced by the patterns established in the parents' families of origin. If the parents were never given permission to separate from their own families of origin, they will experience difficulty in establishing separate ego boundaries between themselves. The new parents will then transmit this need for togetherness to their children, who will also have difficulty separating from them. The implicit obligation in this type of family is to remain devoted to the families of origin. Individuation is not encouraged among family members, and the avenues through which this might take place are frequently blocked.

This blocking behavior is often subtle. It can be seen in the family that permits members to transcend its boundaries but systematically rejects all feedback from such encounters. A typical example is the adolescent who is allowed to interact with systems outside the family but is denied the opportunity to use this experience for personal growth. Families accomplish this denial in various ways. Sometimes they discourage differentiation indirectly by disqualifying the child's attempts at new behavior or expressing fear that great danger is associated with his or her wish to be different at such a tender age. In this way the avenue to differentiation is blocked, and the family goal of maintaining the devotion of its members is supported.

The experience of separateness in relationship is not entirely a physical phenomenon. Boszormenyi-Nagy and Sparks (1973) suggest that actual physical separation is not necessary for one to attain the individuation implied in being separate from the other. Instead, the ability to be separate is realized through the formation of a psychic boundary. With this boundary established, one is not always a product of and dependent upon the family but becomes a separate entity by reason of psychic emancipation. This type of boundary formation is reflected in the work of Laqueur, Labrut, and Morong (1971), who report that as the child develops, primary objects of attachment are gradually replaced. This occurs when the child learns to transfer energies from these primary objects to a widening circle of outside figures, interests, and tasks. As this is accepted by other family members and they assist the child in this growth process, a psychic boundary is formed which facilitates the achievement of a sense of belonging and a sense of being separate.

We believe that one of the most important developments within the family as it passes through its life cycle is the determination of what it will do about closeness and separation in the family relations. Most families are able to establish a workable balance in how its members will come together and support each other and how they will be different and able to be apart from each other. The extent to which this balance is achieved is crucial, and social workers may often find this a necessary target area for their change efforts.

THE COMMUNICATIVE-INTERACTIVE APPROACH

The communicative-interactive approach to the study and treatment of the family developed largely from the work of the Palo Alto Medical Research Foundation Project. The focus of this project was on treating families of schizophrenic patients. Among those who were connected with it and contributed to the basic concepts of the communicative-interactive approach were Gregory Bateson, Jay Haley, Don Jackson, and Virginia Satir. It is accepted in this approach to family treatment that all behavior has communication value and conveys several messages on different levels. The family is seen as a living system that maintains a relationship with the environment through communication which involves the sending and receiving of messages and a feedback process. As a result, family relationships are products of communication. Family members establish rules that regulate the ways they relate to each other and to the outside world. Once these rules are established, the family seeks to maintain the status quo. In other words, the family is viewed as a rule-governed, complex, interactive system, with communication patterns playing a primary role in family functioning.

Satir (1967) refers to communication as all verbal and nonverbal behavior within a social context. This is supported by Watzlawick, Beavin, and Jackson (1967), who maintain that all behavior is communication. This speaks to the complexity of the process of communication. We can readily imagine a simultaneous sending and receiving of messages by gesture, manner of dress, tone of voice, facial expression, body posture, and so on.

In order to understand dysfunction in the family, the communication process operating within family relationships must also be understood. It is important to realize that the way a family communicates, member to member and member to the outside world, reflects the way the family perceives itself and how it will function. The way members of a family communicate with each other shapes the view they have of themselves and the others. This in turn influences the way members report themselves to others, including those outside the family. For example, if the family perceives a member's behavior as good and in keeping with the way it views itself and it repeatedly communicates satisfaction with this behavior, the response will impact on the individual. This member's perception of self will likely be one of value, and this perception will be manifested in transactions with others. If, however, family feedback to a member is constantly negative, the reverse will most likely happen.

If the family decides it is best to rely on its own internal processes for validation of its functioning and it intensifies interaction between members, the freedom to communicate across family boundaries will be restricted. This encourages more communication within the family and more dependence upon one another. If the family is successful in establishing this pattern of behavior, communications from family members will reflect a sameness, and family functioning will likely be characterized by enmeshment.

We support the suggestion of Satir, Watzlawick, and others who believe all behavior in an interactional situation has communication value. This means we believe that the existence of one person in the presence of another sets the stage for communication and, at the same time, assures that the process will take place. This obviously makes possible the act of verbal exchange, which is the most widely understood form of communication. However, both persons may choose to remain silent, and communication will still take place. Messages are conveyed by silence and inactivity as well as by language and activity. The silence of a person who refrains from talking in the presence of another conveys a message to the other, who in turn responds to this silence. Communication has taken place. For example, if the message sent by silence is interpreted as a desire not to engage with the receiver, who respects the wish by also remaining silent, the communication cycle has been completed. The message has been sent, received, and interpreted, and the receiver has responded by the conscious decision to remain silent. And if these two people remain in an interactional situation, despite their silence, they will continue the communication process, with each being aware of the other and through body language, if nothing more, conveying messages one to the other. In other words, as implied by Watzlawick et al. (1967), one cannot refrain from communicating when in the presence of another.

The content and relationship of messages as presented by Bateson (1958), Jackson (1959), Watzlawick and Beavin (1977), and Sluzki and Beavin (1977) provide additional material for social workers in understanding human communication. These authors suggest that every communication carries many levels of information. One of these levels is concerned with the relationship in which the communication occurs; people in communication with each other are constantly attempting to define their positions in this relationship.

Jackson (1959) describes two types of relationships, and the positions of the participants in these relationships, complementary and symmetrical. In the complementary relationship the communication involves two people of unequal status, while the symmetrical relationship brings together two people of equal status. The behavior of each participant identifies his or her status in the relationship. For example:

> In a complementary relationship—the two people are of unequal status in the sense that one appears to be in a superior position, meaning he initiates action and the other appears to follow that action. Thus, two individuals fit together or complement each other.... The most obvious and basic complementary relationship would be a mother and infant. A symmetrical relationship is one between two people who behave as if they have equal status. Each person exhibits the right to initiate action, criticize the other, offer advice, and so on.... The most obvious symmetrical relationship is a pre-adolescent peer relationship. (Jackson, 1959, pp. 126-27)

Double-Binding Communications

Bateson, Jackson, Haley, and Weakland (1956) have suggested the existence of a paradox in human communication which is represented by the double-bind phenomenon observed in the families of schizophrenic patients. The exchange of communication in these families was characterized by the sending of incongruent messages, usually within the boundary of a complementary relationship between mother and son. The incongruency of the double message is reflected in its request that the receiver obey and disobey the message simultaneously. This, of course, cannot be done, and if this type of communication is repeatedly used paradoxical behavior results.

To further illustrate double-binding communication, take the case of an adolescent who wishes to spend the night with a friend. As he and his mother talk this over, she remarks after much discussion, "You know I want you to go and be with your friend; don't worry that I'll be here alone in this big house." This message tells the youngster to go, but at the same time it calls his loyalty to his mother into question and speaks to her fright in being alone, which also says "don't go."

Incongruent messages may become a double bind in certain relationships when a necessary set of conditions is present. The following conditions are set forth as the essential ingredients of double-bind communications by Watzlawick et al. (1967, p. 212):

1. Two or more persons involved in an intense relationship that has a high degree of survival value for one or more of the participants.
2. In this context, messages are given which assert opposing commands, i.e., the assertions are always mutually exclusive which means neither assertion can be obeyed without disobeying the other.
3. The recipient of the message is prevented from commenting on it or walking away from it.

Consider the case of the mother-child relationship. Here the relationship is likely to be intense and to have survival value for the child, who needs nourishment from the parent. This places the child in the position of being unable to comment on the opposing commands of the mother successfully or to walk away from them. As a result, the child is often exposed to the double-bind effect.

Double-bind communication is not peculiar to pathologic families. It may be observed to greater or lesser extent in a wide variety of families, most of which do not require professional intervention. The issue of family pathology may be determined by whether or not the double-binding transaction is repeated sufficiently to become an established pattern in family communication. When this has occurred and the self-perpetuating force of the pathological system takes over, family dysfunctioning results.

It should also be kept in mind that the double-bind process is not a unidirectional phenomenon. The paradoxical behavior that results from the double-binding message in turn creates a double bind for the sender of the message, thus creating and perpetuating pathologic communication (Watzlawick et al., 1967, p. 214).

Metacommunication

Metacommunication is an important part of the communication pattern observed in human interaction. Satir (1967) defines metacommunication as the sending of a message about a message, both of which are sent at the same time. The message conveys to the receiver how the sender wishes it to be received and how the receiver should react to it. Metacommunication also comments on the nature of the relationship between the persons involved, indicating the way the sender perceives the receiver and the attitude the sender has toward the message and toward self. The content of the message, tone of voice, facial expression, body posture, and so on serve to shape and define further what is verbalized by the sender. This adds to the complexity of the communication process and forces the receiver of metacommunicative messages to assess not only the content but the content within the context of the message.

For example, consider an interchange between husband and wife in which the husband comments, "The children really keep you busy." The literal content of the message is that the children are claiming the wife's attention in such a way that she spends a good deal of time responding. However, this seemingly simple statement may carry a number of messages on a metacommunicative level. First, the context within which the message is sent will help the receiver define it. If it occurs in a relaxed conversation after dinner and in a tone of voice that recognizes the wife's many responsibilities it may convey the message, "I value you and I appreciate your accomplishments as a wife and mother." Here the sender's attitude toward the message, the receiver, and himself is one of friendliness. On the other hand, if the same comment is made in a sarcastic manner as the husband restlessly awaits his wife's preparation of dinner, it may well carry the message, "I want you to give greater priority to preparing meals on time." The sender's attitude in this case would likely be, "I am not friendly, you are not treating me in a friendly manner, and the message is a warning to be heeded."

Metacommunication can also be sent on a verbal level. Satir (1967, pp. 76-77) suggests that this occurs when the sender verbally explains the message being sent. This too can occur at various levels of abstraction. For example,

1. It may involve labeling the kind of message sent and telling the receiver how the sender wishes it to be received—"It was a joke" (laugh at it).
2. The sender can verbalize the reason for sending the message by referring to a previous perception from the other—"You hit me. So I hit you back." "I thought you were tired and wanted my help."

The combination of verbal and nonverbal metacommunication creates for the receiver a complex situation from which to determine the meaning of messages received. Making this determination usually requires more attention to the context of the message and the nonverbal metacommunication than to the verbal aspects, as the latter is more explicit. Satir (1967) observes, in her discussion of human communication, "Whenever a person communicates he is also asking something of the receiver and trying to influence the receiver to give him what he wants" (p. 78). Since such requests are not always expressed verbally, those on the receiving end of messages must rely on metacommunication to understand what is asked of them and to determine how they will respond.

CONCEPTUAL TOOLS

Understanding the family as a system requires knowledge of concepts that help explain the interaction of family members within the system. Among these concepts social roles and the function of homeostasis, triangulation, family rules, and family myths are important considerations for social workers and other professionals engaged in treating families.

Social Role

The concept of role within the context of family functioning may be viewed as a prescription for interpersonal behavior, associated with individuals as actors and the status of positions. We agree with Heiss (1976) that role requirements are learned in the process of social interaction and the occupants of a role see it as carrying a specific status for the occupant and for others with whom the occupant interacts. Learning the behaviors expected in various roles involves both observation and teaching.

Learning role expectations by observation may be realized through *role-taking*. Role-taking is essentially imagining oneself to be in the position of another person. This occurs through the process of observing and imitating the behavior of the other, who is usually perceived by the actor as a role model (Heiss, 1976).

In the case of role-teaching information about the role is conveyed by direct communication through which a set of expectations is given to the role occupant by others, thus transmitting what is expected of the occupant of the position. For example, through the process of interaction a husband and wife learn what is expected in their respective roles. If the wife does not make decisions and repeatedly refers all family matters to her husband, her behavior communicates her expectation and the husband learns to make family decisions. As the husband continues to make decisions, he reinforces the wife's behavior and defines her dependency on her husband for making decisions as an expectation of her role as wife. In the meantime, the husband's role is established as the decision maker, and it is expected that he will behave in this way.

If the husband and wife are satisfied with their respective role behaviors, in other words they have harmonized their interpersonal roles around this independent-dependent relationship, *role complementarity* exists between them. In other words, the complementary needs of both are fulfilled by this independent-dependent interaction. And in spite of the appearance of an unequal relationship, this couple may function satisfactorily due to a congruence of roles.

Their relationship would be quite different if an incongruity of roles existed as would be indicated if husband and wife did not agree on the appropriate behavior to be associated with the roles they are to fill. For example, if the husband expects the wife to refer all family matters to him for decision but the wife wishes to share in the decision-making process and refuses to refer all matters to her husband, *role conflict* will result, which is conducive to an incongruity of roles.

It should be noted that "a lack of congruence does not always imply disagreement" (Heiss, 1976, p. 23). Since an individual takes on a series of identities in the process of identifying and developing a self, a lack of congruence might arise as a result of inconsistencies between identities that surface in response to situations experienced by the role occupant. This can be seen when the occupant interacts with various others where existing relationships call forth incompatible identities as in the case of a superior interacting with a subordinate who is also a friend (Heiss, 1976). The identity compatible with exchanges between friends is usually characterized by a *symmetrical relationship* where both communicators behave equally. In the case of communication between superiors and subordinates, the participants exchange different types of behaviors with one (the superior) giving and the other (the subordinate) receiving as is common in a *complementary relationship* (Okun and Rappaport, 1982). While disagreement regarding appropriate behaviors is not involved in this exchange, incongruence develops from the incompatible identities called forth by one actor being in a superior position to the other, who is also a friend. In other words, congruence cannot occur when both equal and unequal behaviors are required simultaneously.

To this point we have been concerned primarily with role as related to various role images. Finally, we will focus on roles from an intrafamilial perspective. Since the parent role is invested with the responsibility for the family system, it represents a logical point at which to begin and will be followed by discussion of the role of children in the family.

Assimilation into the role of parent, as well as the role of child, occurs in the same manner as previously described, that is, through the learning process. The role of parent does not automatically begin with the union of two people as husband and wife, and these roles carry different responsibilities, as previously indicated in this chapter. The role prescription for parent requires the exercise of authority in the interest of the development of children while at the same time providing the opportunity for growth as reflected in separation and individuation. Preferred behaviors for the parent role can be learned through teaching as exemplified in parent effectiveness training. Nevertheless, the first and perhaps most important learning of role behavior comes through observation and role-taking. That is to say, that the child learns parenting behavior from his or her relationship with parents as they move through the life cycle. And much of the behavior demonstrated by parents in association with their children becomes the behavior that the child will demonstrate in the future when he or she becomes a parent. For example, several studies have found that children who are abused by their parents also abuse their children when they become parents. Positive qualities will likewise be transferred to the future parent role.

The role of the child comes with the birth of the infant, and much of the early role behavior is characterized as instinctive and dependent. However, the infant's behavior is also influenced by the responses of the parents in their effort to meet the child's needs. If the child is provided appropriate physical and emotional comfort by the parents and given food when hungry, he or she is likely to respond in ways that reflect contentment. The child's contented behavior pleases the parents and elicits more of the parental responses that produced this behavior, thus defining expected role behavior for both parents and child. The parent role is to provide appropriate nourishment for the child while the child is to behave in ways that reflect happiness and contentment. Even at this early stage of life role behavior is learned through the process of interacting with others.

As the child grows, he or she learns expected role behavior from a number of associations and experiences including siblings, peers, and various adults. One of the most influential sources of learning from adults other than parents is experienced when the child enters school and takes on the role of student. This is a new role, and the child must learn how to behave as a student whose primary objective is gaining specific knowledge designed to facilitate movement through various stages of life. Teaching and observation are again the primary vehicles for communicating what is required of the child in the student role. The teacher communicates specific information and requires the child to demonstrate the extent to which this information is understood and integrated into an orderly body of knowledge commensurate with the child's level of development. In addition to providing information and guiding the child's quest for knowledge, the teacher almost always becomes a role model for the child and thereby enhances the role-taking process through which role expectations are learned.

This interaction defines how the child should behave as a student, that is, that he or she should acquire knowledge under the guidance of the teacher and be able to demonstrate this achievement in communication with others.

Understanding various role sets as experienced by family members and the way in which these roles are defined will greatly assist social workers and other professionals in determining appropriate strategies for intervening in family conflict.

Family Homeostasis

All systems have a self-regulatory mechanism through which a state of equilibrium is maintained. They seek to maintain a steady state, or a desired balance in their existence, through an error-activated feedback process. In regard to maintaining balance in human relationships, Haley (1963) suggests that "when one person indicates a change in relation to another, the other will act upon the first so as to diminish and modify that change" (p. 189). In the case of the family, homeostasis implies that the family acts so as to achieve a balance in relationships. This means that all parts of the system function in such a way that change is unnecessary for realization of family goals.

Most families maintain a balance in relationships through wholesome growth-producing transactions. This implies that permeable boundaries facilitate feedback, and the feedback process promotes adjustments to life-cycle developments which maintain the desired balance. However, family homeostasis may be achieved in a variety of ways. For example, in the 1950s several psychotherapists, including Bateson (1959), found in their study of schizophrenic patients and their families that in some families there was a vested interest in the patient's illness; when the patient began to improve, family members exerted pressure to maintain the illness. In other situations when the patient got well, someone else in the family became symptomatic. This behavior suggests the need for a symptom bearer in the family in order to maintain the established pattern of relationships.

In such cases, the family, in its effort to maintain a homeostatic state, may not always serve the best interests of all its members. Therefore, the worker should keep in mind that in maintaining its emotional balance, the family may try to prevent unwanted change in the system by encouraging role performance that is destructive for the role occupant. Yet, much of the behavior that maintains the status quo within the family is accepted by its members as a legitimate part of the family's operation. This prompted Satir (1967) to suggest that someone outside of the family is most often the first to identify such behavior as deviant and to send out the call for help. For example, the school is often the first to call attention to the deviant behavior exhibited by the child. The family fails to recognize this behavior as deviant because it serves the function of maintaining equilibrium within the family.

To illustrate the homeostatic process further, consider the case of parents who fight in the presence of a child and frequently threaten to separate. The child fears loss of the parents and reacts to prevent this loss by displaying behavior that claims the parents' attention. When the parents focus their attention on the child, they must discontinue their fighting. The threat of loss for the child subsides, and the family remains intact. As this transaction is repeated, it becomes a pattern of behavior in the family; the parents fight and the child acts out to keep them together.

Family Triangulation

A number of theorists have contributed to the development of the concept of triangulation in family relations. The work of Bowen (1966), Haley (1967), and Minuchin (1974) is particularly impressive.

Bowen (1966) suggests that the formation of a unit of three as a way of relating is a process common to all emotional systems. Knowledge of this process is essential to understanding the family as it struggles to maintain itself as a viable system. The triangle, as most commonly perceived, involves three persons (for example, mother, father, child) or two persons and an issue (for example, wife, husband, alcohol). The two-person system, Bowen says, has difficulty maintaining its stability under the pressure of anxiety and tension. When this system experiences intolerable frustration, it triangulates a third person or an issue in the hope of reducing the level of tension. The social worker engaged in family treatment is also a likely object of triangulation, especially when dealing with a two-person system. In a triangled situation the third operative—person or issue—becomes the object of attention for at least one of the original two, and sometimes both engage in a struggle for the advantages offered by the third component of the triangle.

The concept of triangles in human relationships is most often applied as a way of describing the relations of a unit of three. However, more than three persons, or a combination of persons and issues, may be involved, as demonstrated in the family where two or more children alternate as the triangulated family member. In other families more than one child may be brought into the relationship struggle between parents at the same time. As an example, consider the mother whose actions convey to her son and daughter that their father is not interested in the welfare of the family. This encourages them to join with her to ensure survival for the three. It creates a situation in which three have come together against a fourth, and at least four people are actively involved in the triangulation process.

Haley (1967) speaks of the existence of a perverse triangle within the pattern of family relating. This triangle is potentially pathological and so can lead to conflict and possible dissolution of the system. In describing the perverse triangle, Haley suggests that one member is of a different generation (such as parent and child). These two people of different generations form a coalition against the peer of one of the members (for example, mother and son against the father) but deny the presence of the coalition, in spite of behavior that confirms its existence. If the coalition continues and the denial of its existence is repeatedly offered, this pattern of relating is established and a pathological situation exists.

The concept of the triangle in human relationships provides the social worker with a way of viewing the patterns of relating within the family. To illustrate the working of this concept as it is frequently observed in family treatment, a case example from our experience is the H family:

> Mr. and Mrs. H were both 31 years of age. He was a successful executive and she was a housewife and mother. They were married at 21 when both were in their last year of college. Their first and only child was a son, D, who was born one year after the marriage. D had just celebrated his ninth birthday when the family came for treatment.
> The parents were very articulate, and Mr. H's skills in public relations and sales, areas in which he had been quite successful, were readily observed in the early sessions. He explained the family's route to therapy as a mutual decision, coming after D's increasing show of dependent behavior. In school he was demanding more attention, and the teachers thought he was showing signs of insecurity. At home his behavior was somewhat confusing to the parents, as he demanded more attention, yet at times he withdrew from their efforts to engage with him.
> It was learned during the course of treatment that the beginning of this behavior followed closely what Mrs. H described as "rather serious" misunderstandings between her and Mr. H. For the past five years Mr. H had advanced steadily with his company and about one year ago was promoted to a position of increased responsibility. This position required travel and a good deal of entertaining, which forced curtailment of many activities the family had previously enjoyed. Mrs. H was feeling left out of her husband's life, and as both she and the job demanded more and more of Mr. H's time, anxiety and tension developed. In commenting on this Mrs. H stated "the job seemed to be winning" and they had more than once discussed divorce. As a result of the increasing anxiety Mrs. H experienced, she began to do more things with her son, shared her loneliness with him and in various ways conveyed abandonment by Mr. H and their need to be together. This led to a coalition between mother and son, as the son was triangulated by the mother to help in dealing with her relationship with her husband. Nevertheless, this was an uneasy coalition, as D was very fond of his father. When the father also bid for D's attention, D withdrew out of fear of hurting one of his parents. The burden this placed on D was too great to be contained within the family relationship and spilled over into his relationships within the school system.

The family triangle does not necessarily involve the same third person or object throughout the triangulation process, and usually a number of alternatives are available to complete it. In the H case, for example, Mrs. H might also have chosen to attach herself to her parents to help in dealing with her husband or attempted a coalition with the therapist for the same purpose.

It should also be noted that triangulation is not always an indication of pathology in the family. For example, the husband or wife may develop an interest in an outside activity such as volunteer work as a way of spreading out the tension that usually develops in intense intimate relating. It is not likely that bringing this third component into the relationship will become problematic, as long as it does not replace the other principal participant in the relationship. By redirecting some of the energy that otherwise goes into the buildup of tension, both the husband and wife are better able to carry out normal functions.

In summary, triangulation is a predictable way in which human systems handle problems in relating as they seek to relieve the buildup of tension. While it can, under certain circumstances, contribute to family dysfunctioning, it can also be an alternative which leaves the participants in an intimate relationship somewhat more free to function effectively.

Family Rules

Family rules are essentially relationship agreements which influence family behavior. Some rules are explicit and established along the lines of specific roles and expectations of family members. With these rules what is desired is likely to be discussed, which opens the rules to the possibility of negotiation and change. The most powerful family rules, however, are those that are implicit, having been established over time by repeated family transactions. For example, consider the case of a family in which the father is involved in an extramarital love affair. This affair has generated repeated experiences through which family members have come to realize that the extramarital relationship exists. The parents never openly talk about the relationship themselves or entertain discussion of it by the children. As this scenario is repeated, it becomes an established rule that the family will not talk about Father's affair.

The strength of this rule lies in the fact that without discussion, relevant information about the experience is not processed. When this does not occur, the family is less likely to take actions to alter the status quo. The self-perpetuating mechanisms within the family system take over and reinforce the implicit rule, which continues unchanged among family members.

Families also have different ways of enforcing rules in treatment. For example, if the worker seems to be getting too close to a family secret in an interchange with one family member, someone else may enter the discussion with a different idea which changes the flow of information. In another situation, especially where children are involved, a child may suddenly display some form of disruptive behavior. This claims the attention of the group, taking the focus away from the possible revelation of the secret as awareness turns to this new and unexpected activity.

Some families also have rules governing communication around valued areas of family life such as sexual behavior and family illness. Whatever the governing mechanism, when it interferes with the effective course of treatment, preventive measures should be taken.

The Family Myth

The family myth essentially consists of family members' shared beliefs and expectations of each other and their relationships (Ferreira, 1977). It is characterized by unquestioned sharing of beliefs and expectations by all family members, which results in automatic agreement on the myth without further thought by any member. Ferreira gives this example:

> The wife in a family of 16 years' duration did not drive an automobile, nor did she care to learn. It was necessary for the husband to drive her everywhere she wished to go, which he did at whatever personal sacrifice it required. The wife explained her position by saying she was not "mechanically inclined." The husband immediately agreed with his wife and corroborated her statement by adding that she often let things fall from her hands around the house, and had always been that way. He further reported that she also did not trust cabdrivers, while the wife nodded her approval. (p. 51)

The husband so completely shared the belief that his wife was not mechanically inclined and needed his assistance that he not only agreed with her statement but supported the belief by offering an example of her awkwardness. He obviously had no thought of questioning her position.

It is also important to keep in mind that in spite of the irrationality often apparent in the existence of a family myth, it is perceived by family members as an emotionally indispensable and necessary part of their reality. As such, it not only determines the behavior of all family members but it also reveals something about family relationships. It implies the existence of reciprocal roles in the family, which is to say, if the myth is around something someone in the family cannot do, it implies that it can be done by someone else in the family. For example, the wife cannot drive a car, but the husband can.

Watzlawick et al. (1967) describe the myths in family relating evident in the play "Who's Afraid of Virginia Wolf?" Much of the discussion between the characters in this drama, Martha and George, centers around the existence of an imaginary son. Although the son does not exist, both Martha and George believe him to be real and repeatedly express agreement on matters pertaining to him. Watzlawick et al. agree with Ferreira that the family myth serves a homeostatic function and is frequently called into action at times of high tension, which threatens to disrupt family relationships. The myth prevents change in relationships, as do all balancing mechanisms, enabling the family to continue functioning in its customary manner.

SUMMARY

In this chapter we have introduced the idea of family treatment and discussed theory and concepts relative to family functioning. Some of the differences, advantages, and difficulties social workers might encounter in moving from treating an individual to treating the family as a unit are pointed out. A family developmental system is introduced, with emphasis on the structure of the family and various systemic aspects of family organization and functioning. The significance of the struggle for separateness and connectedness among family members is defined, and the process of communication as it relates to family interaction is described. Social role, homeostasis, triangulation, family rules, and family myths are discussed as conceptual tools.

This chapter formulates the foundation of a framework for the study and treatment of the family as a complex and dynamic system. Chapters 2 and 3 will continue the development of this framework by discussing some of the problems that affect family functioning and the task of engaging the family in treatment.

REFERENCES

Bateson, G. 1958. *Naven.* 2d ed. Stanford, Calif.: Stanford University Press.

—————. 1959. "Cultural Problems Posed by a Study of Schizophrenic Process." In *Schizophrenia: An Integrated Approach*, ed. A. Auerback. New York: Roland Press.

Bateson, G., Jackson, D. D., Haley, J., and Weakland, J. H. 1956. "Towards a Theory of Schizophrenia." *Behaviorial Science* 1:251-64.

Boszormenyi-Nagy, I., and Sparks, G. 1973. *Invisible Loyalties: Reciprocity in Intergenerational Family Therapy*. Hagerstown, Md.: Harper & Row.

Bowen, M. 1966. "The Use of Family Theory in Clinical Practice." *Comprehensive Psychiatry* 7:346-74.

Coylo, Grace L. 1962. "Concepts Relevant to Helping the Family as a Group." *Social Casework* 43: 347-54.

Ferreira, A. J. 1977. "Family Myths." In *The Interactional View*, ed. P. Watzlawick and J. H. Weakland. New York: W. W. Norton & Co.

Friedman, E. H. 1971. "Ethnic Identity as Extended Family in Jewish Christian Marriage." In *Systems Therapy*, J. O. Bradt and C. J. Moynihan. Washington, D. C.: Bradt & Moynihan. 1971.

Gomberg, Robert M. 1958. "Trends in Theory and Practice." *Social Casework* 39: 73-83.

Haley, J. 1963. *Strategies of Psychotherapy*. New York: Grune and Stratton.

—————. 1967. "Towards a Theory of Pathological Systems." In *Family Therapy and Disturbed Families*, ed. C. Zuk and I. Boszormenyi-Nagy. Palo Alto, Calif.: Science & Behavior Books.

Heiss, Jerold (ed.). 1976. *Family Roles and Interaction*. Chicago: Rand McNally.

Hess, R. D., and Handel, G. 1967. "The Family as a Psychosocial Organization." In *The Psychosocial Interior of the Family*, ed. G. Handel. Chicago: Aldine Publishing Co.

Jackson, D. D. 1959. "Family Interaction, Family Homeostasis, and Some Implications for Conjoint Family Psychotherapy." In *Individual and Family Dynamics*, ed. H. H. Messerman. New York: Grune & Stratton.

Kempler, W. 1973. *Principles of Gestalt Family Therapy*. Oslo, Norway: A-s Joh. Nordahls Trykkeri.

Klein, Alan. 1963. "Exploring Family Group Counseling." *Social Work* 8:23-29.

Laqueur, H. P., Labrut, H. A., and Morong, E. 1971. "Multiple Family Therapy: Further Developments." In *Changing Families*, ed. J. Haley. New York: Grune and Stratton.

Minuchin, S. 1974. *Families and Family Therapy*. Cambridge, Mass.: Harvard University Press.

Nichols, Michael. 1984. *Family Therapy: Concepts and Methods*. New York: Gardner Press.

Okun, Barbara F., and Rappaport, Louis J. 1980. *Working with Families: An Introduction to Family Therapy*. Belmont, Calif.: Duxbury Press.

Pollak, Otto, and Brieland, Donald. 1961. "The Midwest Seminar on Family Diagnosis and Treatment." *Social Casework* 42:319-24.

Richmond, Mary E. 1917. *Social Diagnosis*. New York: Russell Sage Foundation.

————.1922. *What Is Social Casework?* New York: Russell Sage Foundation.

Satir, V. 1967. *Conjoint Family Therapy.* Rev. ed. Palo Alto, Calif.: Science and Behavior Books.

Scherz, Frances H. 1953. "What Is Family-Centered Casework?" *Social Casework* 34:343-49.

————. 1962. "Multiple-Client Interviewing: Treatment Implications." *Social Casework* 43:120-24.

Sherman, Sanford N. 1959. "Joint Interviews in Casework Practice." *Social Work* 4:20-28.

Siporin, Max. 1956. "Family Centered Casework in a Psychiatric Setting." *Social Casework* 37:167-74.

Sluzki, C. E., and Beavin, J. 1977. "Symmetry and Complementarity: An Operational Definition and a Typology of Dyads." In *The New Interactional View,* ed. P. Watzlawick and J. H. Weakland. New York: W. W. Norton & Co.

Watzlawick, P., and Beavin, J. 1977. "Some Formal Aspects of Communication." In *The New Interactional View,* ed. P. Watzlawick and J. H. Weakland. New York: W. W. Norton & Co.

————, and Jackson, D. D. 1967. *Pragmatics of Human Communication.* New York: W. W. Norton & Co.

2

The Impact of Problems on Family Systems and the Nature of Required Changes

The overview of the family system in Chapter 1 should help social workers to understand many of the processes operating inside the system and provide a partial basis on which to organize helping activities. Further, social workers must be aware of the myriad events and changes which can act upon the family to stabilize or upset its homeostatic balance. These events and their effects must be understood before the plan of action most likely to help a particular family can be formulated.

The presenting problem itself can have disruptive effects. This chapter notes how certain problems affect family organization and interaction and indicates the kinds of changes within the family that are necessary if the problems are to be solved.

THE INTERRELATEDNESS OF FAMILY PROBLEMS AND FAMILY PROBLEM SOLVING

Social workers encounter families in trouble when these families' usual means of problem solving have been of no avail. Several factors may prevent problem solving. The first and most obvious is unavailability of resources, either the family's own or community resources. Even though individual coping, interpersonal relationships, and role performance within the family are adequate, they can be adversely affected by a continuing lack of resources. Lack of medical care, for example, may lead to loss of vital roles in the family or in the external world. Or lack of economic means may deprive the family of necessities including medical care, day care, or other social services.

In these instances, the need for income maintenance, services, and other resources is well established and their lack is obvious. The task of the social worker when resources are lacking is to provide information and to serve as a broker or advocate to connect the family with those resources that will enable it to maintain itself and its members. There may be little need for change in family relationships or process in these circumstances. The activity of the worker in encouraging flagging spirits and in making needed connections may be all that is required.

When resources are known and available but the family does not mobilize itself to make use of them, the problem lies in the way in which the family responds to presenting problems. The means families ordinarily use to solve their problems may hamper rather than facilitate the resolution of a difficulty. In some instances these mechanisms may actually have created the problem. For example, family members may be discouraged from venturing into new positions or maintaining vital roles in the outside world, or at least they may not be supported in their efforts by other members. They may not be able to alter their roles or behaviors due to role assignments within the family system. Thus they are locked by the family into performances that do not serve them well. The family needs to alter its organization and process to motivate or free its members to make use of available resources.

While faulty structure or process may have caused previous difficulties for the family, their operation may have attracted little notice, or, if noticed, efforts to change them may not have succeeded. When a new problem arises, new mechanisms are required. The task for the family is to change in such a way that its members can make use of resources or engage in other behaviors to solve the problem. The solution of the family problem and the alteration of family interaction patterns thus proceed concurrently. If the family can achieve a constructive solution to a current difficulty, its means for solving other problems are also likely to be enhanced.

Awareness of the interrelatedness of problems and methods of problem solving is important. The families most frequently encountered in social work practice do not approach an agency or social worker asking for family treatment or improvement in family relationships. They ask for resolution of a specific difficulty they are facing. We assume that there is some relationship between the problem presented and the set of family relationships that exists and that this needs to be understood (see Leader, 1981). The purpose of family assessment is to be clear about the role of precipitating events and family relationships in the presenting problem. The family treatment plan we suggest begins with the family's request. The worker proceeds to help the family with its goal of resolving the difficulty, recognizing that an effort on the part of the family which is different from its past attempts is needed. This attention to the current difficulty provides a focus for both workers and family.[1]

Thus a current family problem may be seen as a critical phase in the family's development. Unsuccessful coping with the difficulty leaves the family with an additional source of strain, whereas successful coping may put it in a better position to cope with other problems in the future. The problem has injected a new element into the life of the family with which it is required to deal. Whether or not it may be technically labeled a crisis, the resolution of the difficulty is seen as critical to the continued growth and development of individual family members and to the workings of the family as a social organization.

This view of family problems and their resolution through family change efforts can influence the social worker's approach in various circumstances. In the case of a child who needs to leave the family for work or school or to form a new relationship and who is afraid to do so, for example, workers have often considered the child to be conflictfully involved in the parents' marital difficulty and have emphasized the need to work on this problem. The marital problem is presented by the worker as the focus for treatment, although the family's request was to change the child's behavior. In our approach the worker would identify the specific parental disagreement about how to help the child and ask the parents to find a solution to that problem rather than to their marital conflict in general. Reaching agreement on what to do about the child may help resolve the marital conflict or enable the parents to see the need to focus on it.

---

[1]One way this dual focus is incorporated in the initial stage of contact is illustrated in Chapter 3 under the heading "Stage 3: Working Toward Problem Consensus."

Another example is the failure of a handicapped individual to utilize a rehabilitation program. The worker may observe that family bickering and tension have left the handicapped individual angered, discouraged, and preoccupied by family problems, and this interferes with his ability to make use of the program. In our approach the worker would not identify the family tension per se as the problem to be solved but would seek to engage the family in making it possible for the handicapped member to make use of the rehabilitation resource. Achieving that goal would of necessity alter family roles and relationships. We would expect that family tension might be reduced by the solution of this particular difficulty and that other family members might also be freed for growth and the achievement of their own goals. When the system changes, individuals can change.

These examples suggest that in this approach to problem solution the worker emphasis is on the achievement of definite goals rather than the delineation of family problems—more on what is wanted than on what is wrong. As problems impact on family organization and functioning, members seek new mechanisms and renegotiate their roles according to the type of problems with which they are copying.

FAMILY PROBLEMS AS CRISES

The occurrence of a problem poses a demand on individuals and on the family system. It causes varying degrees of stress. Some sort of change or adaptive response is required that may call upon resources or capacities already available to an individual or family. In other instances adaptive responses may not be available to the individual or family, leaving them immobilized, inadequate, or inappropriate for the demands of the situation, a situation then perceived as a crisis.

Crisis theory as it pertains to individuals has been fully elaborated by numerous authors (Golan, 1978; Rapoport, 1962; Wiseman, 1975). We restate just enough of it here to enable our readers to recall how individuals respond to stressful events. We then move on to describe how individual adaptation relates to overall family adaptation, how intrapersonal and interpersonal adaptation mesh.

Individuals need to adapt or adjust internally and in their relationship to others in the family (Rapoport and Rapoport, 1964). They do so in a sequence of phases that have been described in relation to a variety of stressful events.[2] Internal adaptations consist of adjustments in the image of self and of behaviors appropriate to the new situation. These adjustments will vary in difficulty depending on the degree to which the changed situation is perceived as a loss, or as a challenge, or as threatening. The meaning of the change to the individual needs to be processed. When the precipitating event is massive or sudden or both, or even if it isn't either of these, initial reaction typically is denial or shock. One becomes numb or immobile or insists that what is happening is not happening. As the reality of the stressful event and its ramifications become clear, shock and denial give way to protest and anger, and these in turn to an adaptation that is better, worse, or the same as that prior to the event or change. When earlier transitions have not been successfully mastered by resolving feelings and acquiring new behaviors, the present situation is more likely to be interpreted as threat, loss, or challenge, leaving the individual more stressed and incapable of appropriate action. Subsequent sections on each category of stressful events will elaborate and illustrate some of these points.

Individual adaptation occurs in the context of family relationships. While individuals adapt in their own idiosyncratic ways, based on the meaning that the situation has for them, other family members adapt in their own idiosyncratic ways. They also must adapt to each other's adaptation in a reverberating, cyclical way. Perceptions of the situation may vary between members in the extent to which the situation is viewed as threat, loss, or challenge. To the extent that perceptions are similar, members may experience mutual support. To the extent that they differ, members may come into conflict and individual adaptation may be threatened.

. Further, members may move through various phases at differing rates, creating further potential for conflict. The denial of one which encounters the anger of another, for example, brings added stress to the family system. Then when adaptations require new behaviors, there may be disagreement about what new behaviors or new role-taking should be undertaken and by whom. Thus, successful individual adaptation and the equanimity and survival of the family group are interrelated. Means of regulating interpersonal processes in a productive way must be or become available.

Some studies, notably Jackson (1956), have suggested that families as well

---

[2]These phases have been noted and appear to be remarkably similar in relation to death (Kübler-Ross, 1970), to birth of a defective child (Wright, 1976; Wolfensberger, 1967), and to catastrophes (Grossman, 1973).

as individuals go through phases of responsiveness to family problems. While not identical to individual phases, the phases she describes seem congruent with those of the individual. Her discussion seems to imply, however, that all family members are in the same adaptive phase at the same time. This seems unlikely as does the possibility of describing phase-specific sets of family relationships for any particular family problem.

While it does not now seem feasible to describe phase-specific family response sets in adaptation to stressful events, it is possible to suggest family group characteristics that contribute to successful responses to stressful family events. These will be discussed in the final section of the chapter.

A CLASSIFICATION OF FAMILY PROBLEMS

The problems of families that come to the attention of social workers are many and varied. Some of them can be viewed as arising out of the natural course of family events—out of the fact that families are made up of individuals who change and are of differing ages, sexes, interests, and temperaments. Others arise out of life events in the family's engagement with the external world, appearing to be imposed on the family.

Hill (1958) has classified the general categories of problems which arise in families under stress. We have adapted this list, as shown in Table 1, to include problems that are due to both internal and external and normal as well as unusual family changes or events. While the list is not exhaustive, it does cover a large variety of family circumstances known to social workers. The occurrence of any of these events or changes does not necessarily result in a referral for help or a voluntary appeal from the family. Some families may adjust to the problem without external support. The concern is not whether the problem is definable as a crisis, but with the fact that the family appears in need of help.

There are five principal types of family difficulties which may be seen as stressful changes or events. Classified by nature of the difficulty, they are: (1) accession to membership, (2) loss of membership, (3) demoralization, (4) demoralization plus accession or loss, and (5) changes of status.

These problems have consequences which affect individual adjustment, the family group's response to the outside world, and the family's own internal group adjustment through changes in role relationships, tasks, and communication efforts. The ways in which these consequences are felt in various types of family problems are explored in the sections that follow.

TABLE 1
A Suggested Classification of Crises in Families

By Source of Trouble
Extrafamily events such as catastrophes
Intrafamily events

By Nature of the Difficulty
1. Accession to membership
    Marriage or remarriage
    Pregnancy (wanted or unwanted) and parenthood
    Deserter or runaway returns
    Stepparent addition or remarried family combination
    War reunions
    Foster child addition or adoption or foster adult addition
    Restoration to health (e.g., terminated alcoholism)
2. Loss of membership
    Death of a family member
    Hospitalization (illness or disability)
    War or employment separation
    Child leaving home
    Wife starting employment
3. Demoralization
    Nonsupport or other income loss or job loss
    Infidelity
    Alcoholism or addiction
    Delinquency
4. Demoralization plus loss or accession
    Illegitimate pregnancy
    Runaway or desertion
    Separation/Divorce
    Imprisonment
    Suicide or homicide
    Hospitalization for mental illness
5. Changes of status
    Sudden shift to poverty or wealth
    Move to new housing or/and neighborhood
    Change in status of women
    Maturation due to growth (e.g., adolescence, aging, changes due to therapy, or other sources of individual change)

Each event has consequences for:
    Individual adjustment, both psychologically and behaviorally
    Family group adjustment, role relationships, tasks, and communication
    Family group relationship to the outside world

Drawn largely from R. Hill, 1958. "Generic Features of Families under Stress," *Social Casework* 39:139-49.

FAMILY ACCESSIONS AND ROLE CHANGES

In the individual, changing roles requires both an internal, psychological change and a change in overt behavior.[3] As a part of role definition, images and feelings about self and others guide individual behavior. Role images include expectations about behavior related to the role of others (such as mother) and of self in relation to other. They develop in the interaction between family members as the result of members' attempts to regulate one another's behavior. They are, therefore, both consequence and cause of the overt behavior between members.

The addition of a family member requires both the redefinition of existing roles and a definition of the role of the new member. On an individual level, readiness to accommodate and connect to additional or new members must be achieved. A new self-image must incorporate a view of self in relation to the new person. If the incoming member is a child, infant or older, natural or foster, new or returning, the role definition for parent or parents will be enlarged or altered. When both parents are present in the home, the new role definition for Parent A should have the concurrence or consent of Parent B, and vice versa. Similarly, the roles and responsibilities of the added child member need a definition, varied according to the age and need of the child, which has the concurrence not only of the adult members, but of other children in the family. These role definitions are necessary if the enlarged system is to operate in a way that is gratifying to all members and avoids conflict resulting from incongruent role conceptions.

If the added member will occupy a parental role, a similar process is needed. A returning adult member may expect to move into the role as it was previously occupied. This is not likely to occur automatically without some readjustment on the part of the family members already in the system, since their role expectations will have shifted to account for the fact that the reentering member had not been participant in the ongoing activities of the family. The difficulty of reentry will vary according to the status of the individual. Jackson (1956) has detailed the difficulty alcoholics have in reentering the family system upon recovery from alcoholism, largely due

---

[3]Rapoport and Rapoport (1964) discuss both intrapersonal and interpersonal adaptations as essential to successful coping in the honeymoon phase of family growth. This is put forth as a model for adaptation in any kind of family crisis, and these adaptations are seen as essential to individual mental health as well as family functioning.

to the fact that their participation, status, and esteem within the family had ebbed to an extremely low level. On the other hand, McCubbin, Dahl, Lester, Benson, and Robertson (1976) report that prisoner-of-war families which had maintained the expectancy of return and a clear definition of a husband-father role were likely to facilitate reintegration of the serviceman.

Remarried families are another example of the accession of family members. When two partial families are joined, it is not strictly a matter of adding one person to a family but rather of adding two families together. In order to attach successfully to these new relationships, each member must first grieve and detach from lost relationships. The two adults in the family are detaching from their ex-spouses and working out their relationship as new spouses and as parents. Simultaneously, the children are comparing the role-taking of the new adults with that of the now-separated parent. They are reflecting on their own positions vis-à-vis the new parent and their new siblings. In difficult situations, the two families may not become a family but remain as two sets of individuals within the same household. The degree to which they achieve solidarity or remain distant will be a function of the parents' ability to join constructively with each other and with each other's children (Duberman, 1975). More attention will be paid to the tasks of merging and joining such family groups in Chapters 10 and 11 on divorce and family reconstitution.

Another complexity in relation to accession of members arises in foster care situations. The child and the family have the task of connecting to each other while simultaneously being prepared for separation. In addition, each party to the new arrangement is likely to be dealing with separations from prior relationships, the child from his or her family or origin, the parents from a previous foster child. All participants now have to gain an image of themselves and of each of the others in relation to themselves. Meanwhile, the images of prior relationships continue to be real and to guide behavior, however appropriate or inappropriate those images may be to the new set of relationships. Thus both child and foster parents face a considerable adjustment task, one in which they often have little or no assistance. Their efforts meet with varying degrees of success.

There are two additional points in relation to the shifts in patterning of role relationships (both of which will be elaborated later). One is that changes in role relationships occur within and across the different family subsystems. They affect both the hierarchical, intergenerational relationships of parents and children and the relationships in the separate parental and child subsystems. The second point has to do with the communication processes by which these role relationships are altered. If the family has effective communication capability, these changes in family structure can be achieved in spite of tension and turmoil. If effective communication capability is lacking, new role relationships may not be clearly defined and may remain problematic.

MEMBERSHIP LOSSES OR SEPARATIONS AND ROLE CHANGES

Similar considerations apply in the case of losses to family membership. Even temporary losses like extended hospitalization or business trips require readjustment of the expectancies of all members. On an individual level elements of grief or loss come into play, and the relevant feelings need to be dealt with. In general, there is the expectation that remaining members will compensate in some way for the gaps left by the missing member. At the same time, however, the degree of role arrangement required upon loss or departure of a family member depends upon the position and status of the departing member. Fathers, for example, may expect older children to assume household responsibilities during mothers' illnesses. Wives, upon loss of husbands to extended illness or occupational duties, may rely upon children to assume parenting or even spouse roles. Children will look to the remaining parent to carry both parental roles. The departure of a child will have a different effect. The normal departure of a child would ordinarily not achieve problem status in a family, though it may if that child has assumed significant family responsibility. Rosenberg (1975) describes a case in which a daughter's separation from the family for college became problematic because of her role as a peacemaker between her parents.

None of these readjustments comes easily. Remaining family members may lack skills required in adding to their roles, or they may lack the willingness to undertake new responsibilities. Further, the readjustments may entail blurring of generational boundaries or previously adhered-to-sex-role definitions. Since there is an element of loss in the various types of separation, a grief reaction on the part of the remaining individuals may also be expected. "They must mourn not only the loss of exiting family members, but the loss of previous organization of family as well" (Fulmer, 1983, p. 261). Fulmer also points out that normal mourning of losses may not occur because of additional demands placed on surviving members, the feeling that "if I start crying, I may not stop, so I'd better not start." And when a parent's mourning is thus inhibited, children's expressions of grief may be similarly submerged.

Family members may handle their individual reactions to each of these types of readjustment to loss or separations with varying degrees of speed or success. Compounding the individual variations in response is the fact that the readiness of one person to respond constructively may not concur in time with the readiness of others, so that not all members are at the same place at the same time in their readiness to adapt.

Some of the adaptive difficulties following loss or separation of a family member are illustrated in greater detail in the following case material (Deykin, Weissman, and Klerman, 1971). While the loss to the family is due to the psychological withdrawal of a depressive mother rather than physical absence, many of the problems are the same. Such psychological withdrawal may in itself be seen as a function of family operations, but it also affects the response of the family system.

> Even before hospitalization, many families have to deal with the discrepancy between the patient's former functioning and her depressed state. Some relatives are unprepared to cope with role reversals and may themselves become discouraged when their emotional needs are unfulfilled. While this reaction can be seen in any relatives, it is most evident in the patient's spouse. Many husbands develop symptoms similar to those of the patient's, especially somatization. In such marriages, it appeared that both the patient and spouse were vying for the position of the "sick" person. . . .
>
> A spouse who has had to assume many household responsibilities may feel overwhelmed and resentful. Concentrated attention to the patient without any exploration or acknowledgement of the husband's position tends to entrench the spouse's feelings of burden and to diminish his ability to cope with these responsibilities. A simple acknowledgement of the spouse's difficulties may suffice to support him over his trying period. Occasionally, the caseworker has to initiate intensive work which may include helping the spouse to modify his existing living patterns.
>
> The interruption of the characteristic interpersonal family balance, whether it be between spouse and patient or between the patient and other relatives, may have repercussion on all other family relationships. (Deykin et al., 1971, p. 277)

The family's response to the depressive behavior also may serve to exacerbate the anger, despair, and hopelessness already inherent in the patient. The conflict between patient and spouse may reflect an effort to alter, or restore, a previously existent complementarity. Relief from depression might result if greater symmetry could be achieved.

DEMORALIZATION AND ROLE CHANGES

Role and task adjustments are necessary in relation to demoralizing problems in much the same way they are with additions and losses to membership. Here, however, the basis for role reassignment may arise as much from the needs and feelings of family members about the demoralizing behavior as from the actual need for change in the performance of responsibilities and tasks. Role adjustments as a consequence of additions or losses are also accompanied by a great deal of feeling, but they are likely to be more intense if the presenting problem is a demoralizer.

A family dealing with alcoholism illustrates both the feeling intensity and the problems in changing roles. Denial, despair, and anger all make their appearance over time. Apologies give rise to hope, and further drinking brings disappointment, anger, accusations, blame, self-doubt, and feelings of abandonment and loss. Expressions of these feelings are shared, spread among family members, and give rise to further apology, or defensiveness, anger, and counteraccusations. Emotional intensity rises in the exchange.

Concurrently, while the alcoholic's failure to meet family responsibility has given rise to these feelings, things are left undone. Role-taking is affected. The "under-functioning" on the part of the alcoholic requires compensatory behavior on the part of others and often prompts "over-functioning" because of the feelings involved, in ways or areas in which compensation would not be necessary. Such over-functioning reinforces and increases the under-functioning of the alcoholic. Both the over-and under-functioning feed the emotional intensity. How to interrupt this cycle needs to be worked out in each situation. Similar cycles can occur with other problems such as physical disabilities, which, though possibly less demoralizing, also require solution to the problem of how to compensate without overcompensating.

An example of family reaction to suicide serves to illustrate intensity as well as how different sets of feelings can foster conflict. Hajal (1977) describes the efforts of a ten-year-old girl to take over her father's role after his suicide so as to perpetuate an impression of his continuing presence in the family. Her continuing denial put her into conflict with her mother, who had acknowledged her loss and experienced her anger, and was now ready to reorient her life and that of her family to what lay ahead. The daughter's

internal resolution lagged but clearly needed to proceed. Here the intrapersonal and interpersonal are clearly linked.

When there is added intensity of feeling because of presenting problems
in the demoralizer category, several factors are involved. One is the threat
that the problem poses to the family's physical survival, as in the case of loss
of support or the imprisonment of one of the adults. Additionally, the
problem may represent deviations from the family's or society's value system. Infidelity or adolescent unwed pregnancy are examples. The problems
are violations of the rules by which some family members thought the
family was governed. Rejection of the rules may be experienced as a rejection of the family or of persons who made the rule. Or the problem may
be seen as a threat to the image or esteem of the family or of individual
members in the community.

For these and other reasons, feelings of threat, blame, anxiety, and anger
arise when demoralizing problems are encountered. The family should have
at its disposal a means to deal with the intense feelings and resolve the
conflicts that arise.

STATUS CHANGES AND NEW ROLES

This category of family crises is intended to reflect the fact that the world
in which the family lives may change. Change here is less due to intrafamily
events than to external conditions—a new neighborhood, a change in the
job market, a promotion, new views about the role women evidenced in the
outside world. Accessions or losses of membership are not part of the picture. The family nevertheless has the task of adapting to newness and
difference. Upward mobility certainly is more to be desired than downward
mobility, but in either case, changed circumstances require new images of
self and of the family, and new role-taking to accommodate to the changed
status. Family members need to relocate themselves in the social structure,
to see where they fit with their new place in the world. There may be
accompanying pride and self-esteem, new extra-family contacts or, as in the
case of downward mobility, accompanying loss of self-esteem and pride. In
some instances, like moves to a new neighborhood, all family members
share a common task learning their way around and finding new contacts.
The move may be fraught with eager anticipation or fear, or both as in the
case of a move into a public housing project. Where the move is of some
distance, mobility may have separated all members from close ties to friends

and kin and left them bereft, at least until new ties are established. Some highly mobile families, such as military families or those in which job promotions mean moves to new cities, repeatedly face the tasks of dealing with the loss of old ties and establishing new ones. In other instances, such as educational achievement and the change that brings for the individual, other family members are required to adapt to the newness of the individual's role and status. That may be different for each separate member, but it may also require a whole family reorganization as in the case of the family in which advanced education has not been included in its picture of "what our family is like."

Even in those situations in which family members have a common task of adapting to a new social environment, the specifics of the task may be different for each individual member. For some, the task will automatically be facilitated by circumstances such as a good school or a highly evaluating employer. Some members may grieve longer for old relationships and invest themselves more slowly in the new situation. For others, new ways and new conditions are more difficult to accept. The situation of immigrant families offers many useful lessons in this regard. Differences in pace or degree of adaptation may give rise to conflict. Thus it becomes evident that while the family as a group has a common task in adapting to the changed outer circumstances, internal adaptations to each member's adaptation are also required if the family is to cope successfully with the circumstance.

Our discussion here is not exhaustive. We have focused more on some circumstances than others. Doubtless, our readers could identify other circumstances of importance which we have not mentioned. We are also aware of the "miscellaneous" nature of this category which makes principles or issues harder to define and which limits our ability to be exhaustive. In spite of these limits, we hope we have drawn enough attention to nonfamily sources of change to give our readers a basis for awareness of their implication for the family.

FAMILY RESPONSE TO CHANGED CONDITIONS

Factors Influencing Family Response

All types of family problems have a clear impact on family organization and process. The degree to which family members are capable of accommodating themselves to the adjustments required by additions, losses, or other problem events, however, depends on a number of factors. These include: (1) the value placed on the family group in contrast to the priority given to individual goals, (2) the family's authority and leadership structure and rules, (3) the members' ability to communicate and negotiate, and (4) ties to external systems.

Family researchers have for many years sought to identify elements of family relationships and functioning which permit successful coping with stress. Angell's (1936) early studies of family ability to cope with depression and poverty identified integration and adaptability as primary factors. In these studies integration was seen as a sense of coherence, unity, common interests, affection, and economic interdependence. Adaptability was simply the capacity to meet obstacles and shift course. Hill (1949), drawing on his own research with losses of membership due to war separations, also drew attention to these two basic elements.

Cohesion. In a more recent research these same elements have become further defined and elaborated (see Olson, Sprenkle, and Russell, 1979, for a thorough review). Integration (cohesion) has many manifestations and is seen as existing on a continuum between two extremes—complete enmeshment on the one hand and total disengagement of family members from each other on the other. Our discussion in Chapter 1 of the separateness/connectedness dimension captures much of this range. Cohesion is manifest in such things as emotional bonding, mutual inclusiveness, exclusion of nonfamily persons, shared time, space, friends, and interests on the one side and complementary sense of independence from each other. Over-inclusiveness (enmeshment) and over-independence (disengagement) are not known to be conducive to a healthy sense of cohesion.

Members vary in their commitment to the family. Some may see themselves as peripheral and prefer the pursuit of their own goals. Some may feel their own needs will be met by continuing family participation. Others may support or participate in family operations to the neglect of their own interests. These priorities may vary among individuals in the same family. They also vary among families. Where the family has seen the outside world as alien and hostile, as minority families often have had to, mutual support and "family first" may be emphasized, to the detriment of individual pursuits, though putting the family first need not be detrimental to individual growth. Josselyn (1953) reports on the importance for the development of individual identity of a widowed parent's effort to "keep the family together"—an effort in which the value of the family group was primary.

Families in which both individual and family group goals are important should be able to maintain some flexibility in movement to allow for the resolution of particular difficulties. Lacking this flexibility, they will have difficulty when problems arise.

Adaptability. Adaptability has also been further defined in recent research. It is manifest in assertiveness, leadership and control, discipline, negotiation, capacity to shift roles, and rules for behavior. As in the cohesion dimension, there may be too much or too little of each characteristic. Neither extreme is conducive to successful adaptation either of individual members or for the survival of the family as a group. One extreme is inflexibility and rigidity; the other is a complete lack of structure, irresponsibility, and chaos.

Along with the capacity for adaptation, the family also needs to maintain a sense of stability. In this regard Frazer (1984) comments that at "points of pattern change, existing couple or family system constructs are called to task. There is a need now to construe these new pattern variations in ways which both adapt to their new directions while assimilating them under some broad enough umbrella construction so as to maintain the system's general definition of itself as an on-going unit" (p. 369).

We focus specifically here on the elements of authority, leadership, roles, and rules. In some families the pattern is strong parental leadership and control; in others, children participate more actively in decision making. These patterns are derived from the way parents value and define adult and child roles, based on their own prior life experience. Strong parental leadership or control may have caused the problem. It also may exacerbate the problem, stand in the way of its solution, or contribute to its resolution. Similarly, depending on the ages of involved family members, *weak* parental participation and leadership may have caused the problem, may exacerbate it, or may stand in the way of solution.

The abdication of a family role by one of the adult members, or his or her involvement in a demoralizing event, may well limit his or her capacity to provide leadership in the solution of problems. This allows the movement of other members, children in particular, into leadership or parental roles. Another aspect of family leadership is that adults may see a problem and the participation of others in problem solving as a threat to their leadership or authority within the family. Parental leadership which allows for the inputs of child members, however, can contribute significantly to problem resolution.

Closely related to the important leadership and role structure is the operational set of family rules. These serve to prescribe expected behaviors and give individual members a sense of what they can or need to do to alleviate stress and solve the current family problem. It is expected that members of the adult generation will be primarily responsible for setting rules. To the degree that they do so, rules may be many or few, rigid or flexible according to situation, defined with varying degrees of clarity, enforced consistently or irregularly. Here too it is evident that an optimum balance between extremes is desirable.

Communication. The third factor affecting family members' response to a particular problem is their ability to communicate about the changed circumstances and to negotiate about possible responses. In closed family systems, communications may not allow for the assimilation of new information and ideas and may dictate the "one right way" to think about or do things. Differing points of view may be poorly tolerated, even though the occurrence of the problem calls for new ideas and new solutions. Tallman (1970) says:

> What seems necessary is a structure which allows for the expression of a diversity of conflicting views, all of which are subject to evaluation and criticism. At the same time, the integrity of the individual must be protected. A structure which allows for creative problem solving, therefore, should maintain open channels of communication within an evaluative framework which provides for a critical examination of the ideas presented. (p. 95)

The value system must provide for the freedom to communicate differences and to evaluate the ideas presented by others, in order to solve the problems presented to it. In open family systems rules regulating communication allow for expression of intense feeling and different ideas, both of which are necessary for adequate crisis resolution. Members need freedom both to negotiate and to promote change in response to the problem. They also need effective mechanisms for negotiation. Some communications, such as denial, blaming, or withdrawal, are not particularly useful to a family in coping with the tasks at hand and solving the issues presented by a particular problem. Other strategies, such as efforts to understand each others' feelings, values, and goals, may be more useful but may not be available in the family, especially under present circumstances. Additional difficulties may arise if some members verbalize feelings and others wish to withdraw, or if some continue to blame while others seek reconciliation. Individuals respond on the basis of their own needs in the situation. Whether these conflicts are resolved depends on how the family has handled differences in the past and whether they can permit worker suggestions or directions to influence them to develop new responses.

Lacking effective modes of communication, family members may lose their investment in the system and their willingness to contribute to solution of its difficulties. They may attack the system, or fall silent or otherwise withdraw from it. Their potential inputs are lost to the system, as is the system's value to them. The relative value placed on family as over against the individual and the degree of freedom to communicate derive from the family value system, which is largely determined by the adult members.

Ties to External Systems. In times of stress families may need external supports in order to survive and cope. Needed resources may be material, as we suggested at the outset of this chapter, or they may be more for emotional support, which can come from friends and extended family systems. To the extent that these existed prior to the current presenting problem they may be readily drawn upon and contribute to problem resolution. To the extent that they need to be found and developed, problem resolution may be delayed or forestalled.

SUMMARY

This chapter has given major attention to the renegotiation of roles as families experience the impact of increases or decreases in family membership, changes in family members or conditions, and demoralizing events. These events are seen as placing stress upon individuals within the family and upon the family as a whole. We noted that internal adaptation on the part of individual members is required and drew on crisis theory to describe phases of response. Individuals adapt not only to the stress but to each other's adaptation, thus making response an interpersonal and family event as well as an individual one.

A family's ability to survive such changes requires a great deal of flexibility in role definitions and role behavior. Rigid adherence to previously existent role definitions stands in the way of problem solution.[4]

---

[4]Spiegel's (1968) discussion of the resolution of role conflict within the family usefully elaborates what we have in mind here. He suggests that "role induction" is a less useful strategy in the long run than "role modification." The former method is used by self to induce others to take the role as the self would define it. The latter method results in changed behavior on the part of both, or all, participants.

We noted that the concepts of adaptability and cohesion are useful in understanding family response to presenting problems. We described adaptability in role performance as a function of the members' conviction that the family is of value to them and of their consequent willingness to commit themselves to participate in problem solution. Problem solution is further seen as contingent upon family communication capacity. Changing role requirements necessitate a capacity for open negotiation among family members. Family values which provide this freedom and modes of communication which lead to problem solving are both needed. Finally, the family's ability to respond to changed conditions depends on the effectiveness and quality of family leadership. The degree of control and direction provided by the adult members of the family should maintain generational boundaries and enable all members to continue age- and sex-appropriate roles.

The way in which the family accomplishes needed role changes in response to changed family conditions, or fails to accomplish them, demonstrates the interrelatedness of family problems and family problem solving. If needed problem-solving mechanisms are available, family problems can frequently be solved. If they are not available, these mechanisms can be created or improved. This is accomplished in the course of work on the presenting problem, so that solving the problem and changing the family become simultaneous activities. The problems of poverty families addressed in Chapter 4 are a clear case in point.

The introduction of the constructs of this chapter elaborates the discussion on the nature of family systems begun in Chapter 1. Their application and use will become more specific and clear in relation to the particular family problems outlined in the chapters of Part II.

REFERENCES

Angell, R. 1936. *The Family Encounters the Depression.* New York: Scribners.

Bowen, M. 1981. *Family Therapy in Clinical Practice.* New York: Jason Aronson.

Deykin, E., Weissman, M., and Klerman, G. 1971. *"Treatment of Depressed Women."* British Journal of Social Work 1:277-91.

Duberman, L. 1975. *The Re-Constituted Family.* Chicago: Nelson-Hall.

Frazer, F. S. 1984. "Paradox and Orthodox: Folie a Dieux?" *Journal of Marital and Family Therapy* 10(4):361-72.

Fulmer, R. H. 1983. "A Structural Approach to Unresolved Mourning in Single Parent Family Systems." *Journal of Marital and Family Therapy* 9(3): 259-69.

Golan, N. 1978. *Treatment in Crisis Situation*. New York: Free Press.

Grossman, L. 1973. "Train Crash: Social Work and Disaster Services." *Social Work* 18:35-45.

Hajal, F. 1977. "Post-Suicide Grief Work in Family Therapy." *Journal of Marriage and Family Counseling* 3(2):35-42.

Hill, R. 1949. *Families Under Stress*. New York: Harper and Bros.

———— 1958. "Generic Features of Families under Stress." *Social Casework* 39:139-49.

Jackson, J. K. 1956. "Adjustment of the Family to Alcoholism." *Marriage and Family Living* 18:361-69.

Josselyn, I. 1953. "The Family as a Psychological Unit." *Social Casework* 34:336-43.

Kübler-Ross, E. 1970. *On Death and Dying*, New York: Macmillan Co.

Leader, A. 1981. "The Relationship of Presenting Problems to Family Conflicts." *Social Casework* 62(8):451-57.

McCubbin, H., Dahl, B., Lester, G., Benson, D., and Robertson, M. 1976. "Coping Repertoires of Families Adapting to Prolonged War-Induced Separations." *Journal of Marriage and the Family* 38(3):461-71.

Olson, D., Sprenkel, D., and Russell, C. 1979. "Circumplex Model of Family Systems." *Family Process* 18(1):3-28.

Rapoport, L. 1962. "The State of Crisis: Some Theoretical Considerations." *Social Service Review* 36(2):211-17.

Rapoport, R., and Rapoport, R. 1964. "New Light on the Honeymoon." *Human Relations* 17:33-56.

Rosenberg, B. 1975. "Planned Short-Term Treatment in Developmental Crises." *Social Casework* 56:195-204.

Spiegel, J. 1968. "The Resolution of Role Conflict within the Family." In *A Modern Introduction to the Family*, ed. N. Bell and E. Vogel. New York: Free Press.

Tallman, I. 1970. "The Family as a Small Problem Solving Group." *Journal of Marriage and the Family* 32:94-104.

Wiseman, R. 1975. "Crisis Theory and the Process of Divorce." *Social Casework* 56:206-11.

Wolfensberger, W. 1967. "Counseling Parents of the Retarded." In *Mental Retardation*, ed. A. Baumeister. Chicago: Aldine Publishing Co.

Wright, L. S. 1976. "Chronic Grief: The Anguish of Being an Exceptional Parent." *The Exceptional Child* 23:106-9.

CHAPTER 3

The Social Worker's Approach to Family Treatment

The theoretical framework for family treatment from a systems viewpoint is operationalized when it is put into practice by the social worker or practitioner. In making plans for intervention in a family problem situation, the worker must assess the way the family is organized and functions. The underlying issues of family structure and dynamics must be understood before decisions regarding change strategies can be made.

Given the assumption that the family as a group needs to find the means to solve the problem at hand, rather than simply having solutions promulgated by the social worker, one goal of the initial contacts between the worker and the family is to gain the participation of needed family members in the problem-solving process. In achieving this goal the worker must be clear about who the needed family members are and how they can be involved in the process.

TREATMENT FOR THE FAMILY OR FAMILY GROUP TREATMENT

There are three separate but interrelated issues to be addressed in assuring the participation of needed family members. The first is whether treatment for the family and family group treatment mean the same thing. The second raises the question of whether family treatment is appropriate or needed for all problems, or whether there are certain situations where it is contraindicated. The third has to do with the age and family status of persons to be involved.

Conjoint interviews are treatment sessions which include two or more family members. **Family** treatment and conjoint interviewing are sometimes thought of synonymously. In our view, they should not be. Family problem solving *may* make use of conjoint family sessions. They are highly valuable, for reasons that will be detailed shortly, but their exclusive use in problem solving is not required. Individual sessions with various family members, sessions with pairs or triads of family members, and sessions with the entire family all may be productive in altering roles, communication processes, and problem-solving capability. This view, consistent with systems theory, holds that when one member of the family system begins to change, other parts of the family system must also change. A change produced in one person upsets family equilibrium, requiring adaptation (or incurring resistance) on the part of other members of the system. In this vein, Haley (1971) notes that family therapists "realized that traditional individual therapy was actually *one* way to intervene in a family, whether the therapist thought of it that way or not. It was the intrusion of an outsider into a family even if the therapist considered himself to be dealing only with one person's fantasies" (p. 3).

What distinguishes this view from traditional individual therapy is the consciousness of the worker about the consequences that work with the individual may have for that person's behavior in the family and for the family system. When the worker holds a family systems rather than an intrapsychic view of the problem, treatment is more likely to be undertaken with family consequences in mind. The worker can anticipate these consequences, and the client can be prepared in the treatment relationship to anticipate them and to cope with family reactions. Or the client can consciously set new family processes in motion.

There has been considerable discussion in the family therapy literature as to the appropriateness of conjoint family treatment for various presenting problems. Scherz (1962), for example, suggests family treatment for character disorders, but not for adolescent separation problems. Cookerly's (1974) data suggest the usefulness of conjoint sessions for marital problems when the couple is staying together, but not when they intend to separate. Much of the difficulty in such discussion results from the equation of family treatment with conjoint family interviews.

Our position is that all treatment involves the family, but it need not all be family group treatment. In deciding whether conjoint family sessions are the best vehicle for promoting change in a family problem situation, other means of involving the family should also be considered. Family treatment, as we define it, is any treatment that changes the family.

Family members can be involved in treatment constellations other than conjoint sessions. Work on family problems can take place in parent groups, groups for husbands or wives when the identified problem person is one of the family adults, multiple-family groups, or multiple-couples groups, for example. (These are discussed in subsequent chapters.) The individual learning and change that are begun in these groups are carried back to the family. When the identified problem patient is a child, it has not been unusual for treatment to be offered primarily or only to the child's parents. Treatment has been offered less often to another adult when the person manifesting the problem is an adult. An exception is Murray Bowen (1971), who sometimes works with another family adult who manifests more capacity for change with the expectation that this will change the family system. Even with a severe demoralizing problem such as alcoholism, however, some reports indicate that treatment of family members other than the identified problem person has resulted in change, both for the family and for the individual (Cohen and Krause, 1971; McDowell, 1972).

CONJOINT FAMILY SESSIONS

Almost all problem solving in family situations can benefit from family participation. We can think of no category of problems that cannot benefit from family problem-solving efforts. Our theory suggests that no family member is untouched by problems occurring in the family group. Each member is affected by the occurrence of the problem and has some reaction to it. It may alter the person's image of self or of others or of the family group. It may change his or her feelings about self and others. It may alter his or her willingness to participate in family life. These reactions become manifest and enter family interaction and relationships. Or the family member may be a participant in the creation of the problem, or in its perpetuation.

In all instances, with all problems, family participation is needed and useful at *some time* during the life of the case. The purpose of such participation is to help the family members deal with their feelings about the changes occurring in the family group and to enable them to cope with these changes constructively, or to involve them in the creation of change. In this we differ slightly from Perlman (1961), who suggests that only those whose participation is necessary to the solution of the problem should be involved. Our purpose is to see that needed family members are served in some way, while helping them to redefine their roles and positions in the family to promote their own growth and that of the family. This is the critical issue, not the particular mix of conjoint, or individual, or group participation.

Small children may not contribute to the thinking-through process, though this is not impossible in some instances. Their behavior in some sessions, however, can reveal emotional currents or relationship sequences that might not otherwise be noticed. The participation of older children may be revealing, if not crucial, even if they appear at first glance to be detached or may even be living elsewhere. Divorced members have sometimes been involved, even when the fact of divorce would suggest their omission (Leader, 1973). Involved members of the extended family also can be helpful participants. The definition of family is flexible enough to include relevant persons in the family network (Speck and Attneave, 1971), whether they are related by blood, marriage, presence in the home, or social relation to family members.

The emphasis is on the potential contribution of the family member to problem solution, as well as on the gain the family member may experience by participation. Family members often interpret the worker's efforts to involve them in treatment as blaming them for the problem. That is never the intent. While it may often be true that certain members have helped create the problem, there is no advantage to the establishment of blame or causation, and no efforts are expended in this direction. However, if causation is defined as an interactional sequence, it may usefully be understood. All members participate in that process, but this is not the same as ascribing blame.

On all of these issues we approach the position of M-type family therapists as delineated in the 1970 report by the Committee on the Family. In their view, family members may be involved in therapy both individually and in groups. Z-type therapists, in contrast, would meet with the family only as a group, eschewing separate individual interviews. For example, John Bell (1963), a Z-type therapist, says:

> I am absolutely firm about my unwillingness to meet with a part of the family privately. I make it a rule that all relations between me and the family members must be in the group and known to all of them. Being alerted to the deviousness of their efforts to break this rule, I am prepared to affirm and reaffirm my position without apology as the need may arise. This is immeasurably reassuring to the group and protects its solidarity (p. 6).

We agree with Bell that the worker's relationship with all members in the group must be known to all. Continuing secrets and alliances with any member of the family must be avoided.

Workers also need to be clear with family members in advance of separate sessions that for long-term resolution issues will eventually have to be introduced in a conjoint session with involved family members. However, family members may be assisted in separate individual or group sessions to explore particularly painful and sensitive issues, and they can be helped to find ways to bring them up and work them through with the significant other family members. In some instances destructive emotions may be drained and constructive ways of relating identified. There is no doubt that individual family members may seek a devious alliance with the worker, but the worker's awareness of this possibility avoids the permanent creation of such an alliance. It does not seem necessary, in avoiding alliances, to insist on conjoint sessions at all times.

A-type therapists, unlike those who hold Bell's position or ours, maintain a primary focus on the individual. If they see family members, such sessions generally are separate from sessions with the identified patient.

Advantages of Conjoint Sessions

There are advantages to conjoint sessions, some of which we mention here. Others will be discussed in subsequent chapters. One advantage is that they enhance the worker's diagnostic understanding of the family's operations. Given the worker's theoretical position that the family operates as a system, certain observations about the nature of relationships may be more likely in conjoint sessions. We concur with Sherman (1965) that interactional processes "are very involved and not immediately apparent under the best of conditions. . . . They are more likely to be detected when . . . the family members are observed and experienced when physically assembled together" (p. 44). Workers in conjoint sessions may be able to observe interactional sequences, often repetitive ones, between family members of which the members themselves are unaware and which they do not observe and would not be able to report. In conjoint sessions they can see more readily how interactional processes facilitate or disrupt the problem-solving task of the family.

Some workers (for example, Moynihan, 1974) advocate the use of home visits as a means of observing whole-family interaction, as well as a way of engaging family members in the treatment process. The participation of family members other than the identified problem person minimizes individual isolation (Binder, 1971), provides support (Gallant, Rich, Bey, and Terranova, 1970), and permits continued communication (Preston, 1960). Conjoint sessions also provide a greater degree of objectivity to workers who too readily or continuously get ensnared into taking sides, and they minimize the distortion of information which frequently takes place in individual interviews. A similar advantage accrues to family members who may be distrustful of both therapist and other family members. Exchanges that take place in the presence of all can reduce the fears of suspicious members that alliances and plans are being made without them.

Conjoint sessions are especially useful where problematic communication interferes with problem solving. A variety of communication problems occur. Communication sequences are filled with frequent interruptions, changes of topic, and simultaneous talking (Minuchin, et al., 1967). They may manifest incongruencies between the verbal message and the accompanying body language or confusion between the content and command aspects of the message (Satir, 1967; Watzlawick, Beavin, and Jackson, 1967). Wynne (1971) refers to these processes as "bizarre, disjointed, fragmented," reflective of "collective cognitive chaos and erratic distancing" (p. 104). Conjoint sessions allow not only for observation of such sequences, which likely would not otherwise be observable and reported by family members, but also for efforts to interrupt and change them as they occur.

Another communication failure is the lack of sharing of perceptions and information. Family members often hold differing and distorted images of themselves and of each other. Family events are often perceived differently by different members, and often these images and perceptions have not been shared. Conjoint sessions hold the possibility for sharing positive images and feelings along with negative ones, and members may find support along with the opposition they frequently experience. The exchange of perceptions of events can lead to new definitions and to changes in interpersonal behavior. With the worker's assistance, conjoint sessions can provide a sense of safety and can help reticent members express themselves to others when they have not been able to do so on their own. These sessions can also enable members to confront differences which have been denied or deemed unresolvable.

The net effect of such disordered communication processes is serious interference with the family's problem-solving ability. When problems are presented and responded to by distraction, opposition, silence, and distancing, they are never solved. Individual and family goals are not achieved. Tasks are not completed. The use of conjoint sessions enables the family to focus on the problem and to pursue meaningful verbal exchanges until the issues can be effectively addressed, to the satisfaction of all members.

Disadvantages of Conjoint Sessions

There are, nevertheless, some situations in which conjoint sessions are less useful, if not contraindicated. If certain requisites are not present, family members will not participate or may sabotage the sessions. One such requisite is investment in or identification with the family group. Members who value the family's togetherness, cohesiveness, and unity are more likely to participate. In many families this sense of togetherness may have been lost in the tensions created by present or past problems, though it may be recoverable.

The conviction that achievement of personal goals is possible in the family situation is also necessary to the success of conjoint sessions. Family and individual goals are not necessarily incompatible, though they may be in some families, or some members may experience them in that way. The worker's efforts to help the family redefine the problem may help members see that individual and family goals can both be achieved. In the absence of such problem redefinition, family members will refuse to participate, be indifferent, or persist in expressions of hostility and blame. Inability to desist from blaming contraindicates the continuation of conjoint sessions, though the worker will not know until conjoint sessions have been tried whether this is the case.

In some situations the involvement of all family members in treatment may not necessarily be contraindicated, but it may be unnecessary. All members of the family may not be involved in the problem as it is defined at a particular point in time. In different phases of contact, issues between spouses, between a parent and a child, or between siblings may have priority. The way the issue is defined determines who should be involved at any given time.

Family members must be able to agree on the definition of the problem on which they should work. Often family members point to another member as the problem. They are unable to see that family member as reacting to their own behavior, sometimes denying that their own behavior even affects the other. When family members can agree that the behavior affects all of them, that they don't get along very well with one another, they may become willing to address the common problem affecting them all. Some members may be more centrally affected and more willing to participate than others. The participation of all members in conjoint sessions may be necessary to pinpoint or provide a focus on problems, but their continued participation may not be required.

In summary, there seem to be no presenting problems for which conjoint sessions could not be used at some time. The dangers of causing the identified problem person to decompensate, or act out, or the likelihood of general family disruption do not appear to be great. In some instances the continued or sole use of conjoint sessions may be unproductive and therefore contraindicated. Rosenblatt (1975), in his analysis of the Bunkers in "All in the Family," describes the type of family that is not likely to be responsive to conjoint treatment sessions (nor perhaps to any other means of intervention in the family):

> We knew from the outset that the four main characters would always be impervious to change, that in their particular comedy of humors Edith would shuttle between Bewilderment and Right Instinct, and the children would play Young Generation forever, permanently settled into lip-service liberalism and the latest freedom vernacular, their every reaction more predictable than Archie assaults. On the surface, Archie's humor seems more variable. At times he appears as Hate, Stubbornness, Selfishness or Cowardice, but all of these group under the presiding humor of Death itself, which governs every form of immovability, in Archie and in his kin. . . . The Bunkers . . . do not learn from past mistakes. They repeat old jokes and epithets. None seems to have much of a memory for former events which might guide their present decisions. . . . By blocking out the past, of course, they block out the future. (p. 31).

Scherz (1962) and Wynne (1971) seem to concur that families which persist, in spite of the worker's efforts, in such fixed role-taking and inability to respond to the inputs of those about them would not be likely candidates for conjoint family sessions.

ENGAGING THE FAMILY IN TREATMENT

The social worker's desire to include a number of family members in the diagnostic process, if not in treatment, influences the procedures used for the first contact. Certain actions at this time are facilitative and may be undertaken for the purpose of engaging needed members in the problem-solving process.

The process of engaging a family in treatment is both similar to and different from beginning individual or other group treatment. Perlman (1957) appropriately notes that an applicant for service in a social work agency is not yet a client, and the task of the worker in the initial phase of contact is "to engage this client with his problem and his will to do something about it in a working relationship with this agency, its intentions and special means of helpfulness" (p. 113). The person who initiates agency contact may be certain only about the need for help but not about the kind of help needed, or may have a specific kind of help in mind which is different from what the agency and the worker have to offer. Negotiation is needed to clarify how expectations of the applicant are or are not congruent with those of the worker or the agency. In case of the family there are, additionally, differences between family members about what is needed and sought. There are differing reactions to what is made available by the worker and the agency. Before family members willingly engage themselves in a treatment process, negotiations among themselves and with the worker as to the purposes, goals, means of treatment, and the nature of their participation are needed to establish a basis for treatment work.

Perlman (1968) conceptualizes the task of the worker as that of enabling family members to undertake the role of a client. Strean (1974) notes that clients are simultaneously attempting to place workers in a role that reciprocates with their idea of their own role in the treatment process. This is immensely complicated in family work because each family member is attempting to place the worker in a role particularly advantageous to self, a position that may not be at all desirable to another family member. The worker is immediately sought as an ally by various individuals or coalitions of individuals in the family.

Elements of Resistance to Treatment

There are numerous obstacles in the path of engaging family members in treatment. One is the view held by family representatives that one of the members is the problem—not the family as a whole. It is a difficult obstacle to remove if the family has been encouraged in this view by the referring person. Whether such referral sources are inside one's own agency as in the case of a multidisciplinary agency, or are representatives of other agencies, family-oriented workers should educate referring workers to a family systems view of presenting problems. Such a view will put them in a better position to help families accept referrals. The worker also needs to take steps to gain acceptance of the need for family participation by the family member who is the contact initiator.

A second kind of obstacle to family participation in treatment is the view held by many referred families that no problem exists. They contact the family-oriented worker under compulsion from a school, a probation officer, or an employer. They profess no awareness of the reasons for referral, or they see only that others are creating problems for them. They do not know why the school sent them, or why the employer is upset with them. The individual identified as the problem may be willing to keep a proffered appointment to comply with the referring person, but only for that reason. He sees no need for the family to be involved. Or the family may agree to have the identified person come, but sees no need for their participation. The worker, however, may readily sense the need for treatment of the problem and sees the benefits of involvement of the family in treatment.

Families obviously have the right to refuse treatment and to take whatever consequences may come with their refusal. Our concern is to enable the family to establish and maintain contact with helping persons long enough for them to know what it is they are refusing and what the potential gain for them individually and collectively might be. They may or may not be aware of the consequences of refusal for their relationships with referral sources or other community systems.

Work with a family may begin under coercive circumstances. In some situations the agency or the workers may have the authority to force family members into treatment. Such use of authority may be useful in opening up other possibilities for the family or in considering the consequences of no effort to change. Procedures used by the worker in the initial phases of contact may enable the family to move from participation under a sense of coercion to voluntary participation, with an expectancy of personal and family gain. (Other aspects of the use of authority are touched on in Chapters 5 and 7.)

Because so many families known to social workers are of this type, we will devote considerable space to an explication of procedures that help in moving the family into the role of client. The procedures are directed not only at such scapegoating or denying families; they are useful with all types of families. The method described is the process of engagement by means of conjoint interviews. Other beginnings may be made with families, but the conjoint session has special value in the assessment of family functioning, and special usefulness in enabling all family members to see their parts in the family problem-solving process.

The Family Encounters the Worker

The therapeutic situation itself evokes certain responses by virtue of the fact that another person is added to the system. Family members calculate how to adjust their responses to account for the new person in the midst. Each family member has his or her own preferences about what to do and what is needed to cope with the problem. Since the conflicts about possible actions have not been resolved within the family process, there is a natural tendency to seek the support of the worker for one's own position, along with depreciation of the views of others.

These efforts are understandable both in relation to the need of each member to preserve individual integrity and esteem and in relation to the level of caring and trust among family members. There is the expectation that others will not appreciate one's own needs and therefore will not take them into account. There is the expectation that other members will take advantage of expressions of weakness and error. Efforts to blame and demand change in others are a defense arising out of this view of others. The exercise of these actions by family members is accompanied by efforts, observable in the family group interview, to enlist the support of other family members.

As these efforts become manifest to the worker, they are also interpretable as efforts to seek the worker as an ally, to strengthen one's own position vis-à-vis other family members. This is revealed with dramatic clarity in some situations when, in separate interviews, individual members are able to be less defensive and accept more responsibility for family problems than they can in conjoint sessions.

The worker, in response, attempts to establish a caring, understanding relationship with the family members and to value the contributions of each of them. These attempts serve to resist the family pressures to take sides. Family members are forced to take this resistance into account. Failure to take individual responsibility for action is gradually, more or less directly, confronted. Family members may resist the worker's resistance to their usual routines by intensifying their previous efforts; new responses may be found and learned to take the place of the anger and blame.

Thus, while the behaviors that family members display during their contact with the worker are manifestations of familiar family routines, they are not fully interpretable in this light. They also should be understood as responsive to the worker's entry into the family system. It is important for the worker to become a part of the family system, while at the same time not becoming entangled in its usual routines. The family must be helped to accept the worker's entry into the system and to be responsive to the worker's inputs demanding change.

The Worker's Role with the Family

It has been said of family work that the social worker is in charge of the treatment, but the family members are in charge of their lives. The worker's task in treatment, especially in beginning treatment, is to provide the family with a structure that enables problem solving to take place. The worker actively takes charge of the procedures at this beginning stage. He or she has certain steps in mind for the session and asks the family to cooperate. Though the family may appear to have the initiative in the interview, this may be because the worker has asked the members to struggle with a problem in order to see how they go about solving problems. If problem solving does not succeed, the worker interrupts, either to facilitate or move on to other tasks. (While it is conceivable that a family's interaction may not be interruptable, the worker usually has means of gaining the family's attention and cooperation.) The degree to which the worker is able to establish control over the process in the session is a measure of the worker's skill. It is also a measure of the family's ability to gain from participation in treatment, and it thus provides diagnostic information about the family's workability and flexibility.

The diagnostic and treatment efforts should help the family members take charge of their lives. In the sessions the worker requires them to talk about their concerns to the worker and to each other. While it is expected that talking can create new understanding and awareness and can generate ideas about what to do, awareness and understanding are only part of the help available. The worker's requirement that family members engage in different kinds of action in the conjoint sessions vis-à-vis each other sets up new ways of relating that are more productive in problem solving than were their old ways. We expect the family to see the usefulness of the new patterns, learn them, and appropriate them for regular use. But family members are free to accept and make use of, or reject, what they learn in the sessions about themselves, each other, and their interactions with each other.

The worker obviously is concerned about how family members run their lives and may at times offer specific suggestions or directions about what to do. In some institutional settings the worker may even be in a position to tell the family members how to manage their lives outside the sessions and may have some expectation that they will follow the suggestions. It may even be useful to propose courses of action in order to solve a problem or prevent the occurrence of one. The worker's principal task, however, is to structure treatment sessions so that constructive decision making about life issues is possible for the family. While it is important to solve a problem, the worker's goal is not necessarily to solve it for the family, but to make it possible for them to solve it. The beginning phase addresses both aspects. The decision about what to do is the family's.

OPENING PROCEDURES

The first goal of the initial contact is to acquire a firm understanding of the nature of the problem presented by the family and of the workings of the family system that serve to perpetuate the problem or prevent its solution—a picture of how the family is stuck. A second and equally important goal is to gain the family's agreement to participate in a problem-solving process, since the members do not necessarily come with the readiness to do so. A third goal is to set procedures for change in motion. Family members should be able to leave with beginning confidence that they have been understood, that something new is being offered, and that something positive can happen as a result of agency contact.

These goals are interrelated. As the worker acquires understanding, the worker's way of questioning, responding to, and understanding the family's situation provides a different frame of reference for the family. The new information, the new way of looking at things, and the steps that the worker asks family members to take in the initial sessions are themselves the beginnings of change.

Steps or phases in the process of engaging the family in treatment have been identified by both Haley (1976) and Solomon (1977). While there are differences between their approaches, both have elements that we use and have incorporated in our formulation of a procedure to be followed by the social worker in initiating contact for family treatment.[1] As we have noted, these stages are similar to but more complex than the engagement and contracting efforts required in individual treatment.

The steps we outline are for an initial conjoint session, which includes as many family members as seem necessary to problem solution. Most family treatment begins through contact with one family member. The worker takes a position at first contact that the family needs to be involved. Starting with one person and waiting until later to insist on family participation results in lost time and requires a second start. In the initial contact, whether in person or on the telephone, the worker seeks to learn who the family members are. There is enough exploration of the problem to give the worker some sense of agency appropriateness and family relatedness. But the exploration is brief for two reasons. The problem cannot be adequately understood from one person's reporting, and the image of an alliance between the initiator and the worker needs to be particularly avoided in this phase.

Attention therefore shifts rather quickly to the need to engage both the initiator of the contact and other family members in the treatment process. The caller is requested to ask other family members to come and to bring them along to an initial session. The value of the information they can provide and of the suggestions they might offer is emphasized. Family members are frequently responsive to this emphasis on the importance of their contributions to problem solving. If they are not responsive, the worker's efforts must focus on the resistance, rather than on the problem presented by the family. If the problem presenter in the initial contact seems resistant, the resistance should be explored. If the problem presenter attributes resist-

---

[1]For very contrasting ways of beginning treatment, see Satir (1967) and Bowen (1971). Though their treatment methods differ greatly, they both suggest that treatment begin by gaining a historical perspective on the family's development and its problems. Their procedures may or may not require attendance of all family members.

ance to other family members, their anticipated reasons and the presenter's intended means for handling their responses can be explored.

If the presenter's means for handling the resistance of other family members seem inadequate, alternative responses may be suggested. The suggestions are, in effect, new inputs into the family system. If the suggestions are adopted, both the behavior of the initial problem presenter and family processes are thereby altered. Treatment of the family has begun. If the resistance is not strong, family members may recognize that each family member's view of the problem is important if it is to be fully understood, and they may respond to the request that all family members participate at least in the initial exploratory session.[2]

Stage 1: Relieving Initial Anxiety

Once the social worker has succeeded in arranging an in-person meeting with the needed family members, his or her first task in the initial session is to relate to each family member's feelings about having to be there. Family members may have arrived at the appointment with different understandings of what is to take place and what is expected of them. They may be fearful of revealing secrets or expect undesirable changes to be demanded. They may fear blame, punishment, removal from the home, or shock treatment. They may expect helpers to take sides against them.

The worker's overall objective (as in individual treatment) is to establish a safe, nonthreatening relationship with all persons present. The worker inquires about conversations the family members may have had with each other about the appointment, how it has been explained to them, and how they felt about what they had been told prior to coming. This procedure has both communicative and metacommunicative value. On the communicative level it elicits information regarding their anxieties about meeting the worker, airing family problems, asking for help, and revealing themselves to other family members. It provides data about the way family members view both the relationship with the worker and relationships within the family. Family members may have communicated little or much about coming. Clear communication may have gone to some members but not to others. They may feel free to speak in the session or wait for cues from

---

[2]The first example in Chapter 12 illustrates the use of this approach in an in-person walk-in interview.

others. The procedure's metacommunicative value to the family is that it conveys the worker's intention to regard each person's view as important and permits it to be heard and valued. The individuality and separateness of family members is emphasized, while their value to the problem-solving effort is affirmed. The procedure allows for each family member to be heard by other family members. If family members do not spontaneously comment, the worker may ask them if they are aware of each other's point of view or solicit comments on what has been said.

Stage 2: Eliciting Problem Definitions—Questioning that Confuses

After the family members' anxieties about the interview have been reduced, the social worker can proceed to elicit from each one a statement about the problem or problems that have brought the family to the session. There will likely be differences in statements of the problem. For some families this may be the first time that different views have been expressed and heard. The worker's presence may create a tolerance for these differences that was not present in the family's own efforts to deal with the problem. The extent of the members' ability to wait for one another's expressions will offer the worker some beginning cues as to the family's ability to listen and to learn. If they are able to convey appreciation for having heard something from others that they have not heard before, the worker will have an even greater sense of their treatability.

This is not often the case, however. Frequently family members single out one of their number as "the problem." The worker gets the clear impression that the identified person is blamed and isolated and finds little support in the family. The worker may sense little tolerance for the position that the views of each family member are important where the identified problem person is concerned. Such rigidity offers little to support the view that the family can change in order to solve the problem. At this stage the worker primarily is listening and thinking. Only limited efforts are directed at expanding expressions of feelings or changing feelings or problem definition. The important objective at this time is to hear from everyone.

Family members will not always sit patiently to hear what other members have to say. They experience difficulty in remaining in a listener status. There are likely to be interruptions and, if the first speaker does not stop, simultaneous talking. In this event the worker does need to become active to avoid repetition in the session of what the family ordinarily experiences at home. The stage is set for problem solving by disallowing interruptions. At the same time each participant is assured that his or her point of view will be heard. Strenuous efforts by the worker may be needed along these lines in some families. Minuchin, Montalvo, Guerney, Rosman, and Schumer (1967) found it necessary in their experience with severely disorganized families to remove some family members to a position behind a one-way glass when persistent interruptions revealed their inability to listen to others. Even at this beginning stage, the worker's efforts to regulate the conversation may afford the family an experience that they have not had before, and this may enable them to feel that the worker and treatment have something to offer them.

There may also be a reaction to the interviewing situation which is quite the opposite of interruptions and simultaneous talking. Some family members may be extremely reticent to say anything, much less express an opinion, point of view, or difference. The worker will be aware of halting speech, looking down, and looking to other family members for cues, or avoiding involvement. Such reticence can be as much of an obstacle to problem solving as overactivity. The worker may attempt to draw the individual out during this initial phase of the interview by asking for elaboration or may comment on how the situation makes for difficulty in talking, thereby offering encouragement. It may be useful to ask whether other family members can enable the reticent person to speak. These efforts to gain the reticent member's participation become particularly important in the case of the family member whose contributions have not been valued by others. In response to the worker's attitude, other family members may begin to respond differently to the reticent member. The reticent behavior gives diagnostic information about patterns of power, deference, and decision making in the family.

While a prime purpose in this initial contact is achievement of diagnostic understanding, the efforts to elicit information from all members represent a change for family members. For many families this is a requirement that they respond differently to each other. Insofar as they can respond to and benefit from this requirement, treatment has begun for them.

Having said that at this stage the worker's effort is focused on developing understanding of each family member's definition of the problem, we must step back a bit to expand our concept of the worker's role. We intend for the worker's activity to be even more complex than we have just portrayed it. The purpose of this more complex behavior is to gain further understanding of how the family system works in relation to the presenting problem. To this end the worker will ask questions of family members to develop information that will tell whether his or her hunches are right about what is wrong in the family. These hunches may be based on conceptions of constructive communication processes, as was evident to some degree in the preceding discussion. Or they may be based on conceptions of needed family structure, of appropriate modes of handling affect and feeling, of likely causal sequences or circular causality.

We have noted thus far that each member brings to the worker his or her definition of the problem. We have also noted that each family member adapts not only to the problem, but to every other member's adaptation to the problem. Thus, the worker engages in an approach to questioning that is directed by hypotheses about why the family is working the way it is and which assumes and reveals the circular responsiveness of family members to each other. Mother may just have given a description of Henry's behavior. Father may be asked for interpretation of the same behavior and a report of what Mother did in response to it. Judy or Mother may be asked what Father did when Mother responded the way she did. And Mother and/or Henry may be asked what Judy was doing in the meantime. Henry may be asked what prompted him to engage in the behavior in the first place. Consequently it may be revealed that Henry smashed his toys on the floor when Mother was criticizing Father, thereby interrupting the criticism, and that when Mother scolded Henry for being rough with his toys, Father moved to protect him from the scolding. Judy may tell that Father usually gets more angry at Henry when Mother is not around, and Henry reveals that Judy tattles on him to Mother. Questions about context may reveal that Mother's strictness and scolding of Henry has increased in recent weeks and that this is temporally associated with both the death of Mother's sister and Father's taking on a part-time job to bolster family income.

Such new information confirms or disconfirms the worker's hunches about what is wrong and forms a basis for decision about what lines of questioning may still be needed. Even so, both the questions and the answers may produce confusion for a family which brought the view that Henry's behavior was simple obstinacy or an attention-seeking device, undermining their original definition of the problem and providing a new basis for thinking about it.

Our central point at this stage is neither to criticize the family nor to produce change,[3] but to develop a broad understanding on which treatment planning can be based. However, both teaching by the worker and implicit learning by the family occur through this mode of questioning, providing new information and new image which offer some beginning basis for change.

Up to this point in the initial contact procedure, the role we have defined for the worker requires an exploratory, investigative stance. It minimizes commentary on family operations but does require the worker to regulate relations between the worker and family members and among family members as they participate in the interview. The worker values each member's contribution and is thereby supportive of each, but he or she also sets expectations for participation. The pairing of support and participation becomes particularly evident in the next stage of the session, in which there is an effort to define the family problem.

Stage 3: Working Toward Problem Consensus

Social workers often see the problem differently from the way the family does, but they still need to start with the family's definition of the problem. The worker sees the problem presented by the family as evidence of failure of problem-solving processes and thus as a symptom of the problem, while the family sees it as the problem. In the procedure we have outlined, the worker's efforts are directed both to solving the problem and to increasing family problem-solving capacity.[4] The following example will illustrate what we mean.

The problem is presented by parents who are concerned with altering the behavior of a child. In such a case the worker can operate on the premise,

---

[3]For a similar view, see Selvini, Boscolo, Cecchin, and Prata (1980).

[4]Several recent publications discuss work with difficult-to-involve families which emphasize a similar point of view. Chilman (1966) emphasizes this dual approach with very poor families. Larson and Gilbertson (1977) accept parental definitions that the child is the problem but train the parents in a new child-management approach, thus changing their child-management behavior (see also Larson and Talley, 1977). Oxley (1977) describes a residential program for latency-age boys in which parents are required to participate as a condition of acceptance of the boys in the residential program. For some parents this assured only their bodily presence, but many became less resistive and, during a follow-up study, indicated they had benefited from treatment. Both programs required family participation in problem solving, while accepting initially the family's definition of where change needed to occur.

likely to be shared by the parents, that the parents have both the prerogative and the responsibility to regulate the behavior of the child. The worker wants to support them in this and to help them with it. A dual purpose is suggested: The first need is to correct the child's behavior, and the second need is to build the parents' capacity to correct the presenting problem and others that may occur. The family's problem-solving mechanisms have not been working successfully in relation to the presenting problem. Since the family is not asking for help with their problem-solving routines, but only for help in correcting this problem, the effort to change problem-solving routines must be focused on these routines as they apply to the presenting problem.

This should lead the worker to inquire what kinds of efforts have been made by the parents to correct the problem, in order to understand what has not worked and the reasons for the lack of success. Throughout the discussion the parents can be credited for their continuing involvement with their child as a manifestation of their concern for the child's welfare. They can also be credited for not giving up on their child and for their wish to be successful as parents in enabling their child to perform well and to succeed in life. The worker's accreditation of the parent's concern and caring may be something the child has not heard before through all the parents' commands, controls, accusations, blame, and punishment. Such new awareness may make it possible for the child to manifest a wish to have a good relationship with the parents, even if there is not always a wish to please them. Both the parents' and the child's feelings about what has been happening may be aired.

Along with this accreditation of good intentions and recognition of continuing involvement and concern, it becomes obvious that the techniques and strategies used by the parents have not been successful in regulating behavior, as evidenced in the discussion of what has been tried. Having supported the parents' wish to succeed with their child, the worker may now be in a position to suggest that new strategies are needed. If the parents can accept this, a basis for work with the parents has been established.

Of course, the effort of the worker to establish an alliance with the parents may produce a negative reaction in the child. A positive relationship with all family members must apply to the child as well as the parents. The worker will relate both to the child's feelings about being present and to her or his definition of the problem. While feelings of anger and blame are likely to be expressed, the worker may also hear the child's wish for approval and understanding from the parents and the desire for a positive relationship with them. If, by the worker's focus on the positive wish instead of the blame, the parents are able to hear something new from their child, a change in family feeling may be begun. At a minimum, the child may experience enough of the worker's support and concern to enable him to consent to the helping relationship.

In this situation the parents and the identified problem child may be the central actors, but, using the circular questioning method detailed for Stage 2, the worker also solicits views and reactions from others. The worker conveys an interest in what each has to say as a member of the family, valuing their presence and their contributions. Their responses may emphasize support for or blame of parents or their sibling. The worker attempts to understand how they have related themselves to the problem or how they have been affected by it—by becoming involved in trying to solve it or by withdrawal—and how they see themselves and other family members relating to it now.

Acceptance of the problem focus defined by the family at the outset appears necessary to the family's willingness to participate in treatment. At the same time, the requirement that the family participate emphasizes the family role in finding a solution to the problem. Without the latter requirement we would expect no change in family organization and a continuation of the problem or problematic behavior. Oxley (1977) noted that during the treatment of some nonvoluntary families, members other than the identified patient began to focus on their own problems as their comfort in treatment and their self-esteem increased. We see this as a healthy shift from the initial problem focus, an increase in the sense of individuality and separateness of the members, which is necessary to a positive sense of togetherness and solidarity.

In the procedure we have described, the worker is supportive of all family members, even those in apparent opposition to each other. The means the worker uses to provide the support are based on recognition of the need of family members for positive relationships. Communications which drive them apart are relabeled as caring, concern for the well-being of others, and a wish for connectedness. We do not see this relabeling as deception or trickery. It is an effort to identify positive aspects of family relationships. The family members' continuing engagement with one another is seen as an expression of their meaning and importance to one another, however negatively such feelings have been verbalized. Expressions of hostility and blame are common in many families and seem easier than expressions of caring and concern, which paradoxically seem more threatening. They entail a risk of rejection which negative feelings do not. Satir (1967) suggests that low self-esteem lies behind the hesitance to risk the expression of positive feeling. Worker efforts to relabel and thereby promote a positive relationship with the worker and among family members may not have an immediately successful effect. They bear repetition, however; along with other efforts, they will have a cumulative, positive effect.

Stage 4: Focus on Interactional Mechanisms

The fourth stage in the social worker's efforts to engage the family furthers the worker's diagnostic effort. The worker will have gained in understanding how the family works to cope with its problems from the previous stages. The effort at this stage is more specifically directed at understanding the family's ways of dealing with the presenting problem. This stage can be approached in several ways.

Members' Response to Worker's Questions. One approach is for the worker to inquire of family members how they have responded to the problem, how it has affected them, and what they have tried to do about it. Some members will have been more affected, others less so. Less affected members may have remained uninvolved and may show little feeling or reaction. Others, who are more involved, may have attempted to remain aloof but now are willing to manifest their reactions and suggestions. Still others may blame, depreciate, or get angry or aggressive. Some may have attempted to talk it over without productive results. Patterns of involvement and withdrawal, of support and opposition are evident in these differing responses. The worker may comment on the responses to emphasize that each family member does have some connection to the problem, even if he or she has tried to ignore it. This base of connectedness to the problem is the primary incentive for participation in problem solution.

The worker-imposed requirement that each family member hear what the others have to say allows for new information—other members' ideas about a solution—to be shared for the benefit of all. Members who may have already heard other members' ideas for solution can become more conscious of differing ideas about what to do and the reactions of others to their own ideas. They can consider what seems to have helped or hindered solutions and recognize the need for negotiation of these differences. The worker specifically draws such reactions and differences to their attention and asks who in the family does what in the face of differences about how to cope and how each responds to the other's response. Awareness of the difficulty in dealing with differences may ultimately be the basis of agreement to participate in treatment. The wish to do something about how they get along with each other may serve as a common problem definition, a rallying point.

In such a talking approach to problem solving, the worker elicits a response from all present family members, requiring others to listen while one member talks and assuring that each one's turn to talk will come. In some families this regulation of communication may require considerable effort on the part of the worker.

Family Discussion. An alternative approach is to ask the family members to talk with one another about how to solve the problem, while the worker observes what happens when they do. Though the worker may assume that there will be a replay of family operations similar to their usual ones at home, this assumption should be validated. Frequently family members will confirm that this is the usual routine and express dissatisfaction with the process. Often they will report restraint in their behavior due to the presence of the worker, thus confirming the systems theory assumption that the entry of a new member alters the operation of the system. That may be a positive sign about the treatability of the family, but it is not to be assumed that the restraint will necessarily continue in subsequent sessions.

Whether or not family members have been restrained in this procedure, the worker will have acquired some knowledge of the family's mechanisms for problem solving and an awareness of operations that frustrate its problem-solving work. The most observable difficulties are in communications. Communications may be unclear; topics may be changed before issues are resolved, statements interrupted, blame affixed, support offered. Statements may be addressed to nobody in particular, and some individuals may attempt to speak for others. Third parties may enter disputes as peacemakers or allies of one or another member. Various aspects of family relationships, such as levels of respect and caring for others, become evident in this flow of communications. Family solidarity and cohesiveness may be manifest or demonstrably lacking. Each family member also gains a sense, from how others respond to him, of whether he is affirmed, supported, and accepted, and by his own response he conveys to others whether he is affirming and accepting of them, or rejecting and critical.

Communications represent strategies for negotiation and problem solving which have in the past been learned and reaffirmed, and now are apparently in continual use. It is possible that what the worker observes at this point is the simple result of faulty negotiations procedures such as failure to listen intently or respond relevantly, and what is needed is for the family to learn new negotiation procedures. The family can begin to learn from the worker's efforts, beginning with the initial interview, to regulate the conversation.

It may be evident to the worker that family members do not feel very good about each other at this point; negative feelings may be intense with manifestation of undiminished hostility. Struggles for power or control may be revealed, with no one yielding in that struggle, or with one family member accepting a completely one-down position without a struggle. Triads may be tightly locked into position. Verbal and nonverbal communications are evidence that those conditions exist. Changing communication modes or routes may be impossible or may not help. Traces of goodwill and the ability to recall positive feelings are important in the willingness of family members to continue both in treatment and in relationships with one another.

Two-Party Discussing. A third alternative approach for Stage 4 is also diagnostic in effect but has a clearer treatment component. The worker may select a specific issue which has been referred to in the discussion and ask an involved pair of family members to work on it. They are asked to talk to each other to try to solve the problem. Other family members are asked to observe. The worker is in a position to observe what happens between the two parties involved and what the behavior of other family members is.

Both participants usually direct their efforts at getting the other person to see their own point of view. They may both become wider ranging in their arguments, increasingly insistent and intense, or one of them may become insistent and the other withdraw. Both may turn to the worker or to the other members of the family for support when their frustration at gaining the understanding of the other reaches a certain level. The worker may respond to this sense of frustration and hopelessness at being unable to work out their difficulties by helping each participant to become more aware of her or his own feelings of anger and despair and those of others. Noting the strategy that each participant has used in relating to the other and the other's response, the worker may inquire whether they see this description of their interaction as accurate and ask for their estimate of the effectiveness of their actions. In the midst of this awareness of anger and despair, the worker needs to know whether there is also a wish and a hope for change. Some clients may find the possibility of change so inconceivable that they dare not hope for it. The worker's attentiveness to these feelings and accurate description of the participant's interaction conveys understanding and can give rise to hope. Further, the worker's expressions of hopefulness, if warranted, may be useful.

The worker may suggest a brief attempt to continue negotiations between the two participants, with guidance from the worker. Such efforts at guided communication are demonstrations of the treatment procedures and may help the family see that alternate ways of coping hold some hope of correcting the problem it is experiencing. The worker regulates the conversation by requiring (1) that the two participants not interrupt each other, (2) that the other person respond relevantly rather than with a topic change to another issue or a different experience, and (3) that the speakers talk about their own feelings and needs, rather than talking about the other person and what the speaker thinks the other one should be doing.[5]

The emphasis is on the immediate experience in the interview rather than on past events, though past events may be the starting point of the discussion. Thus, A might be talking about feeling understood, or hurt, or lonely, or unsupported by B, not only in relation to an earlier event but in the present discussion of the event. B might respond empathetically or in anger, but focus on the present moment's responses makes the issues more alive and less subject to recall's distortions. The intent is to make it possible for family members to feel that their views and feelings have been heard, an experience they have often not had in their own efforts at problem solving.

Whether the effort succeeds at this point or not, it serves as a demonstration of the kind of work that would take place during treatment. If it does not fully succeed, the worker is clearer about the amount and kinds of effort needed to help. Behind the ineffective negotiation procedures lie the varied needs of the individuals and the reasons that each has for not being able to accept the other's view. They may reflect an effort to maintain integrity and individuality or a struggle for control and power. Such difficult relationship issues will need to be addressed in the treatment.

---

[5]See Kempler (1973), Satir (1967), and Gordon (1970) for development of the use of statements about self rather than other.

While the worker is observing how two family members work on a specific family issue, simultaneous observation of the behaviors of other family members is possible. Other family members may not be able to remain in the observer role; they may become distractors, allies, or peacemakers or otherwise inject themselves into the negotiations. The reasons for such behavior are many and varied. Children may feel threatened by a too tense exchange between parents and act to draw attention away from the argument and onto themselves. A sibling may identify with the feeling of another child generated in the interaction with a parent. A parent may feel strongly about the behavior of the other parent in relation to a child.

However well intended, these behaviors have negative side effects. They inject another relationship into an issue that could, and frequently should have been, resolved by two persons. In effect, the issue is left unresolved rather than resolved. The original disputants are more divided than they were before. The third person becomes occupied in the intervening role and is not free to pursue his or her usual separate activities.

The worker may respond in several ways. The worker may choose to ignore these behaviors at this time, being alert to whether their occurrence is a regular pattern of behavior. The worker may move to block the activity of the third party, indicating that others' observations will be asked for later. Or the worker may comment on the sequence of behaviors among the three family members, inviting discussion of the sequence (not of the problem) by all three. Feelings and reactions of each of the participants to the immediate events then become the focus of the discussion. The worker ascertains whether the family members are aware of the sequence and whether they see it as helpful or not.

Use of any of these three procedures at this stage in the initial contact is likely to be brief, since the social worker is seeking primarily to understand how the family is working and to test quickly whether they can respond to worker intervention. At the same time however, it will be seen that these interventions are useful not only in initial contacts but also in ongoing treatment. Ongoing treatment often proceeds in similar fashion.

Stage 5: Reaching a Treatment Contract

The final stage of the social worker's efforts to engage the family in treatment is achievement of an understanding with the family members about what they want to have changed and what they want from treatment and from the worker. The emphasis shifts from what is wrong to how the family wants things to be, and how the worker can help them get there. The focus is on the effort to define goals and establish a working contract between the social worker and the family about their ongoing work together. Again, the process is similar to but more complex than that required in individual treatment.

The prior stages of the engagement effort have been preparation for the family to approach this one, but considerable work remains to be done. The discrepancies in problem statement now must be resolved into a problem definition to which family members can subscribe as one that they are willing to work on. The shift from what is wrong to how they want things to be moves away from complaining to positive, goal-oriented activity. It is not an easy shift to make. The definition of the kind of help needed from the worker is difficult to achieve, since the family has only the present experience with the worker to go by and consequently knows little about what the worker and agency have to offer. Agreement on the problem definition and how the worker will help are both needed.

In resolving the many issues that arise in contracting with a family about the problems and the goals of treatment, another type of worker activity is required. While previous stages have been worker-directed and structured, they have minimized analytical comment and feedback to the family about the way the worker sees the family working (or not working) together. Worker activity has focused on the process of the family session. In this stage the worker participates with his or her own observations and restatements and focuses on key aspects of the problem.

The worker's effort is directed at achieving a problem definition that is in harmony with the family's needs and wishes. The worker may see a variety of family problems that the family members themselves do not see. He may be aware, for example, that a marital problem exists, and that it interferes with the solution of the problem that the family has presented. The worker may make the connection, but the family may not be able to see this as the problem to be solved. If the presenting problem was a child's behavior, the focus at this stage is not on how the parents can get their marriage together, but on how they *together* can cope with the child's problem. The parents may be able to accept the need to join together to help the child, but they may not see the need to work on the marriage in general. While they may subsequently come to see that work on the marriage is needed in order to help their child, the starting point in treatment is with the problem they see and are willing to try to solve.

The worker's emphasis on what the family would like to accomplish in treatment requires the worker to seek responses from family members about what each wants and is willing to do about the problem. A number of difficulties will be encountered in these responses. One is that goals will be stated in terms of the need for someone else to stop doing something or to be different. Unfortunately, such statements make the definition of the family goal difficult if not impossible. They are statements about expectations of others rather than expectations of self. They concern behavior to be eliminated but not behavior that is to replace what is now occurring. They do not convey an image of what desirable family life would be like. All family members are not likely to find such definitions acceptable. The work of the previous stages of the initial contact should have helped to take the edge off some of these tendencies to blame or scapegoat, but it will not have eliminated them. More work is needed to arrive at acceptable definitions.

Another difficulty is that responses from family members may be in global terms. Either the specifics of change do not become clear, or the proposed changes in the family seem so extensive as to appear unattainable. Demands on others and global expectations reflect the continuing difficulty family members have in defining problems or in communicating their needs in a way that others in the family can accept and agree to. If they had other ways of addressing the tasks that the worker now puts to them, they probably would not need treatment. Specific help is needed.

One means the worker has of helping with these difficulties is the ability to restate or reformulate the problem. The worker may use knowledge of the members and of the group acquired earlier in the session. Knowledge about how members see themselves connected to the problem and about their wish to continue as a group may be used to convert negative statements into positive ones, global statements into more specific objectives. "I want him to stop arguing" or "We are always fighting" may be reformulated to "I wish that we could talk things over." General unhappiness and dissatisfaction may be converted to a wish for family members to "show more appreciation" or to "get along better." In rare instances members may comment about specific things they themselves can do to improve and may show signs of willingness to do them. The worker may offer formulations that express expectations and goals for the family rather than for individuals, or reformulate statements about problems to make them specific rather than global. The general adjustment problem of a family member may be specified in terms such as "planning how things will be when Sally returns home from the hospital," or "what we can do so grandmother won't be so unhappy." Agreement from members to work to solve these problems and achieve these goals is then sought.

Along with the effort to restate goals, the worker draws attention away from individual behavior to focus on the interactive process between members. For example, she or he may offer observations about family interactions which help to clarify for the family the nature of their difficulties. The worker may comment that when members disagree, they become more forceful in their arguments, and the resistance of each stiffens. Nothing changes, and they may therefore wish to consider other means of resolving disagreement. This would be followed by a question about what they wish to do about it. Or the worker may note that when the parents, or any pair of family members, were working on a disagreement, they were distracted by a third member of the family, leaving their disagreement unresolved. This may be proposed as something that could be changed. This attention to the interactive process and the effort to define the problem as one of interpersonal relationships rather than as a problem of the individual serves to reduce defensive behavior and minimize guilt. It should help to free members from resistance to participation in family problem solving.

The worker at this stage also needs to learn what kind of help the family had expected and to define what kind of help he or she has to offer. The worker's means of helping will, in part, have been demonstrated by his behavior in the interview prior to this point, but these means may be very different from what the family wants. There may be a range of expectations of the worker, from removing a member from the home for placement elsewhere; to "straightening out" a member; to getting a member to go to school, or to work, or to a doctor; to refereeing the family arguments; to helping the family find a way to get along or to talk things over. The worker may judge the requests as desirable or undesirable directions in which to move as needed or unneeded, as possible or impossible to fulfill, given the range of his skills or the availability of services in his own or other agencies. A request for placement may be accepted and recommended, or it may be countered with a recommendation of family counseling and an offer of worker involvement in that way. However the family and the service requests are evaluated, the worker's thinking and judgment about both must be conveyed to the family for discussion and decision. The worker needs also to convey his own and his agency's capacity to respond to the requests.

The family's response to the worker's evaluations, suggestions, and offers of help provide further data on which to base judgments about family potential for change and responsiveness to helping efforts. The new information and direction serve to upset the family's usual interchanges. The new inputs may be resisted, in order to maintain the usual balance, or they may be assimilated, in order to promote change.

Whether the family can begin to change or even accept the possibility of change depends on a number of factors, some of which have already been noted. The family's value of family togetherness is one such factor. Even though disaffection and discouragement about the family's situation may be great, there may still be hope that things could be different. Some members, however, may have already lost hope completely, and they cannot be interested in participation in the family. A second factor has to do with the willingness of members to risk. A member's willingness to respond positively to a worker reformulation that says, in effect, "I want you, care about you, wish to be with you," implies a willingness to risk the possibility that other members may not share those desires. Behind this willingness must lie a strong need and perhaps some confidence that other members do care and share the same wishes. Worker sensitivity can sometimes enable a member to claim ownership of such sentiments when this might not under other circumstances be possible.

Another factor affecting members' consent to participate and willingness to change is the fear that the individual will be lost in pursuing the goals of the group, that he or she will be unhappily bound to the family and never be free to leave or to grow as an individual. All the procedures described are intended to convey the worker's support for both individuality and connectedness, and not just for a connectedness that keeps the individual inappropriately bound to the family. If, as a consequence of worker activity, the family indicates a willingness to continue in treatment, it is a sign of their capacity to accept outside contributions to their problem solving, and perhaps also of the worker's skill in conveying helpfulness and trustworthiness.

We have described in some detail a procedure for assessment and engagement of the family at the time of initial contact. The process need not always be lengthy, however. With some families it will be simple and short; with others it may take several hours. If a clear family and worker agreement does not result, the work may have to be carried over into second sessions. Workers may eliminate some stages and still achieve clarity, begin work on a problem, or arrive at a contract with greater efficiency.

SUMMARY

Our concern in this chapter has been to further the understanding of the nature of treatment and the social worker's role in it. Treatment that promotes change in any family member or any set of interactions may be considered family treatment, since it will upset family balance. Conjoint family interviews may be used in treatment but are not synonymous with treatment. A variety of modes of involving family members is possible. Criteria for worker decisions about whom to involve and how to involve them have been suggested.

The worker's task in the initial stages of contact with family members is twofold. The first task is to come to an understanding of the nature of the problem presented by the family and of the nature of the family's difficulty in solving the problem. This assessment effort is concurrent with the worker's second task of engaging family members in the treatment effort. Engagement is complex because different family members may disagree about both definition of the problem and solutions to it, and they may also differ in their willingness to participate in working at solutions. The section on engaging the family has delineated worker activity pertinent to both of these tasks.

While the section on beginning treatment has focused on procedures, we have also considered some of the ways in which the worker's knowledge about family systems is used in assessment and in the worker's contract with the family for further treatment. In our family treatment approach, the worker conceptualizes the presenting problem as a problem of the family system, as one that the family needs to come to terms with rather than a problem of an individual within the family. In this frame of reference, the worker proceeds in a way to help the family think of the problem that way, too. The worker's intent is not to fault the family for the existence of the problem but to indicate that the existence of the problem requires the family to respond and to cope in some way. The worker conveys a willingness to help and to use her or his skills in finding ways of coping, offering hope that constructive solutions can be found which may motivate the family's problem-solving efforts.

REFERENCES

Bell, J. E. 1963. "A Theoretical Position for Family Group Therapy." *Family Process* 2:1-14.

Binder, S. 1971. Zu neueren therapeutischen Ansaetzen bei Alcoholkranken [New Therapeutic Approaches to Alcoholics]. *Psychotherapie und Medzinishes Psychologie* 21:239-47.

Bowen, M. 1971. "Family Therapy and Family Group Therapy." In *Group Psychotherapy*, ed. H. Kaplan and B. Sadock. Baltimore: Williams and Wilkins Co.

Chilman, C. 1966. "Social Work Practice with Very Poor Families." *Welfare in Review* 4:13-21.

Cohen, P. C., and Krause, M. S. 1971. *Casework with the Wives of Alcoholics*. New York: Family Service Association of America.

Committee on the Family. 1970. "Premises about Family Therapy." In *The Field of Family Therapy*. New York: Group for the Advancement of Psychiatry.

Cookerly, J. R. 1974. "The Reduction of Psychopathology as Measured by the MMPI Clinical Scales in Three Forms of Marriage Counseling." *Journal of Marriage and the Family* 36:332-36.

Gallant, D. M., Rich, A., Bey, E., and Terranova, L. 1970. "Group Psychotherapy with Married Couples: A Successful Technique in New Orleans Alcoholism Clinic Patients." *Journal of the Louisiana Medical Society* 122:41-44.

Gordon, T. 1970. *Parent Effectiveness Training*. New York: Peter H. Wyden/Publisher.

Haley, J. 1971. "A Review of the Family Therapy Field." In *Changing Families*, ed. J. Haley. New York: Grune & Stratton.

————. 1976. *Problem Solving Therapy*. San Francisco: Jossey-Bass.

Kempler, W. 1973. *Gestalt Family Therapy*. Hollywood, Calif.: Kempler Institute.

Larson, C., and Gilbertson, D. 1977. "Reducing Family Resistance to Therapy through a Child Management Approach." *Social Casework* 58:621-24.

Larson, C., and Talley, L. 1977. "Family Resistance to Therapy: A Model for Services and Therapist's Roles." *Child Welfare* 56:121-26.

Leader, A. L. 1973. "Family Therapy for Divorced Fathers and Others Out of Home." *Social Casework* 54:13-19.

McDowell, F. K. 1972. "The Pastor's Natural Ally against Alcoholism." *Journal of Pastoral Care* 26:26-32.

Minuchin, S., Montalvo, B., Guerney, B., Rosman, B., and Schuner, F. 1967. *Families of the Slums*. New York; Basic Books.

Moynihan, S. K. 1974. "Home Visits for Family Treatment." *Social Casework* 55:612-17.

Oxley, G. 1977. "Involuntary Clients' Responses to a Treatment Experience." *Social Casework* 58:607-14.

Perlman, H. H. 1957. *Social Casework*. Chicago: University of Chicago Press.

————. 1961. "Family Diagnosis in Cases of Illness and Disability." In Monograph VI, *Family Centered Work in Illness and Disability: A Preventive Approach*. New York: National Association of Social Workers.

————. 1968. *Persona*. Chicago: University of Chicago Press.

Preston, F. B. 1960. "Combined Individual, Joint and Group Therapy in the Treatment of Alcoholism." *Mental Hygiene* 44:522-28.

Rosenblatt, R. 1975. "All in the Family." *The New Republic* 172:36-37.

Satir, V. 1967. *Conjoint Family Therapy*. Palo Alto, Calif.: Science and Behavior Books.

Selvini, M., Boscolo, L., Cecchin, G., and Prata, G. 1980. "Hypothesizing-Circularity-Neutrality: Three Guidelines for the Conductor of the Session." *Family Process* 19(1):3-12.

Scherz, F. 1962. "Multiple Client Interviewing." *Social Casework* 43:120-25.

Sherman, S. N. 1965. "Practice Implications of Psychodynamic and Group Theory in Family Interviewing." In *The Group Approach to Treatment of Family Health Problems*. New York: National Association of Social Workers.

Solomon, M. A. 1977. "The Staging of Family Therapy: An Approach to Developing the Therapeutic Alliance." *Journal of Marriage and Family Counseling* 3:59-66.

Speck, R. V., and Attneave, C. L. 1971. "Social Network Intervention." In *Changing Families*, ed. J. Haley. New York: Grune and Stratton.

Strean, H. 1974. "Role Theory." In *Social Work Treatment*, ed. F. J. Turner. New York: Free Press.

Watzlawick, P., Beavin, J., and Jackson, D. 1967. *Pragmatics of Human Communication*. New York: W. W. Norton.

Wright, L. S. 1976. "Chronic Grief: The Anguish of Being an Exceptional Parent." *The Exceptional Child* 23:106-9.

Wynne, L. 1971. "Some Guidelines for Exploratory Conjoint Family Therapy." In *Changing Families*, p. 104, ed. J. Haley. New York: Grune and Stratton.

CHAPTER 4

Strategies and Goals in Family Treatment

Chapters 1 and 2 conveyed our framework for assessment of family problems. The framework includes understanding various aspects of family structure and process and of the impact of developmental and situational stress on the family. It also provides a basis for defining goals and the means of change—what needs to be improved and how to help the family to make those improvements. Our discussion in Chapter 3 of procedures at the time of initial contact with the family makes reference to a variety of techniques and procedures which not only facilitate worker understanding but can also serve to promote change. The use of these techniques is not limited to initial phases of contact. Our suppositions about the means of facilitating change and the ends to be sought have only been implicit in the preceding discussion. We now seek to be more explicit about them about the means and goals of change.

AN INVESTIGATIVE STANCE

Most theories about treatment emphasize the importance of information gathering during initial phases of contact. Indeed, some theories would seem to convey that information gathering is the only purpose at this phase and that treatment cannot properly begin until information is gathered, filtered, organized, and integrated for full and complete diagnosis. Clearly the worker does need information about the way the family works. The process of gathering the information, the nature of the questions asked, and the kind of data sought are guided by hypotheses about what information is needed to understand the problem and the family's way of dealing with it. These hypotheses are the worker's frame of reference for problem solving, but they are not necessarily made explicit for the family. Information is sought from all family members; each person's view is considered valuable; images of family are elicited from different family members; sequences of member responses to each other become visible out of members' reporting of their behavior; feelings surface which may have been withheld. Information obtained can be about events, behavior, or feelings. It cannot help but alter the system in some way.

From the family members' response to the questioning new information emerges and becomes available to all family members as well as to the worker. The information provides the worker with understanding needed to initiate and promote change. But it is also change for the members of the family (Hoffman, 1981). There is also in the worker's investigative stance an implicit reframing of the family's problem, a new metaphor for their situation, a new way of thinking, of perceiving reality, and of approaching problem solving. The respect the worker shows for each member's views and the information they produce prompt new images of other family members and their contributions. The connections the worker makes between bits of information, the tracing of sequences, and the determination of what is relevant all influence family understanding. Family members now see what others see and understand what others feel. They acquire new images of each other and of events and are prompted to act according to the new images that will in some way be different from previous behavior.

This happens without the worker's explicit expectation for family members to change. At a minimum the new information and worker method may produce confusion or doubt, enough to prompt members' own questioning. It may challenge them to rethink their situation or to alter their behavior. At best they may begin to learn a new approach to problem solving. This is in itself the beginning of change. It is in this sense that assessment and treatment are concurrent. The change will vary in degree from one family situation to the next and in most situations will probably not be sufficient for the family's needs. The model for treatment and the problem-solving process is inherent in the investigative stance and will be repeated and reinforced for their learning throughout the treatment process.

It is important for the worker to retain this investigative stance throughout treatment and not to abandon it after the initial exploration of the family problem. There are several reasons for this. Families are complex organizations in themselves, and ties to systems outside immediate family boundaries are many. Workers need all the information and help they can get from cumulative information, not only about the immediate family, but also about the family's social context, some of which may not be revealed and may even be withheld in initial contacts. It is too easy for workers to come to feel that they know all they need to know in order to help. Continuing an investigative stance minimizes the possibility of forming premature conclusions. It may also serve to promote the family members' own curiousity about their situation.

A further reason for maintaining an investigative stance throughout treatment is that the family members should not come to feel that the worker needs them to change more than they themselves need or want to change. A worker position which pressures for unwanted change arouses unneeded opposition and keeps the family stuck in its unproductive ways. While family and worker both know that their reason for being together is that someone thought that something needs to change, family members and workers likely do not have the same ideas about the necessity of change. In this somewhat paradoxical condition, the worker seeks first to engage family members as allies in the exploratory efforts, hoping that their own discomfort and interest will propel them not only to new understanding of their situation, but prompt them to change on their own initiative.

The worker also does not push specific kinds of change contrary to the family's wishes. He or she investigates what the family members want for themselves from worker and agency and how they want to solve the problems that brought them into treatment. The worker seeks to understand similarities and differences in individual members' views of the problem. Repeated clarification throughout treatment of problem definition and changes sought reinforces the worker's alliance with the family. Where worker and agency definitions of problems and required changes differ from those of the family, these need to be explicated and followed by exploring the possible consequences of their separate views.

EMPHASIS ON HERE AND NOW

Conjoint meetings of family members serve to convey a sense of the here and now of family interaction. We consider it important to be able to observe how family members relate to each other and prefer not to rely on members' reports about how they get along. We assume that what we can observe will give us a fuller view of actual relationships than one member's report of relationships. Though the worker's presence influences, even without trying to, how family members interact, we assume that what we can observe in our presence approximates what happens when we are not present, or will come to reveal critical features of their usual interaction patterns as they grow to feel accepted by the worker. Being there makes it possible for us to comment on the interactions and check out with the family whether what we are seeing is like what goes on at home. They are usually able to tell us, and that offers further understanding about what is wrong and what needs to be done.

Conjoint sessions make it more possible for family members themselves to be made aware of their responses to each other and offer an immediate forum for trying new ways to elicit the responses they want from each other. For example, a family member who has been naming all the things he or she thinks another family member does wrong can come to see that all the criticism is not producing the desired response. This family member may, on the spot, be able to use the worker's suggestion either to speak about himself or herself by talking about the hurt or pain experienced, or to say what he or she needs or wants or to identify positive attributes of the other member. The ability or inability of a family member to use the suggestions become immediately evident to worker and the family as do the responses of other family members. These leave the worker with a clear image of what works and what doesn't, what needs to be worked on, and what else might be tried.

Our focus is first of all on how people treat each other and on the possibilities of their treating each other in a more positive, less dysfunctional manner. We shift to exploring their reasons for treating each other that way only when they prove to be unable to follow worker directives or suggestions for new behavior. Here-and-now exploration in the presence of other family members is in itself enlightening and change producing for other family members, not only for the worker.

THE USES OF HISTORY

Our focus on the here and now does not preclude an interest in family history. In some instances family members seem stuck in their current patterns of interaction, and suggestions, directions, or other worker interventions result in no change. History relevant to current behaviors can be useful in understanding blockages. It is not so much a matter of understanding the evolution of the current state of affairs as understanding the images of roles and patterns of interaction that have been brought to the present from families of origin and seeing how these are being replayed in the current family situation. If husband and wife, for example, are complaining about each other's behavior or telling each other how to behave, it seems useful in some instances for them and the worker to become aware of how their ideas about husbanding and wifing stem from patterns in families of origin, that their families were different in their patterns, that such difference does not mean that either of them is bad, and that perhaps they could now develop some new ideas of their own that fit better with their present situation. Patterns of mothering and fathering can benefit from similar investigation.

It is also useful to understand whether in the past there may have been significant events that have been transitions into states of lesser productive functioning in the family. The most immediate past transition would be the events that prompted the referral or application for treatment. A loss of a job or taking a new one, a death, a move to a new location, an illness, the arrival of a new family member, and all the attendant ramifications of these can often be identified as significant events in shifting family relationships. Often families are not able to identify any such events, but with some persistence on the part of the worker, it may be possible to ascertain that the meanings that family members attach to current events reflect lack of resolution of such events in the past. Viewing current behavior of other family members as threats of separation, may, for example, reflect unresolved grief. A tendency to view other family members as critical even when they are not may be attributed to an experience of loss of self-esteem consequent to a specific event or relationship in the past.

Our principle guiding the acquisition and uses of history is one of selectivity rather than comprehensiveness. History should help to understand the specific interaction, problem, or difficulty being experienced and acted out in the family relationships at a given point in time. Needed and useful history relates little to complete chronology and more specifically to key events and relationships that bear upon the present problem. It does not attempt to answer the question of "who started this" but is focused on the meanings that past events have for present relationships. Such recall may evoke strong feelings about past events that have not been fully resolved, such as lingering grief over losses. Or recall may develop clearer images about old relationships in families of origin that are being reenacted in one's present family. Awareness of such old feelings and images can provide a basis for redirection of family behaviors. And, lest this sound completely like a foray in promoting individual insight, we emphasize the importance of developing this kind of history in the presence of other family members, so that all may gain from the information and expression of feeling that accompanies it, and participate in the reordering of family interaction that is warranted by it.

CHANGING FEELINGS AND CHANGING BEHAVIOR

The debate about whether feelings about other family members have to change before one can change behavior toward them, or whether behavior change can occur without prior feelings change is not an either/or proposition. Both routes can be helpful. In many instances family members may be able to follow worker suggestions by trying new behaviors, given an awareness that present behaviors do not serve them well or, in the absence of such awareness, as an experiment to see how things go. These suggestions may range from a simple new behavior such as saying something differently to a more complex directive about tasks to undertake between sessions. When suggestions are not followed, new tasks may be suggested or it may be useful to explore the feelings that enter into the failure to try the new behavior. Often such feelings have to do with the anticipated responses of other family members. When these feelings are drawn out in the presence of other family members, the reactions and different feelings of others can immediately be noted. When new behaviors are tested, positive responses on the part of other family members can lead to change in feelings and attitude on the part of the members which can in turn stimulate the trying of other new behaviors. Negative responses from other family members are of course possible, in which case worker suggestions to the responding member to try a different response may be the best route. In other situations the alternate route of exploring the reasons for the negative response and the initial actor's response to the negative response of the other would also be useful.

We are clearly focused on here-and-now feelings and are interested neither in unnecessarily stirring old disappointments and resentments nor in the catharsis of accumulated negative affect, particularly not in the presence of other family members. Such discharge of affect serves more to arouse defensiveness, blame, and counter-hostility and only replays in the worker's presence the family's everyday experience. In some instances of intense emotion separate sessions can be useful to drain negative affect and allow the worker to begin to structure a more positive approach to the relationship. A separate session may also enable a less defensive response and provide opportunity for the worker to help the member to act less defensively in subsequent conjoint sessions. In other instances family members may be helped in dealing with negative feelings in conjoint sessions by reframing the feelings in a more positive way or by the use of other procedures which serve to regulate communication. And we are interested in making it possible for family members to express positive feelings about each other because they have often neglected to offer each other such self-affirming messages. These too are new behaviors and can stimulate new responses from other family members.

L'Abate and Frey (1981) argue for an approach to practice similar to ours that includes recognition and expression of emotions in addition to emphases on rationality and behavior change. They say it is in the awareness and expression of hurt, emptiness, loneliness, and pain that one can fully experience separateness and individuality and that this experience allows individuals to come together in a more complete relationship. Recognizing and working through feelings and acquiring a new way of thinking about the situation are both needed emphases in a thoroughgoing model of treatment. We can also affirm along with Bowen (1978) that where everything is so highly emotionally tinged and charged, there needs to be a strong emphasis on rationality. Both emphases are congruent with our approach to treatment.

PROMOTING POSITIVE INTERACTION WITH THE FAMILY'S ENVIRONMENT

Of all professionals who work with families, social workers are probably most aware of the effects of extra-familial forces on the internal functioning of families. It is repeatedly noted that dysfunctional families are under stress from lack of needed social supports and from material, social, or psychological burdens placed upon them by their environment. They may be isolated by lack of meaningful positive connectedness to important external systems such as kin networks, organized groups, social agencies, schools, and places of employment. At worst, external systems can create stress, and at best they often provide no relief, respite, or support. The family's lack of connectedness also leaves them isolated from the standards, guidance, and restraints that society offers and that could provide information and direction for structuring family life. Social workers' efforts to bring the resources of the community to bear upon the family in a constructive way are clearly needed to reduce stress, to provide positive support, and to promote family responsiveness to these outside sources of support and direction. Several examples will illustrate what we mean.

The availability of income, from whatever sources, or lack thereof has consequences for the family's survival as a body, for the esteem of the family in the eyes of the community and of the members themselves, and for the members' esteem for each other. In some instances efforts to insure income maintenance may do more for internal family operations than any other form of intervention. Restoring the breadwinner's role as breadwinner may restore not only his or her self-esteem but enhance capacity to provide the leadership and structure needed for effective functioning as parent and partner. The provision of services that restore health or increase capacity to handle disability may serve similar purposes.

Reconnection to relatives from whom the family has been distanced may open avenues for support that is badly needed for understanding and acceptance, for acquisition of new ideas, or for something as practical as relief from child-care responsibility. Kin networks are sometimes burdensome and controlling and need a social worker's intervention to interdict negative effects or to produce positive ones. Where, for example, the extended family has serious problems for which the present family has had to assume responsibility, such as serious illness of a parent or sibling, and where this has resulted in marital or parent-child discord, assistance in coping with extended family may be what helps most in resolving the marital discord. Or where overly close ties to the family of origin serve to interfere with the integrity of the family group, the worker may need to involve both families in working out a new accommodation.

Religious and ethnic connections can also have profound effects on family functioning, infusing not only the family's values but also the rules by which it operates. An ethnic or religious value that promotes strong paternal control and leadership, for example, can have the effect of overcontrol of spouse or children. A worker's effort to engage a religious leader or trusted friend with the family may do more to mitigate possible negative consequences or promote positive ones than if the worker sought to work only with the family.

In all the connections we have mentioned it is important for the various extra-family systems to provide support for the family to fulfill its functions to its members. Where that support is not forthcoming, worker interventions need to be directed at insuring it. Conversely, the family needs to be open to feedback from the community about its operations and for information and direction relevant to its tasks. In their thinking, workers should seek to enable the family to maintain its separateness and integrity as a unit while at the same time insuring a positive sense of relatedness and connectedness to the community.

In this latter regard we note the special situation of the multi-problem, multi-agency family. Such families are so subject to multiple agency directives and influences that the sense of the family's own directedness is lost. While failure of self-directedness was most probably the initial reason for multi-agency involvement, such families need worker assistance in sorting out multiple demands and taking control of their own destiny.

The means for dealing with the complexity of family-community relationships are many. A telephone call to or an in-person contact with a significant other which suggests contact of a directed kind with a family member may in some instance be useful. In other instances, the inclusion of various significant others in one or more conjoint sessions with the family may be needed. For the multi-agency family an interagency conference is necessary to reduce the contradictory and often overwhelming demands placed on the family. Such meetings may profitably include members of the family as well. These interventions with significant others, though time consuming, are clearly necessary if the family is to be restored to adequate functioning. Worker purpose in these interventions is variously to activate natural helping systems, to minimize negative elements in the family's network of significant others, and to promote understanding of the family's situation and cooperation on its behalf of all elements in its life space.

REGULATING COMMUNICATION

Family communications must aid the process of problem solving rather than hinder it. The problem about communications is not that they do not occur, because "no communication" is not a possibility. The problem is that communications that do occur do not, for a variety of reasons, lead to problem solving. On the content level, verbalizations may not convey a clear understanding of what the person meant to say. Verbalizations may be confounded by dissonant body language. Tone of voice may accentuate difficulties by conveying heavy affect or great insistence on the rightness of what a person is saying and the necessity for all others to agree. Individuals may be interrupted by others before they are finished. They may not be heard because of the simultaneous talking of others. They may be responded to with a topic change as though they were not heard. Some members' points of view never get aired, much less heard and taken into account. Consequently topics are not pursued until they are understood, till differing points of view have been adequately aired, and until plans are made or disagreements have been resolved. And the family remains stuck in its dysfunctional state.

Given such a state of affairs, family relationships deteriorate. Individual members feel disrespected, misunderstood, and alone. They may respond by further withdrawal or greater insistence or heavier affect, escalating the unproductive cycle. Distance between family members may increase, and power struggles or physical conflict may ensue. Caring and investment in relationships is decreased.

The need for new patterns of communications thus becomes evident. Worker activity needs to insure that individual points of view are heard, understood, and responded to relevantly; that family members get the help they need in saying what they intend to say; that they are enabled to say what they themselves need and want and to express positive feelings rather than only airing anger, criticism, and blame. Worker re-regulation in the here and now of dysfunctional communication processes requires active, on-the-spot worker intervention and serves to promote problem solving as well as the development of more positive relationships between family members.

STRENGTHENING FAMILY STRUCTURE

Elements of family structure are observable in the communication processes of the family. Who speaks to whom; who listens to whom; whose ideas are adopted; who gets put down, shut out, or ignored; who seldom or never speaks are aspects of communications that tell of role, status, power, control, affection, and distance regulation in relationships. Communications contribute to the shaping of family structure, and family structure in turn serves to shape the pattern of communications. Other aspects of structure that need worker attention in the helping process are factors of stability and changeability, family hierarchy, family subsystems, and distance regulation.

Changeability. One concern about structure is that it should not be so rigid as to prohibit variability and change. At the same time it should be sufficiently stable, so that members can experience the family as dependable and predictable enough to provide some guidelines by which the individual members can be clear about what roles and behaviors are expected. On the other hand, structure should also not be so changeable as to be chaotic, with no clearly defined roles or rules for behavior, with only vaguely defined subsystems within the family and no sense of leadership and control. For individuals, subsystems, and the family as a whole to function properly, subsystem boundaries, roles for individuals, and rules of the system need to be clearly defined without being permanently fixed, subject to change as the needs and demands upon individual members and the system as a whole change. Achieving clarity about boundaries, roles, and rules in the interest of stability and at the same time enabling the family to allow for needed change is a central task in the treatment process.

Hierarchy and Subsystems. Family systems and individuals function best when the parents provide leadership, direction, and rules for behavior for the children, whether there is one parent or two in the home. Consider the mother who permits her oldest son to intervene repeatedly in correcting the behavior of his younger brother; he becomes an authority to the younger brother and creates a structure that defines the older brother as the disciplinarian and the mother as incompetent in controlling the behavior of her children.

The object of change in this situation is to restore the mother to her rightful place in the family hierarchy, which is the position of control of family operations. To realize this the social worker must find ways to help the mother define her role as it relates to the behavior of both of her sons. For example, she might be helped to tell the older son that she will correct his brother's behavior whenever she thinks it necessary, or direct him to inform her if he observes behavior that should be corrected and she will handle this with his younger brother. As this pattern of behavior is repeated, it will establish a new structure with mother and children having different levels of authority. Her adult partner's support in bringing this about will serve to insure further the operation's success and the family's growth.

Consider also a situation in which the parents are constantly fighting when they are together. The father comes home and exchanges unpleasant greetings with the mother, which signals distress and the children intervene by misbehaving. This claims the parents' attention and prevents them from having to deal with each other, and everyone is protected from the open conflict of the parents. These sequences of events are structured within the family's transactional patterns and most likely will change only if the basic structure of the family is changed. Social workers may alter family structure by initiating alternative patterns of interaction. At such points the worker's attention is directed toward rebuilding and strengthening the relationship of the marital and parental pair. Encouraging the partners to spend time together in relaxing activity without the children or by asking them to plan together how to regulate the children's behavior may both serve the purpose.

In the example just given, our concern was to protect the boundaries around the parental subsystem from inappropriate cross-generational alliances or interference. Similarly it is sometimes important to protect the subsystem of children from unneeded involvement by the older generation. This can be seen, for example, in repeated parental intervention in disagreements between children and making decisions for them regarding the issues involved. Such action does not allow children the opportunity to learn how to negotiate and settle disagreements within the boundary of the sibling subsystem. The parents' intrusion in this way is a violation of the subsystem boundary which is supposed to protect the children from this kind of interference from parents. On the other hand, children are sometimes allowed to intrude into the domain of parents such as interrupting the parents' conversations or entering their bedroom and sleeping with them whenever they wish. In each case the boundary around the subsystem is not functioning properly, as it does not prevent intrusion from outside the system.

Rules. Family transactions are also governed by a set of covert rules within the family structure. The manifestation of these rules can be observed in various ways depending on the family members involved and the context in which it occurs (Nichols, 1984). Such rules may focus on the dependence of family members upon each other or the joining of members to protect each other. For example, a teenage daughter is planning to shop for a picnic and is offered transportation by a friend but does not accept because her father plans to go shopping and would also like her to go with him and help select a gift for her mother. In this instance, the unspoken rule is that family obligations take precedence over nonfamily relationships.

REGULATING DISTANCE

As indicated in an earlier chapter the balance between separateness and connectedness among family members is important as the family carries out its various functions. Boundaries surround not only the subsystems just discussed, but also the individuals within the subsystems and serve to regulate the distance between both individuals and subsystems.

Serious boundary problems are seen when distance between individual family members is not properly regulated by boundary protection. This most often takes the form of extreme closeness or extreme distance in interpersonal relating among family members. These extremes of boundary functioning are identified as *enmeshment* and *disengagement.* The presence of either of these conditions indicates difficulty in the way family members perform tasks and carry out responsibilities.

Enmeshment. Minuchin (1974) emphasizes the necessity of clear subsystem boundaries for proper family functioning. This means the boundary around a subsystem should be well defined, allowing subsystem members to perform necessary functions without interference from others. However, maintaining a clear boundary does not presume an impenetrable wall, but a state of permeability which allow members of a subsystem to have contact with others. When movement across boundaries is not allowed, closeness in relating within the subsystem becomes central and enmeshment is likely to follow.

Consider the example of a mother and daughter who over time have turned to each other for emotional support and understanding, gradually shutting out the father and labeling him as an outsider. The boundary between mother and daughter becomes diffuse with no clear separation of roles and identities and a loss of the ability to act individually. As this continues, they become more and more dependent upon each other and increasingly unable to communicate across the boundary that surrounds them. This is an enmeshed state and also represents an intergenerational boundary violation, as both mother and daughter, who are of different generations, are locked in a common boundary.

A state of enmeshment may also envelop the family system as a whole. Minuchin notes that some families center activities so much among their own members that they "develop their own microcosm" (1974, p. 54). This makes for increased communication within the family and decreases contact with others outside the family circle. As a result, members are drawn closer to each other and boundaries are blurred.

A major deficit associated with enmeshed subsystems or families is that although there may be an increased sense of belonging shared by those involved, members also give up the ability to act alone. With this loss of autonomy subsystems will not likely be able to explore, take chances, and solve problems that normally fall within their range of activity. Likewise, enmeshed families find it difficult to adjust to change under stressful circumstances (Minuchin, 1974).

Change efforts in cases of enmeshment may vary depending on the severity of closeness demonstrated and other circumstances surrounding the problem. However, the goal of change activity is to strengthen individual subsystem boundaries, as indicated, and restore autonomy. This will allow communication outside of the confines of the family and its subsystems and help to reverse the pattern of turning inward for all of the support needed for daily living.

Disengagement. In contrast to the diffuse boundaries of enmeshed families, disengaged families experience inappropriately rigid boundaries, and members become disengaged with regard to their patterns of interactions. These rigid boundaries make communication between subsystems difficult, counteracting the development of a sense of closeness and belonging. As a result, disengaged individuals and subsystems become isolated. Nevertheless, they may develop a strong sense of autonomy, which supports independent functioning.

Disengagement in families limits the normal protective functions of the family and sharply decreases feelings of loyalty and the capacity to share with other members and request help from them when needed (Minuchin, 1974). The emotional distance between family members does not allow the stresses experienced by one member to be shared by other members except in instances where stress is unusually high and persistent. In other words, the disengaged family is an individually oriented family with each member being primarily concerned about his or her own interest.

When social workers encounter disengaged families, the primary objective is to restructure boundaries in such a way as to open them up to communication across subsystems. This will help to promote interdependent interaction between individuals and introduce the opportunity for increased closeness in relating.

Separation-Individuation. Distance in emotional relating within the family might also be viewed from a developmental prospective. While each family is primarily responsible for the way in which distance is regulated among its members, we should not overlook the fact that the parents as architects of the family bring to this task the experiences of development in their families of origin. And this experience will have some influence on the way differentiation takes place in the new family they create. If the developmental experience was one in which the parents were allowed to grow and move toward independence as children, chances are good that the climate for growth will be positive for their children. On the other hand, if they were subjected to experiences that discouraged their own efforts to effect emotional separation from their families of origin, it is likely that the situation will be less encouraging for children seeking to develop their own individuality.

It is useful to keep in mind that the separation-individuation process occurs gradually over time. At birth the infant is physically dependent upon the mother for existence but shows signs of wanting to experience separation as soon as he or she is able to crawl away from the mother to explore new territory. The distance of separation is not very far at this stage, and the child always returns to the mother. This perhaps provides the first test of how distance is to be regulated among family members. For example, a mother who must watch over and guide each move the child makes as he or she crawls around the room might not find it easy to allow more freedom later when walking could take the child out of her sight. This is not to minimize the importance of early attachment between mother and child, which is critical to healthy development in later stages of childhood and even into adulthood. Yet, there has to be a willingness to allow children to separate and explore the world around them, even in early childhood.

The regulation of emotional closeness and distance among family members surfaces in a more observable manner during late adolescence and early adulthood when confrontation is likely around conflicting issues. It is also at this point in family development that the determination is made regarding "how much of family life is to be regulated by considerations of authority" (Hess and Handel, 1985, p. 44). This must be answered by parents, who have to decide to what extent they will impose their wishes on the children. Flexibility on the part of parents as reflected in the ability to rethink their position and adjust their objective for the children in the interest of a wholesome balance in the separation process is an important factor.

When problems in regulating distance occur in relation to separation/individuation, social workers intervening in these situations must look for the way in which authority is used and explore the objectives parents have for their children. Do parents want the children to behave like adults or remain dependent and childish? Do they push the children toward desired objectives or restrain them from movement toward individuation? How do parents define themselves and the children? Understanding how the family functions in relation to promoting appropriate autonomy for its members will usually provide an acceptable point of entry for the introduction of change strategies.

Another factor that influences closeness and distance in family relationships is the extent to which there is a congruence of images among family members. In the process of living together each individual develops an image of what other members are like. This image includes realistic and idealized components derived from the personalities of both the holder and object of the image. It involves experiences with each other and evaluations by parties outside of the dyadic relationship. In addition to the image each member holds about the other, each individual also has an image of the family. This image expresses the relationship of the image holder to the family and the impact the family has on the holder (Hess and Handel, 1985). For example, an adolescent may conceive of his or her family as an excellent environment in which to live and grow, or a prison that restrains and confines.

It is important to realize that a congruence of images among family members is not based on how similar they are to each other, but the extent to which differences and similarities are mutually acceptable (Hess and Handel, 1985). Consider a husband who does not allow his wife to carry any responsibility for the family, and she perceives this as his concern for her welfare and recognizes his control as a strength, while he sees her passive contentment with his actions as support for the welfare of the family. The differences here are mutually accepted, and there is congruence of the images they hold of each other. We agree with Hess and Handel, who suggest that family relationships are shaped by the interlocking meanings derived from the perceived images that exist between its members, and these images determine in large measure the closeness and distance members will experience in relating.

SUMMARY

Our emphasis on an investigative stance in treatment is in harmony with the social work principle of starting where the client is and with the need to involve the client family in the problem-solving process. Our clear preference for focus in treatment is on here-and-now behavior and feelings determined by a selective investigation of history, with both events and relationships, often serving a useful purpose in the production of change. Since families live in a social context, we see that it is important to build effective linkages between family and other systems when other systems undermine or fail to support the family or when families fail to use the support and guidance of those systems.

Areas of focal attention in the treatment process are the family's communication patterns, its structure and its regulation of interpersonal distance. Families and family subsystems need boundaries and a balance of leadership, direction, rules, hierarchy, separateness, and belonging for effective functioning, and constructive communication processes which clarify all of these for family members. In some cases, all these aspects of functioning may need work; in other cases, only some aspects will need improvement.

Families coming to the attention of social workers present a broad range of problems in functioning. The treatment approach which we have described draws on several treatment models and is, we think, broad enough to be applicable to a variety of family situations.

REFERENCES

Bowen, 1978. *Family Therapy in Clinical Practice.* New York: Jason Aronson.
Hess, R., and Handel, G. (ed.). 1985. *The Psychosocial Interior of the Family*, 3rd ed. New York: Aldine Publishing Company.

Hoffman, L. 1981. *Foundations of Family Therapy*. New York: Basic Books.
L'Abate, L., and Frey, J., III. 1981. "The E-R-A Model: The Role of Feelings in Family Therapy Reconsidered." *Journal of Marital and Family Therapy* 7(2):143-50.
Minuchin, S. 1974. *Families and Family Therapy*. Cambridge, Mass.: Harvard University Press.
Nichols, M. 1984. *Family Therapy*. New York: Gardner Press.

Part II

Intervention Strategies

Part II consists of seven chapters focused on intervening with families to change dysfunctional patterns of interaction. In this part the theory and concepts presented in Part I are operationalized in work with specific populations. The populations we have chosen to discuss by no means form a definitive group, and their inclusion does not imply preference with regard to other populations seen in family treatment. They simply represent a sampling of the kinds of families and family problems that social workers encounter in contemporary practice. The choice resulted from our own practice experiences, discussions with practitioners in social work agencies, and information provided by students in fieldwork placements. We readily acknowledge that there are many other populations involved in treatment, and we hope to contribute to the discussion of these populations in the future, along with other educators and clinical practitioners.

The first chapter in this part, Chapter 5, addresses the problems of poverty families and the techniques for treating this population in contemporary society. The impact of external systems in shaping the structure and functioning of these families and the role of the social worker as advocate and broker in meeting family needs are emphasized. The uniqueness of this type of family in relation to communication, rules, and expectations is highlighted. Procedures for intervening with the problem poverty family are discussed, with emphasis on the value of home visits, working with extended family members, and maintaining a suitable climate for effective intervention.

Chapter 6 focuses on the shifting roles of adult children and their aging parents. The difficulties encountered when adult children must take a major role in decision making relative to the welfare of their parents are brought clearly into view. We take a look at existing attitudes toward the older members of society and the process of aging as conceptualized in theory. The significance of earlier parent-child relationships and life-styles of the parents is discussed, and problems encountered in engaging a family composed of adult children and their parents are explored. The impact of role reversal, spouse-parent relationships, and adult sibling relationships and how to deal with them in treatment are also examined.

Chapter 7 is concerned with the treatment of families involved in cases of child abuse. We offer an understanding of the abusing parent and discuss the necessity of meeting the unmet needs of parents who abuse their children. Establishing a relationship between worker and parents that is free of blame for the abuse is emphasized, as well as the necessity of involving the child in treatment. Suggestions are made for working with the parents and the abused child separately in the early phase of treatment.

Chapter 8 discusses intervention with the black family. While much of the material presented is useful in work with all families, the primary emphasis is on the middle-class black family. We expand on the framework presented in Part I to examine what is unique about the black middle-class family structure and how the family carries out its functions.

Recognition is given to the importance of the history of the black family as it has affected the roles of husband and wife, their pattern of relating, socialization of the children, and so on. This chapter provides an understanding of this growing population and suggests the tools to be used for successful intervention.

Chapter 9 describes treatment of families with alcoholic members. Most of our attention is given to alcoholism of the adult male family member. However, there is also some discussion about situations in which the wife/mother or an adolescent in the family experiences problems with the use of alcohol. A systems approach to treatment is suggested which calls for the involvement of spouse, children, and extended family to promote necessary change.

Chapter 10 is focused on the family as it struggles through the process of dissolution, culminating in divorce. The phases of family dissolution and the impact of social forces on the breakup of the family are discussed. A variety of issues that must be addressed by family members and social workers engaged with them in affecting change are also presented.

Chapter 11 is concerned with remarriage after divorce or widowhood and the adjustment of the stepfamily that is created by this union. The stepfamily is viewed from a systems perspective, and various family patterns are discussed. The problems stepfamilies are likely to encounter, the adjustments necessary for satisfactory functioning, and some suggestions for treatment are included in this chapter.

CHAPTER **5**

Family Treatment for Problem
Poverty Families

In the large body of literature on families in poverty, the terminology in reference to the family's needs and problems is often different from the terminology describing general family treatment. The difference does not appear to be accidental but rather to represent variant ways of conceptualizing the family. Our emphasis with poverty-level families is on the family as a group, which represents a primary difference from other approaches to poverty families. Those who treat malfunctioning poverty-level families, and the families themselves, may benefit alike from this effort to bring together knowledge and insights from family practice and work with poverty-level families.

Our approach to the problem poverty family views the family as an organized system of internal subsystems which is engaged in varying ways and degrees with external systems. Events inside the family system are seen as affecting the nature of transactions with the outside world; conversely, events in other systems are seen as influences on internal family relation-

Note: We are extremely grateful to Leonard Press, Associate Professor, School of Social Work and Community Planning, University of Maryland at Baltimore, for his review and constructive suggestions of this chapter.

ships and events. The behavior of external systems is viewed as particularly important in the internal operations of poverty families. Further, we pay primary attention to the ways in which family members engage each other in seeking to have their needs met, to gain cooperation, establish order, negotiate differences, or otherwise regulate family activity. While knowledge of early life deprivation or training is relevant to understanding behavior, as in traditional casework, more attention is paid to the way that current problems evoke, and current patterns reenforce, nonproductive modes of relating and problem solving. Individual behavior is viewed in the context of family and external system events.

The problems poverty families face have all been noted in the literature on problem families.[1] They include problems in marital relationships, including those of single parenthood; in parenting; in household management; in role performance at school or on jobs or in other aspects of community life; in family isolation from relatives, friends, community organizations, and other support systems; and in lack of health, material means, or education and skills. The focus of this chapter is on the way in which the poverty-level family is a participant in the development of these problems of functioning, and on how it can promote or be assisted in promoting their resolution.

POVERTY FAMILIES AS PROBLEM FAMILIES

Problem poverty families have variously been labeled "disorganized," "multi-problem," "hard-to-reach," and "hopeless." The labels prompt images of the kinds of parents and children that inhabit the families, of the kinds of relationships they have with one another, of the ways they cope with family life in general and their own specific problems, and of the ways they engage with the outside world. Though these labels may in a sense be accurate, they are in another sense more appropriate to the ways social workers and other practitioners have thought about and responded to them. As Wiltse (1958) has noted, the sense of hopelessness resides in the social worker as well as in the family: "Disorganized" is an appropriate label only in the sense that social agencies and helpers have not understood the kind

---

[1]The literature is replete with descriptions of poverty families. Wiltse (1958), Geismar and Ayres (1959), King (1967), Bandler (1967), and Hallowitz (1975) are particularly vivid or detailed.

of organization that occurs in families and have lacked the concepts necessary for understanding. "Hard-to-reach" follows at least in part from inadequate conceptualizations and a related lack of skills and techniques.

The conceptualizations of problem poverty families offered here will
provide new understanding (and perhaps new labels) that should help social
workers feel less hopeless about them and more able to find ways to enable
their responsiveness and growth. Given the present deficits in services to
poor families, we also hope that agencies will gain new understanding and
become more willing to commit needed resources and services to the effort.

Families in poverty do not all fit the images. Many poverty-level families
function well in spite of great adversity; marital relationships, child rearing,
and performance in the outside world proceed satisfactorily and with success. It is important to know that such families exist, and it would be
extremely useful to know the factors that account for their survival and
success. Such knowledge would enable workers to deal more effectively with
the problem-ridden families about whom we are concerned here, and enable the family members to succeed as families and individuals.[2] Thus, we
will be discussing a subgroup of poverty-level families—those that do not
function well and therefore come to the attention of social workers in social
agencies.

Nevertheless, there is a relationship between poverty and the problems
of these families. Chilman (1975) sees poverty as clearly a cause of family
problems, particularly where the family has lived in poverty for a generation or longer. The problems of the family may become the central handicap in its ability to extricate itself from poverty or its other problems.

> These poverty conditions contribute to such attitudes and behaviors as
> fatalism, alienation, distrust between family members, separate male and
> female worlds, little communication between mates and between parents
> and children, and punitive and authoritarian methods of child-rearing.

---

[2]Ideas about why problem families do not function well have for the most part been
developed out of clinical work with these families. Such work could, by inference, give rise to
descriptions of healthy families, but few attempts have been made to lay these out
systematically, especially in regard to poverty families. Studies designed to understand
well-functioning families in general are few in number. Some efforts have been made to
compare families which function well with those that do not. The work of Lewis, Beavers,
Gossett, and Phillips (1976) is a particularly good example of such an effort. They compare
family processes in physically healthy and nonhealthy families. H. McAdoo (1977) and J.
McAdoo (1977) are studying successful black families in an effort to account for their difference
from the stereotype of lower-class black families.

> Attitudes and behaviors of these kinds growing out of long term, severe poverty, tend to further the problems of poor families, adversely affecting family relationships and developmental outcomes for both parents and children—especially the latter. (Chilman, 1975, pp. 58-59)

The problems of family functioning in poverty-level families will not be resolved without some change in the family's poverty status. Income maintenance by itself does not appear to be a sufficient solution however. Bishop (1980) notes that while unemployment is clearly disruptive to marriages, the provision of income maintenance either in the form of AFDC-U or a negative income tax has also increased the rate of marital dissolution. Thus, though the provision of income is necessary for family functioning, some changes in family functioning must also occur if the family is to be extricated from the perpetuation of individual and family problems, and from poverty status. Further, adequate external system supports, such as the worker orientations and agency commitments described below, are essential to motivate change in poverty families and to forestall the repetition of present patterns in succeeding generations. Extrication from the poverty status rests not only with the family but also with a change in the perspectives of the external systems which affect it. We are concerned with facilitating change at both levels.

EXTERNAL SYSTEM/FAMILY SYSTEM OPERATIONS

We see the poverty problem family as a bounded system, subject to inputs from external systems. The limitations of material means are, initially, limitations in the support provided by external systems for the family. The economic system has not made available opportunities for employment and income production to meet the family's needs. Where these are lacking, the social system, because of public attitudes and consequent public policy, has not provided adequate alternate means of support for the family, either in income or in services. Limited resources and restrictive agency policies are the measure of society's attitudes. These limited inputs from external systems diminish the family's ability to maintain itself materially. They also affect the status and role assignments of family members, particularly those of the family breadwinner.

Further, negative attitudes and sometimes outright hostility toward the poverty family may be manifested by the public, by agencies, and by workers. Middle-class values lead to expectations of certain responses from the family and to disparagement and rejection when the family does not manifest these responses. The feedback to the family depreciates the family's image of itself and of its individual members. When the family is lacking in self-enhancing feedback from the outside world, the esteem of family members for each other suffers. Self-esteem, useful as a source of strength and motivation, is diminished, and the burden of promoting it is left totally to the already overburdened family.

Another negative impact that external systems have on the poverty family is the existence of policies that divide families rather than bring them together. In some states policies are still in effect which provide support for mother and children when father is not there, but do not support them when he is present but unable to provide financial support. This serves to divide the family and inhibit family strength and growth. Kaslow (1972) has drawn attention to the way such policies work against the strengthening and integration of the family and the family effort to promote these results.

Other agency policies also serve to divide and fragment the family. Examples are service to the health or mental health needs of some family members but not of others, or attentiveness only to the physical or mental health of a family member without attention to the family circumstances that affect health.

Agencies which require the family to conform to agency policy operate as though the family is an extension of the agency, subject to its bidding. Instead of providing support to the family's own problem-solving efforts, the policies of agencies and the actions of workers often serve to inhibit the capacity for independent thought and action. In conceptual terms, the family loses its boundaries as a separate system and becomes incorporated as part of the agency system, thus increasing rather than decreasing its dependency. Families known to more than one agency, as Hoffman and Long (1969) suggest, may find themselves faced with contradictory requests which may result in breakdown of family structure or family boundaries.

Family interaction with other, less official or public systems may operate similarly. The extended family, the siblings or parents of the adult family members, sometimes provides little or no support. In poverty families these persons are often psychologically or materially not in a position to be supportive and are themselves in need of support. When a relationship exists, extended family members often see the members of the poverty family as people to be controlled or directed or drawn upon for their own support. Consequently, the inputs to the family system from the extended family leave it diminished in capacity for independent operation.

Extended family members, however, can be helpful in providing supports, sometimes financially and materially, sometimes in services such as child care or homemaking during illness. Stack (1974) has noted the particular means of helpfulness of kin and kinlike networks. When such relationships are tenuous, family members can sometimes be helped to strengthen them, to their own gain.

Often problem poverty families simply lack connection with the outside world. Friendships are meager or nonexistent. Encounters with institutions such as churches, schools, and health services are dreaded and avoided. The potential for connectedness, interest, and self-affirmation is not available.

In these and other ways, external systems can affect the processes operative within the family and leave its members alienated, depreciated, distrustful, and hostile toward the outside world. They are thus more intensively dependent on one another for affirmation and rewards and are subject to heightened interpersonal tension. Fewer exchanges with external systems mean that family members often lack awareness of the standards and expectations of the outside world (King, 1967). There is a lack of knowledge of what may be available to them or how to make use of what is available. Agencies sometimes even operate to make such information inaccessible to family members. Therefore, problem poverty families often lack the repertoire of appropriate knowledge and behaviors available to them. The family system has in effect been closed off to inputs from the outside world which could be potentially helpful in solving the family's problems. Because of deficits of information and skills, contacts with social institutions often end in failure and disappointment. In Chilman's (1975) view, such family limitation may be a function of the duration of poverty status over extended periods of time, especially when it continues into a second generation.

Thus, a negative interaction occurs between the poverty family and external systems. Over time, relationships deteriorate unless processes are set in motion which alter the behaviors of either the family or external systems, or both. The failure to achieve the desired positive connections must be attributed to the stance of the outside world *and* to the family's limitations. New behaviors initiated by the family or by the external systems affect the interaction between them and offer hope of improvement in the family and in its relationship with the outside world. If new information and resources are made available, the family has to be able to respond to make effective use of them. It may need assistance in learning to respond to the altered situation, since its responses have been tailored for the external systems as they had been behaving. Treatment, therefore, must contain a substantial element of advocacy to change external systems. In other instances, the limitations in the family's knowledge and coping skills should be the focus of treatment.

Since there is a reciprocal influence between the family system and the systems external to it, transactions within the family system between family members will be affected by the transactions with outside systems. Similarly, changes within the family will alter the transactions with the outside world. Present patterns of transaction may have developed and persisted over time, but they represent adaptation to current circumstances. A systems viewpoint emphasizes the need to understand what is occurring in the present as each system responds to inputs from the other. This is true whether the family is responding to the requirements of external systems or to the appearance of new problems. Further, to the extent that present behavior is determined by past experience, it is determined by learning rather than by psychological conflict. That is, people cope in present transactions because they have learned to cope that way and have not learned other ways which might now be more useful to them (Cade, 1975; McKinney, 1970). This emphasis on here-and-now transactions, which is reflective of family treatment in general, is especially useful in helping families who have immediate material needs as well as problems of individual and interpersonal functioning. The emphasis is on what is to be done rather than why the family is in a particular situation. As a focus of treatment, teaching and asking the family to try out new behaviors takes priority over understanding and insight into past causes as a means for promoting behavioral change.[3]

INTERNAL FAMILY SYSTEM OPERATIONS

The nature of the problem poverty family's boundaries, rules, communications, and identity follows from the nature of the family's relationships to external systems. The negative nature of the relationships with external

---

[3]Research by Reid and Shyne (1969, pp. 82-93) shows that even though psychoanalytic theory suggests a focus on the development of insight into causes of behavior, caseworkers have nevertheless focused more on current interactions of the client with the family or other systems.

systems for these families has been defined; there is little in them to offer either adult or child a sense of positive meaning or affirmation. As bread-winners or as clients of an income maintenance program, adults feel depreciated and find no status; children receive minimal affirmation or recognition for their efforts in school. Consequently, for gratification of their personal needs, each member turns to other family members. The need to seek all gratifications within the family places undue stress on internal family operations. Unsatisfactory patterns develop and persist as long as the family's position in the community persists.

The internal operations of problem poverty families are viewed in relation to family structure, which incorporates generational boundaries and family rules, and to family communication processes. These elements are not totally separate from one another, though we do describe them separately. These aspects of family functioning relate to the family's integration, solidarity, and sense of identity, which in turn are important elements in its structure and process.

Boundaries

Family boundaries define the various subsystems in the family structure (see Chapter 1). The marital pair first forms a marital subsystem, which may become a parental subsystem. Family operations and strength depend in large measure on the ability of the adults to form a strong bond with each other. Satisfaction in their own relationship derives from that bond, as does the ability to support each other in child rearing. In problem poverty families, however, the relationships between the adults are characterized by distance, conflict, and transiency. They interact with each other primarily as parents, minimally as spouses.

While communicational and interactional problems (which we will describe shortly) are primary sources of the inability to form a strong marital bond,[4] the structural outcomes must also be considered. When relationships do not work partners may withdraw from them, psychologically or physi-

---

[4]The parents' inability to provide love and affection for each other and for their children has been attributed to their individual need for love and affection, due to the deprivation they have experienced in their own growth and development (Bandler, 1967; Lance, 1969). While this is no doubt a factor, other factors enter in. Current material limitations reinforce the parents' sense of deprivation. Current communicational and interactional modes (which we describe subsequently) frustrate their efforts to obtain satisfaction from each other.

cally or both, and the withdrawal may be temporary or permanent. Or they may engage in overt conflict, verbal or physical or both. In families with children a parent may withdraw from the parenting function as well as from the spouse role. Withdrawal from the parenting function represents the relinquishment of parental leadership. The role of the withdrawing spouse/parent may thus become more that of a child than of a parent. The usual generational lines are crossed.

When the failure of marital bonding results in conflict which cannot be contained within the bounds of marriage, a second form of generational boundary violation may occur. A parent may seek a member of the child generation as an ally, sometimes to gain support for self, sometimes as a means of attack against the spouse. If both parents have remained in the home or are significant for the child, the child is placed in an untenable position between them.

The child who responds to this boundary breakdown by moving to comfort or support one of the parents increases his or her isolation from the other parent. Thus he deprives himself of the support of the other parent and may thereby accentuate the conflict between the parents. He may seek to reconcile parental differences, a function which places him more in the parent generation, or he may actually take on parental functions. Or he may develop other emotional, physical, or behavioral symptoms because of this uncomfortable positioning. Cues from the parents will suggest to the child the ways in which he is needed.

The breakdown in parental leadership is manifest also in those instances in which children move into parenting roles with other children. Such movement may be prompted by the parent, and it gains parental approval. While it often results from parental conflicts or default, it may in other instances often be necessary for a child to perform in the role of a parent, as for example when work, illness, or errands leave both parents unavailable. This becomes even more likely in single-parent families. An older child may take on a child-caring role with younger siblings during after-school hours, before the parents return home from work. Or they may be asked to undertake extra household tasks during an illness of one of the adults. Troubles may arise when parents have not provided sufficient direction.

> An older girl was left in charge of several siblings who began fighting with each other. Having no instructions from the parents about what to do about this behavior, she separated them and did not allow them to play

together until the parents returned home. The younger sibs complained to the parents who, in turn, chided the girl for her actions. No instructions were offered about what to do if the behavior recurred. The girl was left with negative feelings toward her siblings for causing her trouble and toward her parents for not supporting or directing her. The younger siblings were likewise left with angry feelings and a reduced need to be cooperative.

In these circumstances the parents failed to provide a clear, unambiguous structure within which the parenting child and the other children could relate, leaving cause for disagreement and fighting. Where parental leadership is clear, all children will know their limits and responsibilities during a parent's absence.

The likelihood of a child's becoming a parental child seems greater in problem poverty families than in other families. The parents' poor position in the outside world, as we have suggested, leaves the parent with reduced need satisfaction, self-esteem, and status within the family. These factors combine to reduce parental assertiveness and leadership. Seeking affirmation and status, they may more readily seek a child as an ally or yield to the wishes of a child, especially when these needs are not met by a spouse who may have similar needs and may be unable to meet the other's needs. Furthermore, in single-parent families, which many of these families are, the tendency to rely on parental children increases.

Rules

Closely related to a lack of structure evidenced in generational boundaries and parental leadership is a lack of clear and consistent norms and rules for behavior. In problem poverty families, parental responsibilities in setting limits to behavior often are not fulfilled. What is a limit today may not be a limit tomorrow, or even ten minutes from now. A limit defined by one parent may not be held to by the other parent. Behavior is regulated by injunctions on a particular piece of behavior but with no further explanation about why it should be stopped, about circumstances under which it is permitted, or about what desirable behavior should be substituted. Children consequently have no consistent guides for behavior which they can internalize and thereby become self-regulating, either in the parent's presence or away from them. Parents are constantly required to regulate the activity of the children, leaving them totally enmeshed and absorbed in child care and less free to meet their own needs. They feel overburdened and over-whelmed.

The parents' abdication from regulation or their total withdrawal from the family, either temporary or permanent, leaves relationships disrupted and reenforces the sense of inconsistency and instability. Parental behavior in this area is also attributable, at least in part, to the parents' limited status outside the family and their own and family members' reactions to that status. Where the parents have themselves been raised in similar families, these behaviors are learned in their families of origin.

Such interaction of course interferes with the growth and development of the children and the parents. The process does not allow for individuation and separation of family members but instead keeps them dependent upon and bound to one another. It is a kind of being "stuck" together that is very different from being able to see oneself as an individual, but an individual who takes satisfaction and enhances her or his identity out of belonging to the family. The "stuck togetherness" is similar to the situation of "enmesh-ment" described by Minuchin and Montalvo (1967) and to the "undifferen-tiated" family situation described by Bowen (1971).

Similar, but less often described, is the lack of clear expectations and rules about marital behavior. Dissatisfaction with marital relations may result. Adults may think of themselves primarily as parents and devote little atten-tion and effort to their roles as spouses. Frequently spouses are unsure of themselves as males or females. They become aware of their spouse's expec-tations primarily when they fail to meet them, not through transactions which result in explicit definitions of what is expected and desired. Com-plaints are frequent; the freedom to say what "I want, need, or would like" is lacking, as is the means for expression. As in parent-child relationships, it is easier for spouses to learn what is not wanted than to learn what is wanted. Role performance cannot be achieved with confidence. Since role expectations are not clearly defined, the interpersonal process leaves spouses feeling insecure and lacking in self-affirmation.

Communications

When clear and consistent rules for behavior are lacking, communica-tions are likely to be dysfunctional to family stability and problem solving. Communication is characterized by interruptions, simultaneous talking, topic changes, and unclear meanings. Members do not really listen to each other and frequently do not really expect to be heard. When others respond, it is often to make a counter point of their own, rather than to respond to what has been said. Voices escalate in volume in an effort to be heard, and in the noise, affect rather than content is communicated. The verbal message is lost and is not responded to. Interaction reveals affect and feelings rather than information and ideas, and the interpersonal aspect of the message predominates over the content aspect. In some instances limitations of language ability affect the ability to achieve understanding and solution of a problem. The families are thereby impoverished in their attempts to generate information and solutions to problems.

These characteristics of communication in poverty families, as contrasted to other problem families, differ in intensity, not in kind. Intense need and seeking on the part of family members are implied. In such families, consequently, efforts at problem solving by means of verbal communication are unproductive. Nothing in the family changes as long as communications operate in this manner. Furthermore, the members' frustration with one another and their sense of isolation are increased. They get no sense of being listened to and really heard. They do not obtain understanding, self-affirmation, or nurture from the unresponsiveness or arguments of others.

The communications thus reflect family relationship and structure. The isolation or lack of support within the structure that one or more members may feel becomes evident through the lack of supportive communications and the volume of negative messages directed at them. Members feel isolated from other family members or fear that others are allied against them. For example, when a child communicates as though he or she were a parent, one of the parents may feel as if the other parent and the child are allied against him or her. Or parent communication may seem to derogate a spouse in favor of a child.

Thus the communicative effort at both the content and the relationship levels serves to perpetuate the unsatisfying relationship rather than to change them. A homeostasis is reached, and problem solving does not occur. Family structure is maintained in its disabling form. The family system is stable (morphostatic), but in a form that gradually leads to less rather than more effective functioning.

Identity, Integration, and Solidarity

A number of writers have attested to the importance of a sense of family identity in family coping and problem solving. In our view, this is both consequence and cause of the problems in family functioning.

Hess and Handel (1959), in their research on normal families, refer to the image members hold of the family as a group with a particular past and future. This group identity has meaning for the individual and is seen as important for individual growth and role taking within the family. The image may take various forms, such as "the people that I live with" or "the family that I belong to." Holland (1970) and Laing (1967) also identify images of the group and of the member's place in the group as significant for individual identity and role taking. The term "family" contains within it a sense of integration and solidarity, factors which Angell (1934) found to be significant for the family's ability to manage the stresses of the depression of the 1930s.

Wiltse (1958) takes the position that the concept of family identity is significant in problem poverty families. He defines it as "a mutual relation in that it connotes both a persistent sameness with a family (family character) and a persistent sharing of some kind of essential family character with other families like it" (p. 21). Rabinowitz (1969) observes that it is this sense of being a group which is lacking in poor, multi-problem families:

> Researchers participating in the Wiltwyck study were struck by how little these families seem to be recognized by their members as groups of people who belong together. Parents seem to disassociate themselves from each other and from their children. They seldom have conversations with each other or with a child. . . . Both enjoyment of family life and any positive valuing of family relationships are notably absent. . . . Although they maintain a family form they do not develop a family consciousness. (p. 180)

Having a sense of the family and of belonging to it is as important to individual functioning as is the sense of separateness of self. But it is difficult to develop a positive image of the family in the midst of the structural and communication deficits found in poverty families. The modes of coping with problems and of handling relationships have served to drive members apart rather than to promote a sense of unity and harmony. The family's material status also has its effect. It becomes easy, when material necessities and the means for acquiring them are lacking, to doubt, argue, and blame, and over time to come to feel alienated and apart from the group. The group, in turn, holds insufficient meaning or value for the individual, since it is not a source of nourishment or support. Members are not likely to be committed to preserving it or making an effort to improve it.

We have observed the opposite effects in certain cases, however. In some families the children are able to become upwardly mobile. Such families seem to be characterized by a family theme, defined by the parents, which conveys that though the external world is hostile, the family can succeed if everyone joins together. Goals of survival and achievement are emphasized. Parental leadership is strong, and rules are explicit and clearly enforced. Long-term family survival is given priority over immediate individual goals. Staying together and working together are essential to survival. Under these circumstances, individuals can achieve and advance despite poverty. The individual is enhanced through the *esprit de corps* of the family group. In some instances, however, the individual may experience a sense of rigidity and overcontrol and have difficulty achieving individuality or separateness from the group.

It usually is not possible to identify all the possible difficulties in any given problem poverty family. Social workers need to be generally aware of the stresses on the family, of the behaviors and responses of other systems toward the family, and of the way the family reacts to, copes with, or processes its experience with the outside world. They face the task of identifying the varying degrees to which the problem-solving effort needs to be directed toward external systems, or towards family structure or family process, and of deciding how their efforts should best be directed.

To some degree, the worker's efforts should be directed toward both external systems and the family itself. Modes of intervention related to external systems, to changing family structure, and to changing the communication process are suggested in the following section. The choice of intervention, as always, depends on the worker's judgments about the family's needs and capacities. The primary emphasis is on working with the family as a group, but this does not mean that work with individuals is not possible or necessary. Our particular purpose, however, is to show how work with the family as a group is undertaken.

FAMILY PROBLEMS AND FAMILY PROBLEM SOLVING

All too often, social workers and other helpers have concluded that reality problems such as income, housing, and health care must be solved before obvious problems of individual and family coping can be addressed. Workers make heavy investments in obtaining needed services for families, and, in spite of considerable frustration, these often result in improvement for the family. But they become disappointed when the family does not then show improvement in its coping capacity, in parenting, in sibling relationships, in individual adaption in the family or outside of it, or even in a willingness to try to wrestle with these problems. It seems, when work on one aspect of the family situation is delayed until work on the other is satisfactorily concluded, that the family is lost before work on the former begins. To avoid this dichotomy, it is necessary to focus simultaneously on the problems and realities posed by life and external systems for the family, and on the way in which the family manages its relationship with them.

Umbarger (1972) discusses this dual focus and concludes:

> A family therapy approach oriented toward the ecological systems that form the context of behavior can attend *simultaneously* to the realities of poverty and to intrafamilial issues. The tactics necessary for assistance with poverty problems, such as home visits, school visits, agency visits, and work with the extended family, are the occasion for restructuring relations within the family unit. The management of poverty is part of the treatment procedure context, and not simply an effort to remove obstacles so that the "real treatment" might then begin. The therapist works at the interface between the family and non-familial systems, using typical poverty events—such as unemployment, legal troubles, unpaid rent, or housing difficulties—as the occasion for interventions into the affective, communicational, and structural aspects of family organization. Every new external emergency is an opportunity for restructuring the psychosocial interior of the family. (pp. 156-57, italics ours)

These emphases are congruent with our position about the interrelatedness of family problems and the family's problem-solving mechanisms (see Chapter 2). The solutions to the very real problems of employment, housing, health care, and school performance are achieved, at least in part, by focusing on the way in which the family works at the solutions. Interactions between family members which encourage or discourage, help or hinder, speed or slow progress are a concurrent focus for family work.

The orientation to families described by families described by Umbarger (1972) and Cade (1975) is consistent with an emphasis that has long existed at some places in social work practice. Perlman (1957) writes that the social caseworker has the dual task of achieving solution to a problem and increasing the problem-solving capacity of the persons being served. She delineates how this is accomplished in work with individuals, though the work she describes with individuals is done on behalf of the family as well as of the individual. We will emphasize the means for developing the problem-solving capacity of the family group through efforts on behalf of the group as well as the individual.

CONJOINT FAMILY TREATMENT

The balance of this chapter is concerned with treatment. Some of our formulations for working with problem poverty families, along with strategies that have been described in the literature, are presented, and various ways of working with the family are noted. In the mix of techniques and methods, three themes give coherence to all of the worker activities: (1) the view of the family as a system in interaction with other systems, (2) the concurrent focus on solving problems and improving the family's problem-solving process, and (3) the conjoint effort of the members. The work reported was done in a variety of family and mental health services.

The treatment approach presented here envisions work with all members of the family, often in conjoint sessions of members with the social worker. The advantages of conjoint family work named in Chapter 3 apply to problem poverty families.

McKinney (1970) notes that work with the entire family serves to promote a sense of family cohesiveness and strength:

> Family group casework, with its emphasis on transactions and communication within the family and with significant others, focuses immediate attention on the family as a unit. This point needs stressing because often the multi-deficit family is seen as an amorphous collection of individuals vying with each other for attention or for the immediate meeting of their own needs, often at the expense of others. This attention to the family as a constant, allows the worker to be flexible in giving importance, when indicated, to family members as individuals within the context of family, to parental functioning, and to parent-child and sibling relations.
>
> Worker activity is guided by the premise that the family as a group can develop more strength to cope with maturation and family roles and tasks by an emphasis on transactional processes within the family rather than by casework with individual family members. (p. 327)

Thus, engaging all family members in the problem-solving task is useful in engendering in the family members a positive image of themselves as a unit. It conveys the idea that each may gain from common effort and work on problems that affect them all. The conjoint effort serves to stimulate motivation for participation in treatment and in family problem solving. Wiltse (1958) says, "By actively promoting family identity the social worker can exploit its force to give greater cohesiveness and direction to a family's development, and therefore the power of the family as the basic socializing agent in the life of its individual members is enhanced" (p. 21).

BEGINNING TREATMENT

As the "hard-to-reach" label often given problem poverty families attests, traditional approaches in family agencies, mental health services, and public social services have not been successful in meeting needs or gaining cooperation in treatment efforts. Social workers and their supervisors and consultants have frequently concluded that these families are unmotivated for help or change. Recently, some new ways of looking at the families have changed worker attitudes and have resulted in the development of special means for engaging them in the problem-solving effort. These means involve: (1) efforts to relate to the family's own special needs and concerns, including material ones, rather than those of the worker, (2) meeting the family at home rather than an office, (3) being available when not scheduled to be, and (4) engaging in activities with the family, as well as talking.

While these strategies have been used with a variety of families, their use with poverty families is especially necessary for successful engagement. In these aspects of beginning the treatment and continuing throughout the treatment effort, the worker acts to meet real needs, both material and psychological, while also working to develop trust, to teach and educate by instruction and demonstration, and to alter structure and interrupt dysfunctional interactive processes between family members. Such activity implies not only special efforts, orientation, and attitudes on the part of workers but also a special commitment of agency purpose and resources that is not always required in treatment of other families.

These efforts are similar in some ways to commonly accepted treatment practice with individuals. The similarities lie in the simultaneous emphasis on developing a positive relationship, defining the problems that the client wants solved, and finding ways to achieve a solution. The differences stem from the effort to involve all family members in the process and from the focus on transactions between family members.

Worker Orientation

Describing these families as hard to reach seems to be another way of saying that as family systems they have been closed to inputs from external systems. Family system boundaries are impermeable, and members are unreceptive to the expectations and help of others. Clearly, ways must be found to make them more responsive to the inputs of the outside world and more accessible to the help that is offered.

Two identifiable factors affecting success in engaging troubled poverty-level families in treatment are the conceptual stance and the attitudinal orientation of the helper. It is first necessary to conceptualize the problems as problems of the family rather than of an individual and to be able to identify what the family needs. Sager, Masters, Ronall, and Normand (1968) report that success in reaching low-income mental health center clientele increased when staff members were trained to see the relevance of the family to the psychiatric problem and when they could acquire a different image of the needs of the family. It was noted that families expected immediate response and offers of clearly defined help. When the clinic changed its intake procedures to expect family participation at the outset, to eliminate the delays resulting from screening, history-taking interviews, and transfers to other workers, successful engagement of families increased.

The Sager group report indicates that the negative attitudes of workers can be reduced by training that places behavior in the context of the family system and improves their ability to see behavior as adaptive to the social situation. It is also evident that when the worker's negative attitudes are replaced by the ability to manifest respect and trustworthiness (Freeman, Hoffman, Smith, and Prunty, 1970), and to "tolerate the dependency" of the family (Lance, 1969), successful engagement with the family can occur. Since negative attitudes on the part of external systems have a deleterious effect on the problem poverty family, changed orientations and responses are needed in agency systems as well as in workers to produce responsiveness and change in these families.

Problem poverty families often exhibit behaviors that test the worker's attitudes, interest, and concern. Previous experience with workers may enhance the family's doubts about the worker's interest, reliability, and concern. Families often report experiences of not being responded to, being rejected, and being controlled by workers and agencies. Repeated and consistent responsiveness is needed to overcome the family's wariness and lack of trust. During the initial phase families distance themselves in various ways, such as absence at the time of scheduled appointments. Workers have responded by seeking clients at other locations if they were not home at the unexpected time. When they are home, families often leave the radio or television on at loud volume or have friends, neighbors, or relatives present. Such behavior may continue over many months, though it decreases over time as workers persevere and family members become convinced of the worker's interest and dependability.

In the worker's efforts during beginning stages to join the family and establish a good working relationship, it is important to remain aware of the harsh realities confronted by poor families. Workers' willingness to help families deal with these realities by seeking to understand their living conditions, cultural patterns, value systems, and goals needs to be conveyed. Gwyn and Kilpatrick (1981) emphasize this as being of particular value in working with poor black families. Sherman (1983) also stresses the effort of the worker and family to identify, clarify, and achieve goals that are important to the family in dealing both with material and interpersonal problems. Developing tasks related to these roles and building skills needed to complete the tasks are important aspects of the worker's and family's agenda. These activities serve both to solve problems and increase family problem-solving ability. Worker bridging and advocacy with school systems, for example, conveys willingness to help with practical issues while also developing the family's ability to handle them (Aponte, 1976). Respecting family autonomy in setting goals and in seeking their active participation gradually decreases the likelihood of the unresponsiveness described above. Rabin, Rosenberg, and Sens (1982) found that efforts to create an atmosphere of familiarity were particularly helpful in establishing a working relationship with the family. They work to become known as family members through informality and the sharing of personal experiences and feelings, including anger. They also made extensive efforts to know the resources, practices, and values of the community and to become known in it. These efforts enabled families to be in more positive contact with the world beyond the immediate family and to reduce its sense of isolation.

Viewed as an interactive, intersystems process, this changed agency and worker orientation to seeking out and reaching out appears in numerous instances to have had the capacity to induce family cooperation and participation.

Home Visits, Activity, and Talk

There is persistent reference in the literature on family treatment to the value of home visits in acquiring a clear picture of how the family works (e.g., Moynihan, 1974). These visits benefit the worker's understanding; they also serve to make the family more accessible to worker input. Home visits seem more natural to problem poverty families and serve to avoid the negative connotation that some groups have about using mental health services (Levine, 1964). They lend themselves more readily to approaches which are not so specifically suggestive of treatment but allow the worker to be seen as friend and member of the family, images which appear less threatening to the family's already low self-esteem. Home visits also use approaches that are oriented to activity and doing (to be described shortly), as well as to talking. They also enable the participation of more members of the family than referrals to separate services for the individual problems of family members would.

Workers have engaged in a variety of activities with family members. Art, crafts, games, fixing toys and furniture, repairing or making clothing, cleaning house, and setting hair have all been reported. In addition, workers have participated with families on outings and trips to agencies and clinics. These activities have been successful in promoting participation in treatment and change in family functioning.

Levine (1964) has found that activities quickly reveal the nature of family interaction. For example, when parents competed with children in games, they had difficulty in playing according to the rules, as did the children. They were unable to provide consistent rules and structure. In fixing toys and furniture, parents lacked skills and confidence. The worker would undertake to enforce game rules and demonstrate how to fix, modeling these activities for the parents and encouraging them to take over.

Scheinfeld, Bowles, Tuck, and Gold (1970) also introduced games and toys, inviting all members to participate. Activity sometimes began with only one or more of the children participating, though the interest of others was gradually attracted. Parent participation was sought as a means of promoting parental interest in the child's growth and learning, though sibling participation also allowed workers to help with these relationships.

They report particular difficulty in getting fathers involved in activities with the children, which they attribute to cultural conditioning which sees fathers as having a minimal role in the socializing of children. Most studies suggest that the father's role in the family is an important one, but this observation implies that participation does not have to be manifest in this particular way.

Bandler (1967) likewise reports that the worker's participation in low-income family-life activities—becoming a member of the family—was crucial to the family's involvement. In that project, the worker engaged initially in discussion with the family rather than in activities, in an effort to identify problems that were not too anxiety provoking and held some promise of solution. Workers "moved toward solution of the problem before identifying it." At later stages, after more trust of worker had developed, more explicit efforts were made to identify problems and establish priorities for the problem-solving effort.

Like Bandler, Lance (1969) is also explicit about efforts to work with the parents. Both gave relatively less attention to engaging the children in the initial phases of contact, though they appear to do so at later stages. They, along with King (1967) and McKinney (1970), are very concerned to meet the material needs of the families, and they minimize the fear that meeting needs will result in insatiable demands. The needs are real, not just a manifestation of psychological dependency. Meeting needs is essential to the functioning of the family on the material level. It is also important psychologically in conveying a sense of being valued and cared about.

Even though the worker often enters these families initially due to referral because of the needs of the children rather than the needs of the parents, the meeting of children's needs takes into account the parents' rivalry with their children for attention and affection. Therefore, worker efforts in initial stages convey that the worker is there for the family, not only for the children. There is no necessity for a parent to feel that workers are concerned about the children "but not about me." The worker is in a position, in the conjoint sessions, to be responsive to the needs of all by being responsive to their communications and moving to meet needs as they are expressed. The worker's regulation of his relationship with the children, as with the parents, provides a structure which can offer relief and hope to the parents. As Levine (1964) and Scheinfeld et al. (1970) report, this has accomplished more by demonstration and modeling and less by telling or taking over. Parents are supported as adults and as parents by these means in the group.

There is a range in the responsiveness of poverty problem families to worker contact. Success is predicated on the family's willingness to continue contact with the worker, even though the members may be reluctant to allow the worker any power of influence in the family system. In other instances there may be total refusal of contact, except with authoritative pressure.

The authority to require family participation may be necessary in some instances. While the application of authority is a complex effort, we suggest its use in the initial phase primarily to require continuation of contact with the worker, rather than to require family members to engage in specific actions toward each other or with other systems. Where necessary, it can be valuable in allowing the worker time to establish credibility, trustworthiness, and interest so that the family can experience the worker as someone who can be useful to them. The inducement of specific behavior is better left to later contacts, when the family may be more ready to accept the worker's suggestions and try out new behavior.

Authoritative pressure and home visits may both be useful, but with some families they are not necessary for successful engagement. In the experience of Sager et al. (1968), some families were not only willing to continue but kept office appointments. Powell and Monoghan (1969) were successful in engaging families—mothers, identified child patients, and siblings of identified patients—by use of a multiple-family group, which they saw as less threatening than work with one family at a time.

Assessment of the family's ability to cooperate is necessary to determine whether authoritative pressure, home visits, or office visits are initially most likely to result in family engagement or when shifts from one to the other technique may be needed.

In summary, initial contacts are characterized by the worker's efforts to become part of the family and thereby gain the trust of family members and their willingness to work on problems confronting them. Worker participation involves being available when needed, arranging to meet the family at home, encouraging the participation of as many members as possible, and being responsive to needs, problems, and process as they occur. The worker may participate through discussion or activity, or both. Activity covers a wide range, from games to tasks in the home to accompanying family members on visits to an agency, a clinic, or a school.

This emphasis on participation in the family is highly congruent with the activity orientation and the here-and-now emphasis of the family therapy field. The worker is placed in a position from which it is possible to alter the actions of family members by introducing information and behavior which the family itself does not generate, in order to achieve more favorable outcomes. Less emphasis is placed on insight and awareness than on trying new behavior and ways of relating. Worker participation makes support, information, suggestions, and other interventions possible when assessment indicates that they will be most meaningful. Proposing change in the midst of process offers opportunity for immediate tryout. The worker's intention is to provide nurturance and to demonstrate new coping skills which the parents may emulate and adopt as their own, activities which Wiltse (1958) has called "parenting the parents."

Problem Focus

In the initial phase, little time is devoted to making explicit the nature of the problem. The worker manifests interest and is responsive to the needs and concerns of the family as they are able to reveal them. Bandler (1967) has the worker making moves to meet needs without explicit joint definition of a problem. McKinney's (1970) examples indicate that problems or concerns identified by the children may be the basis for beginning work. In all instances, the response is to problems defined by the family rather than to concerns brought by the worker. Worker concerns may indeed be legitimate, but the family experiences presentation of them at the outset as yet another criticism from the hostile world rather than as a manifestation of caring about what the family cares about.

Some problems and concerns are revealed in the family's telling of them to the worker. Others are revealed in the interactions between members observed in the worker's participation with the family members in various activities. There are problems for the family to solve and problems in the problem-solving process to be corrected. Worker activity is directed to both.

Minuchin (1965) demonstrates one way in which work proceeds on both levels. In the early part of each session, specific concerns that have arisen are defined. Involved family members are asked to work on that concern while other members observe. The worker directs the interaction between family members in the problem-solving process. Within the overall definition of problems in family relationships, different problems may be addressed in each meeting with the family. These moves gradually make the definition of the problem to be solved more explicit. The problem to be solved becomes the problem in the family's problem-solving process. An example from our practice serves to illustrate what we mean:

> A sequence began with the father's expressed concern about the inability of the high school graduate daughter to mobilize herself to find employment. Father was pushing mother to get the girl to "move." Her compliance would help with material needs and would serve as self-affirmation for him. Mother was defending the girl's inactivity, experiencing father's demands as an attack on her. Father became angry and discussion ended.
>
> The worker focused attention on the parents' communication about the problem. Both agree that the sequence was typical, and both were dissatisfied with the outcome. The worker agreed that the daughter's unemployment was a valid concern but promoted discussion between the parents so they could, as a parental subsystem, join together in helping their daughter. Both parents valued the opportunity for further discussion, particularly for the further expression of their respective points of view. Each of them felt the other had heard them in a new way. Mother could sense father's feelings of helplessness in helping the daughter. Father became aware that mother, beyond her defensiveness, shared his concern for the daughter's immobility. The interaction could now shift from "attack-defend" to "what can we do."

Thus the worker in the initial phase seeks to be responsive to family definitions of problems, without necessarily making them explicit. As the family's trust in the worker grows, the worker may take initiative in defining problems and even in ordering priorities among them. While work on the problems proceeds, the worker also attends to the problems in the family's problem-solving process which may increasingly become the focus treatment work.

INTERVENTIONS IN FAMILY COMMUNICATIONS

The interventions described in this section are directed to the family's problem-solving operations which have resulted in ineffective responses to internal or external problems. Some of them have been introduced in the discussion of initial engagement of the family, when they are indeed useful and often needed.

When family communication patterns are faulty, they do not result in decisions to change or undertake new action. Things are left hanging when attention is diverted, or there is overt disagreement and no way to resolve it. As the family persists in its unproductive ways, positive feelings shared among members dissipate. The worker's role in regulating the family's communications must therefore be an active one.

Satir (1967) suggests communication procedures which apply in treatment of problem poverty families, and Minuchin (1967) offers rules for the regulation of communication in treatment sessions. The worker's activity regarding communications in poverty families is not notably different in kind from that used in other families. The need to persist in regulation due to the family's intense persistence in familiar modes is increased, however.

The worker may attempt to state rules of communication at the outset, though this is not generally effective, or may simply attempt to regulate communications according to the rules. The particular topic or problem under discussion may be money, schoolwork, employment, going out, housekeeping, caring, or obedience. Any topic or presented problem serves the purpose. The worker's attention is directed to the way in which the family works on the problem.

The first rule for such communication disallows interruptions. The worker conveys an interest in what each member has to say, making clear that other members will have their chances to be heard. The worker may block interruptions in various ways. A verbal intervention may be used: "I want to hear what mother is saying. Then I will hear from you." Sometimes a hand motion directed to the interrupter and a body inclination toward the speaker will serve the same purpose. In other instances the worker may need to move himself between the speaker and interrupter to block the interruptions. Though the non-interruptions rule is useful when there is much simultaneous talking and interrupting, it is not absolute. Interruptions for purposes of seeking information or clarification have been found to be useful (Alexander and Parsons, 1973), and worker directives may permit or encourage such interruptions.

There are other forms of interruption. Two members discussing an issue may be interrupted by a third. The third person may be diverting attention to his own needs or may, in the midst of intense disagreement, take sides or assume a peacemaker role. While this is interruption of process rather than of speech, it leaves the situation unclear and lacking in resolution. The worker who becomes aware of the pattern therefore may draw attention to the process or block its reoccurrence. The worker may give recognition to the interrupter's anxiety and the reasons for it or may return to the original speakers to encourage them to work on the issues at hand.

The worker also seeks to have family members be specific about the person to whom a communication is addressed, and what it is that the person is being told. Thus, if a parent is complaining about the children that "they never" or "they always," the worker may determine which child is of particular concern and ask the parent to address that child about a specific behavior. Similarly, in response to a generalized complaint about a spouse, the worker might suggest talking to the spouse about a specific incident. One intent in this procedure is also to help family members talk to each other rather than to the worker. Talking to the worker rather than to the family members carries a message about the inability of family members to talk usefully with one another, and thus it represents an impasse in their communication. A second intent of this procedure is to begin the process of separating persons out as individuals. It makes clear that persons have separate identities and are not simply a part of the family mass.

The language deficit in problem poverty families may mean that members have difficulty putting into words what they feel or want. Workers can usefully put things into words for family members, being careful to check that this expresses what the individual wishes to convey to others. Rephrasings are often necessary to capture the meaning intended and to enable the person being addressed to understand. Failure in comprehending may be neither lack of clarity of expression nor lack of understanding, however. Rather, the hearer does not like what is being said. Once it is certain that the hearer is clear about what is being said, his or her disagreement or agreement with it may be pursued.

Many communications reflect a continuing tendency to express blame, anger, or hostility. Behind angry communications lies an unexpressed wish for relatedness and self-affirmation. Angry expression defeats the fulfillment of the wish and does not gain the end desired. For example: "You never take me anywhere" sounds like an accusation, which arouses defensiveness. The wish for companionship and relatedness is not revealed. If it were revealed, it might serve to bring the sender and the receiver of the message together in a new way. Similarly, a parent's command to a child may be perceived as hostile or controlling, but it may be due to concern about what may happen to a child in the present or the future. The child hears only the command and resists, but if the caring or concern can be identified and labeled, a new, more responsive relationship might develop. The worker may relabel or rephrase such negative communications to draw attention to the wish imbedded in them and to the self-defeating aspects of their continued use. This activity alters communication processes as well as the relationships among family members.

The injunction to address remarks to someone specific implies an expectation that the person addressed will respond relevantly. If the communication has been clear, relevant responses are easier, and irrelevant ones are easier to detect. Topic changes are the most frequent form of irrelevant response. These often come in the form of countercomplaints or the raising of another issue that takes precedence in the eyes of the respondent. Though it may be a defensive maneuver, it has the overt effect of substituting a new issue for one already stated, which is then left unresolved. The worker may regulate the irrelevant responses in several ways. He may comment that the response did not seem to connect with the original comment. He may ask the speaker whether the response was what he wanted the other to comment on. Or he may ask the respondent to reply to a specific aspect of the previous remark.

These directives require family members to convey clear, explicit messages, and to listen. Since verbal expression and active listening are frequently not part of the family's repertoire, compliance with the worker's directives will not be easy, automatic, or prompt. The intense and immediate need of family members to be heard and recognized will promote the persistence of established patterns. However, if the need to be heard and recognized is to be gratified, it is important that the old patterns be interrupted. There may be extreme difficulty in interrupting them. Minuchin (1965) has removed some family members to another room behind one-way glass with another worker to make certain that their listening status is enforced. Most interviewing situations, either at home or in an office, do not allow for such separation unless there are coworkers for the family. In that case separate discussion may be possible, though separate listening or observation is not. Even then, space limitations may prevent the separation. In the most difficult situations, workers may have to schedule separate interviews for different family subsystems.

The worker's efforts to enable the exchange of information that is useful to problem solving also have the effect of reducing the negative affective component of the communications and enhancing positive messages. Over time, as issues are dealt with and members feel heard, the noise level is reduced, and the aggressive, hostile overtones become minimized. The atmosphere becomes more conducive to positive feeling about other members and about the family group.

In problem poverty families there is frequently a need to reduce the negative affective component of communication in relation to the informational or content aspect. In this regard they appear to contrast greatly with other families, in which the communication of feeling and information has been inhibited. However, feeling may also be inhibited in some members and some problem poverty families. In that event, worker activity seeks to draw out the member who is silent or who avoids expression of feeling in what she or he says. This effort enables that member to produce missing information or to express feeling for family reaction and processing.

The worker's regulation of the family process through these rules of communication blocks or alters existing processes within the family. The underlying assumption is that effective use of language to convey information and meaning is essential to problem solving. When meanings and exchange about the problems become clear, effective problem solving can take place.

The worker's regulation of the communication process during the interview also provides family members with a different experience with one another. New information can alter the images they have of one another and provide them with new understanding. The experience of being listened to and understood provides affirmation of self and a greater readiness to listen to and appreciate others. The communication process the worker requires in the interview can be modeled by family members for use in day-to-day exchanges when the worker is not there. In addition to correction of the family problem-solving process, specific family problems such as school attendance, finances, health, or employment are also being solved.

INTERVENTIONS IN FAMILY STRUCTURE

Interventions in structure are designed to do several things. They serve to support the adults as parents who can provide the direction and structure needed by the children for adequate socialization and emotional growth. In this there is an implication that there will consequently be less need for the children to function as parents or for generational boundaries to become unclear and diffuse. Interventions in this area also seek to strengthen the marital relationship, if there is one, or to provide the single parent with some source of satisfaction of the need for growth and emotional support outside of the relationship to the children.

The first aspect of worker intervention in structure relates to family rules.

Engagement with the family in activities or in interviews ensures the worker's presence during parent-child interactions, which reveal the inconsistencies about rules and expected behaviors. A worker engaged with a child in a game or activity can make his or her expectations of the child's behavior in the game clear and consistent. Parents may observe and use the worker as a model, or the worker may be able to discuss with parents what has happened, what the parents might have done if the worker had not been there, and whether the parents see the intervention as useful. Discussions can elicit what behaviors parents want from their children and can clarify whether the means the parents use are successful in obtaining those desired responses. Their wish to be good parents and to have children who know how to behave, to be responsible, and to succeed is identified and openly supported. Parental directives to a child, even when they sound hostile or attacking, may be redefined, for both parent and child, as an expression of parental concern. Parents may be more readily able to acknowledge such wishes and concerns as they feel the interest and support of the worker. If a parent, for example, responds with an angry "no," the worker may label this as the parent's concern to provide guidance for the child. This relabeling provides the child with new information about the parent's behavior and also increases parental awareness of the caring component of his or her own behavior.

The worker may also clarify whether the parental directive is just for the present situation or for other similar occasions also. If it is also for other occasions, the parent may be encouraged to provide explanation or further instruction. Rewards for compliance and consequences of noncompliance are discussed in advance. If the parent does delegate household or parenting tasks, the parent may be helped to be explicit about the exact duties, how much authority the child has over the other children, and what they are to do when other children do not cooperate. Such discussions assume that parents are operating out of a deficiency of knowledge and skills about parenting and can gain by awareness and specific direction (Wiltse, 1958; Levine, 1964; McKinney, 1970). They also, by implication, leave the parents in control of the structure provided for the child. The child can be gratified by parental attention. As his behavior becomes more consistent and tests the parent less and less, he can also be gratified at the fewer occasions for hostile outbursts. Parents can be relieved that the child has become clear about the rules for behavior and welcome the reduced need to regulate it.

Another aspect of worker intervention in structure relates to the role of the parental child. The delegation of responsibility to a parental child has served to provide the parent some needed support. It also puts the child in a special position with the parent. Both parent and child may therefore have difficulty in relinquishing the special relationship. The parental child needs to feel that other activities and relationships can be rewarding. The worker therefore acts to move the child back to a child's role and to connect him with his peers, as well as to connect the parent more explicitly to the adult generation.

In the sense that parents compete with their children for recognition and attention, they operate more as members of the child generation and less as an adult subsystem. The worker's attention, therefore, needs to be directed to enabling both parents to move back into the parent generation. They need to feel that becoming more active as parents can produce results and be gratifying. If needs for self-affirmation and affection have been met by the child, the worker moves to connect the parents with other sources of adult support.

Where both parents are present in the home, this means work on strengthening the marital relationship, in addition to strengthening parental functioning. Work on the relationship between the parents, similar to any such effort in marital counseling, can be productive. Work on communication processes, on clarification of roles and expectations, and on finding ways of gratifying and supporting each other is useful, as it is for any other couple. Achievement of some success as parents may also reduce the stress on the marriage. Successful involvements outside the home, such as a satisfying work situation, can also be useful in relieving the burden on the marriage for satisfaction of emotional needs, putting the partners in a better position to be responsive and giving to each other.

Where only one parent remains in the family, the worker similarly seeks to reduce the parent's dependence on the children for support, gratification, and self-affirmation. Relationships with other adults are encouraged, and if none exist, the worker may provide a bridge to new associations with peers or peer groups. Single-parent associations, therapy groups, or family life education programs may provide both support and guidance. Encouragement of the parent's participation with peers in recreational, educational, or community-directed activity has specific value of its own, but it also emphasizes to the parent his or her worthwhileness and provides needed separateness from the children.

WORK WITH THE EXTENDED FAMILY

While not an immediate part of the family system, extended family relationships are a problematic aspect of family experience and have a strong impact on family structure and functioning. Orcutt (1977) has drawn attention to the ways in which the problems of the extended family become the problems of the family. In problem poverty families, the need to help family members deal constructively with the problems of their kin may mean enabling them to connect with needed services. In Orcutt's example, the worker helped with the psychiatric hospitalization of a parent. When relieved of these burdens, the nuclear family began to cope more effectively.

In other instances, the problem is more one of conflicted relationships. The parent or parents have not separated and are overconnected to families of origin. They are still struggling with issues of control or being cared about and find themselves unable to maintain their separateness from parents or siblings. Material dependence may inhibit individuation and achievement of psychological independence. Their lack of material and psychological independence from the family of origin leaves them in conflict with spouses. Or the struggle over separateness draws the children in, leaving the child distanced from a grandparenting relationship which might otherwise be gratifying. In other instances, a grandparent may compete against a natural parent for a child's favor. The social worker assists the parent in achieving individuality and separateness from his or her parents. In Orcutt's example, the achievement of psychiatric hospitalization likely required the resolution of ambivalence between the older two generations and achievement of some capacity for separation of self and other. Work on these problems may be undertaken conjointly, as is the work within the nuclear family group, or in separate interviews.

Minuchin et al. (1967) comment on the "nonexistent grandmother" often found in problem poverty families. This role is taken by the mother in a three generation family in which the middle generation is an adolescent daughter who has borne children and still lives in the same household with her parent or parents. She herself has not achieved sufficient emancipation and separation from her parent or parents. She is still dependent on them for guidance, direction, and control. She is both child and mother, and caretaking reponsibilities for her child are ill-defined. Expectations and role definitions of grandmother/mother and mother/daughter are unclear. Treatment work needs to clarify these with much the same procedure used to make explicit any of the family's roles, rules, and expectations. Duties can be defined so that the grandchild is not neglected and so that a reduced amount of conflict occurs between mother and grandmother.

The "man in the house," another member in problem poverty families who often suffers from role ambiguity, may both be and not be a part of the family. The family therapist sees his presence as an important element in the family system and therefore includes him in the problem-solving process. This male figure often offers real support of both a material and a psychological nature. He may provide the affection and satisfaction that the mother needs so that she can lead the family or reduce her inappropriate leaning on her children in general or a parental child in particular. Kaslow (1972) notes that this person's presence gives rise to an issue for family treatment in public social services when his integration in the family may mean a reduction in the financial assistance provided it. This tenuous position may interfere with his effective integration.

Other factors also attest to his not being an integral part of the family. His position vis-à-vis children to whom he is not father is often ill-defined. The mother conveys contradictory messages about whether she does or does not want him to assume parenting responsibility, preventing him from disciplining the children, even if they are left in his care. The lack of clarity about his role creates conflicts for him and for the children. What to do becomes an issue of work in treatment for her, for him, and for the children. This is accomplished by resolving ambivalence and by clarification of roles and rules of the relationships.

The definition of family for treatment purposes should include all those who are significantly related to the family, whether by blood, physical presence, or social contact. Activity among any of these persons in the network of relationships affects the functioning of the family for better or worse. Worker-induced change any place in the network may bring about significant improvement in the life of the family.

REDUCING FAMILY ISOLATION

Because the problem poverty family often lacks constructive contact with community institutions, it may not make use of the resources that are available. Children are not enrolled in day-care centers or after-school free-time programs. Parents themselves do not use available enrichment or educational groups that could offer them psychological support as well as direct guidance and help for the family and thereby reduce the stress on the members and their relationships. Therefore it is an explicit goal of family work to establish connections to community institutions (Bandler, 1967; Scheinfeld et al., 1970). The bridging effort often requires the worker to accompany one or more family members to new locations to establish contacts with the workers providing those services or with members of other families who are participating. Since some family members may be more ready than others to participate, the worker must direct attention to the way some members undermine the efforts of others to relate to new services or individuals.

The family's increasing openness to these new relationships may be attributed to the trust they acquire in the worker. It is also, in part, a function of the restructuring of the relationships and communication processes. The family's use of these resources offers more natural support for the family and may reduce over time the amount of worker investment required.

REORIENTING EXTERNAL SYSTEMS

In the systems frame of reference only part of the family's isolation in the community and lack of positive relations in the community may be attributed to the family itself. We have suggested that the operations of external systems often work to the direct disadvantage of the family, through policies that divide the family or restrict the resources available to it. In addition, as Hoffman and Long (1969) suggest, agencies sometimes work at cross-purposes, further undermining the performance of individual members and the integrity of the family group.

Family members may learn, when they don't know how, to relate to external systems in ways that produce advantage for them. But direct worker intervention is often needed to help loosen interpretations of restrictive policies or to coordinate when policies of different agencies are at cross-purposes. The worker's interpretation to agencies of the functioning and needs of the family is one direct way of intervening. Case conferences with several agencies are often needed. Joint conferences between the family members and workers from several agencies may also be helpful. These are particularly significant when a given agency is acquainted with only part of the family and is unaware of or does not understand significant aspects of the family situation. The effort of the family worker is to orient all personnel involved with the family to the family as a whole.

Worker brokerage on behalf of the family brings full circle the range of interventions with poverty problem families. More complete discussions of this function have been undertaken elsewhere (Orcutt, 1973; Grosser, 1965). Though we have directed our attention primarily to work with the family itself and to the need to participate with the family in engaging agencies, we do not thereby minimize the importance of the worker's roles of broker and advocate for the family.

NOTES ABOUT COWORKERS AND AGENCIES

The work with problem poverty families suggests a number of reasons for the involvement of more than one worker with a family. The first has to do with the need for the ready availability of workers. The family's sense of urgency as well as the immediateness of some needs often require quick responses, when a specific worker may not be available. A second worker involved with the family may be able to meet these needs or to help them cope with the issue.

A second reason for the involvement of more than one worker is for simultaneous work on family issues by subsets of family members (Mostwin, 1974). Subsets of family members may be separated to work simultaneously on the same issue, or to continue work on a separate issue by one subset of persons. Parents and children may be separated into subsets for work on a particular issue, or a parent and a child may become a subset, while other children are withdrawn to observe or work on different problems. These arrangements are more feasible if more than one worker is engaged with the family.

A third reason for using coworkers is that simultaneous work on the involvements and concerns of more than one member of the family as they affect the family may be necessary. The extent of worker activity required would sometimes exhaust the time, if not the energy, of a single worker. The multiple problems of problem poverty families require that some problems be given priority over others, but long delays in the work on any of them may not be possible. The involvement of a second worker may avoid the necessity of leaving work on a particular problem incomplete while another crisis is addressed.

Coworkers of different sexes are suggested, to offer models of the ways males and females can work together as well as the ways two adults can work together. While their work together can generally be expected to be harmonious, it may also demonstrate conflicts. Family awareness of these conflicts is not destructive if the workers can also demonstrate means for the resolution of disagreement.

The presence of a second worker can provide support for a family member when, in the midst of all that is going on, the other worker may not be as aware of the need. A male's support of the wife's position may offer something new to the husband. A female worker's support of the husband can have similar effects. Disagreements with persons of the same or opposite sex and efforts to resolve them may also provide a new experience for family members. Besides being advantageous for the family, a coworker's presence may be an advantage to a worker who has become overidentified with a member of the family and has thereby lost the ability to be effective with the group. A coworker can sometimes spot such pitfalls and help extricate the therapeutic effort from them.

The involvement of more than one worker with the family requires substantial agency, and thereby community, commitment to the family. Intervention with problem poverty families also requires agency commitments to change in attitudinal orientation, information supply needs, scheduling arrangements, and adequate provision of services and resources to help these families. Such commitment of personnel and services on behalf of the poor is largely lacking. Unless increased commitments are made, it will be difficult to know how much of the despair and conflict in individuals and families can thereby be lifted, and how much more direct work on the family's organization and process will be needed.

TREATMENT PROGRAM EFFECTIVENESS

The techniques and strategies described here have been tried and found useful in a variety of settings with problem poverty families. They have been shown to work where other types of efforts with similar families have produced minimal or no change. Our experience, and that of others we have referred to, does not suggest that this approach and these techniques always produce change. It only suggests that the conceptual orientation and techniques may in some instances be more effective than other strategies.

There is no systematic research on the application of these techniques to problem poverty families. Such research would require before-and-after measures of family performance and would match the change against change in families which had not experienced treatment. While some of the efforts reported have attempted before-and-after measures and could assert with confidence that change took place, it is possible that the change might also have occurred without treatment, since no control families are reported in any of the studies.

In this sense, family treatment of problem poverty families suffers the same defects of evaluation that characterize the family therapy field in general (Wells, Dilkes, and Trivelli, 1972; Briar and Miller, 1971). Other kinds of efforts with problem poverty families have been evaluated much more thoroughly and extensively. Geismar (1971) reviews the evaluations of effectiveness of a number of those projects. He concludes that efforts to help such families must attend to the material as well as the interpersonal aspects of the family situation and that multifaceted intervention has an edge over single-method efforts. Resources as well as treatment must be available. Though the facets he defines are not necessarily the same as the efforts we have described, we also advocate multiple modes or points of intervention. He concludes that intervention with problem poverty families has been shown to produce positive change. With this we also concur.

Without minimizing the need for further systematic evaluation of the family group approach, we do assert that the approaches we have described can be effective in producing change. The projects that have undertaken before-and-after assessment of the families offer one basis for such an assertion (Levine, 1964; Minuchin et al., 1967). There is a further basis in the report of Sager et al. (1968) that change to family system strategies resulted in greater continuance in treatment of the population served, though not necessarily of the same families.

Further research is needed to identify which aspects of theory and technique account for the usefulness of a family group approach. It should ascertain that successes are attributable to the theory and techniques rather than to the talent of particularly skilled practitioners who might have used other techniques with similar success. It also needs to isolate the characteristics of families that enable them to respond under these conditions of treatment. And finally, research should identify more explicitly the mix of external system change and internal family change that is needed to provide relief from poverty status and to improve in general the functioning of the family group and its individual members.

SUMMARY

The poverty families discussed in this chapter are those with multiple problems. The focus on the family as a group as it is affected by external systems differentiates our approach from much other work on this category of families. Problem poverty families are heavily affected by their negative position in relation to external systems. The failure of external systems to provide material or psychological support, status, or information leaves the family to its own resources, with negative effects on the relationships among family members. Parents experience losses in self-esteem, lack status with each other and with their children, and abdicate their leadership roles within the family. Generational boundaries become blurred, with children taking on parental roles. Communication processes do not contribute to problem solving. Both family structure and process are inadequate to the problem-solving effort.

Treatment for problem poverty families is a complex effort. Solving the family's problems and improving its means of problem solving are concurrent, not sequential, tasks. The social worker approaches the whole family so that each member can feel the worker's interest without having to vie for the worker's acceptance and recognition. The worker moves quickly to meet material as well as emotional needs. Home visits, participation with the family in a variety of activities, and talking are vehicles for interaction with the worker. The worker moves to strengthen the parental subsystem, to change communication patterns, and to enhance the family members' solidarity and cohesiveness, in the context of work on problems presented by the family. Since family members are often socially isolated, the worker helps connect them with the extended family, recreational resources, social contacts, and agency supports. Agency attitudes and practices frequently have a negative impact on the family, requiring the worker to serve as broker and advocate for the members.

Coworkers are recommended for the family because of the multiplicity of tasks for and with the family. Changed agency attitudes and practices are seen as necessary for effective intervention. The treatment procedures we outline have been tested in practice. However, there is a paucity of research about the effects of treatment for problem poverty families.

REFERENCES

Alexander, J. F., and Parsons, B. 1973. "Short-Term Behavioral Intervention with Delinquent Families." *Journal of Abnormal Psychology* 81:219-25.

Angell, R. G. 1934. *The Family Encounters the Depression*. New York: Scribners.

Aponte, H. 1976. "Family School Interview: An Eco-Structural Approach." *Family Process* 15:303-11.

Bandler, L. 1967. "Casework: A Process of Socialization." In *The Drifters*, ed. E. Pavenstedt. Boston: Little, Brown.

Barnes, C. G. 1978. "Working with the Family Group." *Social Work Today* 4:65-70.

Billingsley, A. 1969. "Family Functioning in the Low-Income Black Community." *Social Casework* 50:563-72.

Bishop, J. H. 1980. "Jobs, Cash and Marital Instability: Review and Synthesis of Evidence." *Journal of Human Resources* 15(3):301-34.

Bowen, M. 1971. "Family Therapy and Family Group Therapy." In *Comprehensive Group Psychotherapy*, ed. H. Kaplan and B. Sadock. Baltimore: Williams and Wilkins.

Briar, S., and Miller, H. 1971. *Problems and Issues in Social Casework*, Chap. 11. New York: Columbia University Press.

Cade, B. 1975. "Therapy with Low Socio-Economic Families." *Social Work Today* 6:142-45.

Chilman, C. 1966. "Social Work Practice with Very Poor Families: Some Implications Suggested by Available Research." *Welfare in Review* 4:13-21.

————. 1975. "Families in Poverty in the Early 1970's: Rates, Associated Factors, Some Implications." *Journal of Marriage and the Family* 37:49-62.

Freeman, H., Hoffman, M., Smith, W., and Prunty, H. 1970. "Can a Family Agency Be Relevant to the Inner-Urban Scene?" *Social Casework* 51:12-31.

Geismar, L. L. 1971. "Implications of a Family Life Improvement Project." *Social Casework* 52:455-65.

————, and Ayres, B. 1959. "Evaluating Social Functioning of Families Under Treatment." *Social Work* 4:102-8.

Grosser, C. 1965. "Community Development Programs Serving the Urban Poor." *Social Work* 10:15-21.

Gwyn, F., and Kilpatrick, A. 1981. "Family Therapy with Low Income Blacks: Tool or Turnoff." *Social Casework* 62(5):259-66.

Hallowitz, D. 1975. "Counseling and Treatment of the Poor Black Family." *Social Casework* 56:451-59.

Hess, R., and Handel, G. 1959. *Family Worlds*. Chicago: University of Chicago Press.

Hoffman, L., and Long, L. 1969. "A Systems Dilemma." *Family Process* 8:211-34.

Holland, D. 1970. "Familization, Socialization and the Universe of Meaning." *Journal of Marriage and the Family* 23:415-26.

Kaslow, F. W. 1972. "How Relevant Is Family Counseling in Public Welfare Settings?" *Public Welfare* 30:18-25.

King, C. H. 1967. "Family Therapy with the Deprived Family." *Social Casework* 48:203-8.

Laing, R. 1967. "Family and Individual Structure." In *The Predicament of the Family*, ed. P. Lomas. New York: International Universities Press.

Lance, E. A. 1969. "Intensive Work with a Deprived Family." *Social Casework* 50:454-60.

Levine, R. 1964. "Treatment in the Home." *Social Work* 9:19-28.

Lewis, J. M., Beavers, W. R., Gossett, J. T., and Phillips, V. A. 1976. *No Single Thread: Psychological Health in Family Systems*. New York: Brunner/Mazel.

McAdoo, H. 1977. "Development of Self Confidence and Race Attitude in Black Children: A Longitudinal Study." In *Third Conference on Empirical Research in Black Psychology*, ed. W. E. Cross, Jr. Washington, D.C.: U.S. Department of Health, Education, and Welfare.

McAdoo, J. 1977. "Relationships between Black Father-Child Interaction and Self-Esteem in Preschool Children." In *Third Conference on Empirical Research in Black Psychology*, ed. W. E. Cross, Jr. Washington, D.C.: U.S. Department of Health, Education, and Welfare.

McKinney, G. E. 1970. "Adapting Family Therapy to Multi-Deficit Families." *Social Casework* 51:327-33.

Minuchin, S. 1965. "Conflict Resolution Family Therapy." *Psychiatry* 28:278-86.

————, and Montalvo, B. 1967. "Techniques for Working with Disorganized Low-Socio-Economic Families." *American Journal of Orthopsychiatry* 37:880-87.

————, Guerney, B., Rosman, B., and Schumer, F. 1967. *Families of the Slums*. New York: Basic Books.

Mostwin, D. 1974. "Multidimensional Model of Working with the Family." *Social Casework* 55:209-15.

Moynihan, S. 1974. "Home Visits for Family Treatment." *Social Casework* 55:712-17.

Orcutt, B. 1973. "Casework Intervention and the Problems of the Poor." *Social Casework* 54:85-95.

————. 1977. "Family Treatment of Poverty Level Families." *Social Casework* 58:92-100.

Perlman, H. 1957. *Social Casework*. Chicago: University of Chicago Press.

Powell, M., and Monoghan, J. 1969. "Reaching the Rejects Through Multi-Family Group Therapy." *International Journal of Group Psychotherapy* 19:35-43.

Rabin, C., Rosenberg, H., and Sens, M. 1982. "Home Based Marital Therapy for Multi-Problem Families." *Journal of Marital and Family Therapy* 8(4):451-62.

Rabinowitz, C. 1969. "Therapy for Underprivileged Delinquent Familes." In *Family Dynamics and Female Sexual Delinquency*, ed. O. Pollack and A. Friedman. Palo Alto, Calif.: Science and Behavior Books.

Reid, W., and Shyne, A. 1969. *Brief and Extended Casework*. New York: Columbia University Press.

Sager, C., Masters, Y., Ronall, R., and Normand, W. 1968. "Selection and Engagement of Patients in Family Therapy." *American Journal of Orthopsychiatry* 38:715-23.

Satir, V. 1968. *Conjoint Family Therapy.* 1967. Palo Alto, Calif.: Science and Behavior Books.

Scheinfeld, D. R., Bowles, D., Tuck, S. J., and Gold, R. 1970. "Parents' Values, Family Networks, and Family Development: Working with Disadvantaged Families." *American Journal of Orthopsychiatry* 40:413-25.

Sherman, R. 1983. "Counseling the Urban Economically Disadvantaged Family." *American Journal of Family Therapy* 11(1):22-30.

Stack, C. 1974. *All Our Kin.* New York: Harper & Row.

Umbarger, C. 1972. "The Paraprofessional and Family Therapy." *Family Process* 11:147-62.

Wells, R., Dilkes, T., and Trivelli, N. 1972. "The Results of Family Therapy: A Critical Review of the Literature." *Family Process* 11:189-207.

Wiltse, K. 1958. "The Hopeless Family." *Social Work* 3:12-22.

CHAPTER 6

Treatment of Elderly Parents and Adult Children as A Family Unit

When we think of the physical structure of a family the configuration most often visualized is that of parents and children living in the same household. In this family the parents are the adult members and occupy the hierarchical position that carries with it the executive authority for family operations. However, this is not the only family composition social workers encounter in professional practice. Some families are headed by only one parent; others include relatives outside the nuclear family, friends of long standing, and so on—all of whom interact with each other in ways that form a functioning unit.

One family makeup with which social workers are familiar consists of elderly parents and their adult children. The members of this family do not usually live in the same household, and executive responsibility for the family system is not necessarily carried by the parents. In fact, the reverse is most often the case. When adult children are involved in planning and providing for their parents' needs, it is usually because the parents are unable to carry this responsibility for themselves. Subsequently, the children, in most cases, occupy the position of final responsibility. This is not to say that the aging parents have no part in the decision-making process, but the adult children assume a major role in assuring a viable existence for their parents.

ATTITUDES TOWARD THE AGED

An awareness of the increasing number of older citizens and their need to participate in society in meaningful ways is well established. Yet, underlying attitudes that are somewhat derogatory toward the elderly and the aging process are prevalent in many areas of society. Some of these attitudes seem to grow out of our well-established belief in individuality, self-reliance, and productivity as symbols of a preferred life-style. This lends support to the value placed on youth and leaves little room for reward to the aged who, for various reasons, may be no longer completely independent or able to make a substantial material contribution to society.

Studies have revealed a number of stereotypes about older persons in our society. Spence, Feigenbaum, Fitzgerald, and Roth (1968) found that medical students perceived old people as "more emotionally ill, disagreeable, inactive, economically burdensome, dependent, dull, socially undesirable, dissatisfied, socially withdrawn, and disruptive of family harmony than youth or adults" (p. 979). Wolk and Wolk (1971) report similar attitudes among student social workers and other professional practitioners.

Research, however, has found most negative stereotypes about the elderly to be untrue. For example, the belief that the aged person loses intelligence and cannot master the learning of new material was not substantiated by the findings of Dennis (1966) or Butler (1967). Some also hold that the older person is a nonproductive member of society. This was not supported by Soddy (1967) and others who have compared age and productivity. For example, most of the studies regarding age and output in the work situation have shown a slight positive relationship between output and age, or none at all (Soddy, 1967, p. 87). The same was generally true with regard to such work-related factors as absenteeism, accidents, and illnesses.

The health of the aged is questioned by many who believe their physical condition renders them susceptible to frequent illnesses that limit most of their activities. In addition, it is widely assumed that the elderly are usually disengaged from their families and live in relative isolation. Neither assumption is supported by research findings. A National Health Survey (National Center for Health Statistics, 1964-1965) showed that most persons in this group were able to perform in their major activity roles. And Shanas,

Townsend, Wedderbrun, Friis, Milhoj, and Stehouwer (1968) reported frequent contacts between a large majority of older persons and their relatives.

Social workers and other professionals intervening in situations involving the elderly should be careful not to fall prey to these negative attitudes. Instead, they should view the aged differentially as individuals, the same as other clients, and proceed to meet their needs in the manner most appropriate for each situation.

THE AGING PROCESS

In order to work effectively with the family that includes adult children and their elderly parents, it is essential to have an understanding of the aging process and how it affects both parents and children. Although growing old is a normal phase in the individual life cycle, it is often the most difficult to accept by the older person who experiences it, as well as by their children who witness it. In various ways aging represents an ending process frequently associated with loneliness and dependency for the elderly. It is also a constant reminder of one's own mortality to younger persons who observe the aging of their elders.

The continuing desire to understand the aging process and its impact upon individuals and society has attracted numerous researchers. Havighurst and Albrecht (1953), Cummings and Henry (1961), Tallmer and Kutner (1969), Lemon, Bengston, and Peterson (1972), and Maddox and Douglass (1974), to mention a few, have all addressed various aspects of the aging process. From these and other studies a number of theories have been suggested as a basis for understanding the process of growing old and the behavior shown by old people. While there is far from unanimous agreement among researchers, it seems fair to say that there is general agreement that older people display behavior which supports the belief that they tend to disengage from the interactional processes of society. However, the extent of disengagement and the causal factors underlying this process remain in question among researchers.

Up to this time most attention has been focused on two theories of aging: the theory of activity and the theory of disengagement.

Activity Theory

It is widely assumed that aged persons become increasingly less active and withdraw from some of the roles they have customarily fulfilled, or have these roles withdrawn from them. Many researchers have looked to activity among the aged for answers to the problems of adjustment in later life. Havighurst and Albrecht (1953) studied the activity of this group and reported a positive relationship between social activity and satisfaction. A number of researchers have also reported corroborative findings. For example, Burgess (1954) found that persons with a high level of adjustment spent greater amounts of time in participation with social and voluntary organizations. Kutner, Fanshel, Togo, and Langner (1956) reported a significant relationship between high morale and a high level of activity.

Activity theory, as it relates to the aging process, grew out of these findings. It is based on the assumption that the social self is evidenced and sustained through interaction with others, as manifest in the performance of various life roles. It is specifically centered around the importance of social role participation as a means of realizing a satisfactory adjustment in later life.

More recent research by Lemon et al. (1972) tends to limit the applicability of activity theory. For example, their findings did not support all interpersonal and noninterpersonal activity as contributing to life satisfactions. They did not find a significant relationship between life satisfaction among the elderly and solitary activity such as watching television or reading a book. Social participation in formal organizations was also found to have no significant influence on feelings of satisfaction. However, significance was found between life satisfaction and informal activity with friends. This supports an earlier finding by Lowenthal and Haven (1968):

> It is clear that if you have a confidant, you can decrease your social interaction and run no greater risk of becoming depressed than if you had increased it. Further, if you have no confidant, you may increase your social activities and yet be far more likely to be depressed than the individual who has a confidant but has lowered his interaction level. Finally, if you have no confidant and retrench in your social life, the odds for depression become overwhelming. The findings are similar, though not so dramatic, in regard to change in social role: if you have a confidant, roles can be decreased with no effect on morale; if you do not have a confidant, you are likely to be depressed whether your roles are increased or decreased (though slightly more so if they are decreased). In other words, the presence of an intimate relationship apparently does serve as a buffer against such decrements as loss of role or reduction of social interaction. (pp.26-27)

Therefore, based on more recent findings, it seems safe to assume that older people can benefit from access to someone in whom they can confide, and having a confidant is perhaps more important than engaging in activity per se.

Disengagement Theory

In studying the aging process, Cummings and Henry (1961) presented findings which indicated that the existence of older people was characterized by withdrawal from participation in the interactional processes of society. They defined this withdrawal as disengagement on the part of the aged, supported by the decreasing number of people with whom the aging individuals were involved and the amount of interaction they experienced with these associates. Underlying this decrease in involvement with others was a change in the personality of the elderly person which resulted in increased preoccupation with the self. This formal presentation by Cummings and Henry set forth the early framework of disengagement theory.

Over the years since these findings were reported, a number of researchers and writers have focused their attention on this theory. Bell (1976) is among those most recently concerned with the theory of disengagement, which he explains as follows:

> By and large, the theory posits a functional relationship between the individual and society. The fact that individuals age and die and that society needs a continual replacement of "parts" is a fundamental tenet of the theory. In this view, both the person and society comprehend the necessity of the situation. As a consequence, the individual who can no longer produce effectively is expected to withdraw (i.e., disengage) from the on-going social life about him. . . . The disengagement processes which eventuate in a self-oriented personality are held to contribute to the maintenance of psychological well-being in late life. (pp. 31-32)

Thus, disengagement theory suggests that disengagement from active society by aging people is a natural phenomenon from which both the individual and society benefit. Society gets a "new part" which enables it to continue at an optimal level of functioning, and the disengaged individual finds satisfaction in a new self-centered role. It is further implied that social and psychological withdrawal by older people from active participation in the social life around them may be a necessary part of a successful aging process.

The suggestion that the elderly person wishes to withdraw from social life as a normal consequence of growing old has been challenged by other researchers, including Tallmer and Kutner (1969). They suggest that certain concomitant life stresses associated with aging could produce the withdrawal reported by Cummings and Henry. In replicating the Cummings and Henry study, they studied the relationship of three independent variables—ill health, widowhood, and retirement—to the disengagement process. Their data provided substantial evidence that disengagement is not caused by aging but is the result of the impact of stresses, physical and social, and these stresses may be expected to increase with advancing years.

Both activity theory and disengagement theory have claimed the attention of many researchers, but there is no consensus as to the relationships of various factors operating within the framework of these theories. Based on the research that has been done, we agree with the view that disengagement is a differential experience of older people which has a strong relationship to the conditions of life as experienced by the individual. In the case of activity theory the people involved, the nature of the activity engaged in, and the degree of confidence shared among the participants seems to be of paramount importance in promoting feelings of well-being among the aged.

While we will not undertake to examine further or clarify these theories, we will borrow from both in accordance with the above statement. Role theory will also be drawn upon later in the chapter to promote understanding of some of the dynamics of relationship and to consider intervention strategies.

LOSSES EXPERIENCED BY THE AGED

Underlying the disengagement process of the aged is the experience of loss in several areas of functioning. Schwartz and Mensh (1974) speak of natural losses which occur over time in a more or less gradual manner. This includes functional deterioration with regard to vision, hearing, central nervous system functioning, use of body muscles, and so on. They also mention "culturally determined and circumstantial losses such as the breaking up of one's social network, economic loss, loss of assigned roles, and loss of options and/or privacy" (p. 8). In order to understand older people in their situations, social workers must be familiar with these losses and their potential effect on the life circumstances of this group.

Physiological Aging

Physiological aging is an area of medical expertise involving biological processes of the body, and we will deal with it only briefly and in relation to a few physical changes that can be readily observed. This is a significant part of the life cycle and perhaps the most noticeable process of change among older people. Signs of physiological change may vary to some extent among individuals and are most noticeable as the body begins to be somewhat less efficient in the performance of its customary life-sustaining functions. Among these changes is a gradual dehydration of muscles and other deteriorations that affect the normal functioning of body organs. This is usually accompanied by a loss of physical dexterity and feelings of tiredness. Some increase in blood pressure may also be experienced. Recovery from injuries and the healing of wounds are relatively slower among the elderly. Visual and hearing impairment, together with central nervous system changes that can result in forgetfulness and some decline in mental alertness, may occur.

While these physiological changes are recognized as a part of the aging process, they do not indicate an automatic onset of illness or the need to curtail older persons' performance of major activity roles. To the contrary, most people are able to continue their major activities in spite of physiological aging.

The elderly themselves are painfully aware of these changes, which come at a time when they are usually involved with fewer people and less frequently than in earlier life. It is well for the social worker to be aware that older people may mourn the loss of physiological functioning in the same manner they experience the loss of a relative, a position, or a status in life.

Studies (Bartko, Patterson, & Butler, 1971; Kannel, 1971) have also shown that good physical health is related to activity. For the elderly activity is at least one means through which they can maintain contact with the world around them, and good health may be the key to sustained activity.

Psychological Aging

The process of aging psychologically is not completely separate from the biophysical process of aging. Indeed, it is very closely related in many ways. Biophysical influences are recognized, for example, in the tendency of older people to show a decrease in memory for more recent events, while at the same time demonstrating vivid recall of events and experiences which occurred many years before. This shift in memory to past events usually reflects on a period in the life cycle of aging individuals when they perceived themselves as more successful. Since a number of changes occur in later years that tend to threaten the self-image of the older person, perhaps this is one way of connecting with the experience of usefulness.

Among the losses experienced by old people the most inevitable is the breakup of their social network. Schwartz and Mensh (1974) suggest that one of the prices for surviving into the later years of life is the likelihood that most friends and associates, and sometimes many family members, are eventually eliminated, for various reasons, from the network with which the elderly interact. Included in this process are the disruptions usually brought on by retirement. The social network of the retiree as it relates to economics, status, and roles represents perhaps the most significant disruption. In terms of economic loss many older people, upon termination of gainful employment, are faced with a change in the standard of living to which they were accustomed. For those who were able to maintain a barely adequate standard of living while fully employed, the loss of income by retirement frequently plunges them into poverty with all of the psychological implications of this status. For example, the elderly couple who manages to live independently, by careful management of the husband's income, might find themselves needing to depend more upon their children for financial assistance after his retirement. This is likely to interfere with feelings of independence and contribute to a sense of growing insecurity for the older people.

Certain social losses also accompany disengagement from gainful employment. The reality of retirement usually means the end of a number of social and collegial activities such as lunches, attending conferences, union meetings, picnics, and so on. The older person does not easily replace these associations and in many cases may well drift toward a life of increased loneliness.

The emphasis of society on a youth culture imposes some limitation on the coping ability of the aged population. Physical attractiveness, strength, and success in competition are important attributes of a youth-oriented culture. However, these attributes diminish with age, and the elderly can no longer compete successfully for rewards which demand these attributes. Bowman (1956), in pointing up the relationship between physical changes and emotions, suggests skin wrinkles, loss or greying of hair, and other physical indications of aging may contribute to inferior feelings. If there is a decrease in sexual capacity or less enjoyment from the sexual experience, this too can contribute to feelings of depression in aging individuals. However, there is considerable disagreement among researchers and writers with regard to change in the sexual capacity of older people.

Intelligence and learning receive a good deal of attention from those who study and work with the elderly. It is generally accepted that a close relationship exists between these attributes, but some studies of intelligence show a decline with age, some show no change, and still others show an increase in intelligence among older people. The reason for the disparity may be the measuring processes used. The instruments used to measure intelligence in the elderly in many situations have drawn much criticism. Carp (1973) suggests that one of the problems with existing instruments is in the standardization of intelligence tests, which are based on the results achieved by younger people. The aged do not share common experiences with the younger group on whom most tests are standardized. Therefore, they cannot be expected to respond in the same way to material drawn from the experiences of young people (Carp, 1973, p. 119). As a result, an accurate measure of intelligence among the elderly is not likely to be obtained by the use of such instruments.

Carp also found a general lack of interest among the elderly in taking intelligence tests. Most of them think these tests have very little intrinsic value. This usually results in low motivation for taking such a test, which is likely to have a negative influence on the outcome.

Thus we conclude that a true determination of change in intelligence among older persons has not yet been achieved. In regard to learning, there is little evidence of change in learning itself among the aged. Nevertheless, learning in older people may be affected by interest and motivation in relation to what is to be learned. In other words, the degree of learning may be reduced if the new knowledge or experience is not in keeping with individual interest. Learning scores are also reduced by a slower rate of responses, which might be caused by disease or other biological dysfunctions common to the aging process.

According to Botwinick (1973), role relationships between men and women change during later years, as evidenced by women demonstrating more assertiveness and men showing more of their submissive impulses (p. 66). It is well to keep in mind that such changes can be problematic, especially when they involve a marital relationship. Consider the case of a husband who retires from his employment after many years of working and providing for his family. His retirement income is much less than his previous earnings, so his wife accepts a part-time job as a nursing aide and becomes involved in her work and the collegial atmosphere of the hospital. In addition to elevating her status to that of employee and breadwinner, she is the beneficiary of social gains no longer shared by her retired husband. By reason of his own change in role and status, the husband may experience serious damage to his self-esteem, and this can find expression in a deterioration of the marital relationship. Often, the deteriorating marital relationships of aging couples somehow manage to involve one or more of the adult children. The struggle that is likely to follow can soon escalate to a point where the family can no longer cope with the conflict, and help is sought from outside the family group.

WORKING WITH THE FAMILY

The focus in this section is on family transactions as experienced by adult children and their aging parents and the underlying dynamics of the functioning of families of this composition. The interactions between adult children and their parents must be understood before intervention into the dysfunctional processes that may occur as a result of these interactions can be undertaken.

We cannot overemphasize that the elderly are members of families, and their problems can best be viewed in the context of family interactions. Contrary to popular belief, ties between parents and their adult children are not always severed. Instead, contacts between them are quite frequent in most cases. Therefore, family therapy involving adult children and their parents is not only appropriate but necessary in many situations where the aged members are experiencing difficulty.

We agree with Brody (1966), who believes adult children generally behave in a responsible manner toward their parents. When they do not, the situation is often complicated by a constellation of personal, social, and economic forces. Therefore, in order to work effectively with adult children and their parents, the social worker must make a careful assessment of the existing situational and emotional factors as they relate to the transactions occurring between the two generations.

Within the broad guidelines of this assumption, we will consider some of the forces operating in extended family relations.

Defining the Problem

The assessment begins with some notion of how the presenting problem might be viewed. Savitsky and Sharkey (1972) report that there is little difference in the way a family presents itself to the social worker when it comes for help, whether the problem is aged parents or a rebellious adolescent. In either case the problem presented is frequently not in itself the problem with which help is most urgently needed. This is not to say the worker should ignore the problem as initially defined by the family. It is obvious that what the family presents is what they have singled out as their present concern, and this must be addressed in a way that is acceptable to them. We are suggesting, however, that when the problem presented concerns the aged parents, the worker should not overlook other possible aspects of the problem. For example, aging parents can create a great deal of anxiety for their children as a result of their inability to function independently or to accept altered roles in relation to the children. Adult children may also be experiencing guilt over their own inability to meet the needs of their elderly parents effectively.

When such underlying concerns are interfering with the problem-solving process, it may be necessary to focus on these concerns as a way of helping the children find the true source of their discomfort, en route to a more appropriate view of the parents' situation. The following case from our files demonstrates what a family may bring to the worker and what often lies beneath their expressed concerns.

> The daughter requested and was granted some time for herself and her husband with the social worker at the nursing home where her 76-year-old mother was recently admitted. They had been seen during the admissions process, at which time both expressed satisfaction with the care the nursing home purported to provide. Nevertheless, the daughter was now complaining vigorously, with support from her husband, about the care her mother was receiving. She described her mother as a very neat person who was accustomed to clean surroundings and having her food prepared as she liked it. The daughter reported that on her last visit she had found her mother wearing clothes that were not clean, and she did not finish her meal. She was sure the food had not been properly prepared.
>
> Finally, the daughter wondered if it had not been a mistake to place her mother in the nursing home. When questioned about this she was able to reveal a great deal of fear and concern about her mother's poor health; the demands her presence in their home had made on both her and her

husband; and how much they had tried to provide the care she needed but had failed in these efforts. Nevertheless, the daughter still felt responsible for her mother's care and was not sure they could entrust this responsibility to the nursing home.

There was no objective reason for the complaints offered by the daughter about her mother's care. Further exploration revealed the primary problem was not the mother's care in the nursing home, but the anxiety her disability had created for the daughter and the guilt generated around the family's inability to care for her. A part of the work to be done here was to help the daughter and her husband cope with their feelings about themselves in relation to the health and physical needs of the wife's aged mother.

Relationships

Knowledge of the relationship that exists between adult children and their parents is crucial in work with the extended family. This is so, regardless of the problem presented. The social worker will find it useful to obtain some sense of the kind of parent-child relationships experienced during the developmental stages of the adult children, and how this relationship developed over the years. Leach (1964) suggests:

> The quality of a person's childhood relationship with his parents strongly influences his feelings toward them throughout his life. If it promotes his independence while meeting his normal dependency needs, he is better able to resolve his conflict between dependence and independence and to move away from his parents without guilt and crippling anxiety. At the same time he has no need to renounce the relationship; it remains warm and friendly. . . . A child so reared expects and wants to share his and his children's life with his parents and to plan with and for the parents whenever they need his help. (p. 146)

This means that if the adult son or daughter shared a relationship with his or her parents during the early years which provided for growth and was experienced as satisfactory, the current relationship is likely to be sufficiently strong to make constructive problem solving a successful undertaking. On the other hand, if the earlier parent-child relationship was characterized by conflict and this conflict was not resolved, efforts to work with them at a later time are likely to be very difficult. This past unresolved conflict may return and interfere with the adult child's ability to help the parents and the parents' ability to accept help from the child (Leach, 1964, p. 146).

Bringing the adult child and parent together in a therapeutic situation when earlier conflicts have not been resolved, therefore, can produce undesirable consequences. For example, the child may see it as a chance to get revenge for what were perceived as earlier injustices from the parent. And the parent might view the coming together as an opportunity to renew the struggle to control the behavior of a disrespectful child. Sometimes guilt is encountered over past failures on the part of both parent and child. In any case, when the aging parent cannot function independently and needs the assistance of the adult child, the worker must act to resolve the conflict, if at all possible, and provide the help needed by the elderly family member.

It is usually helpful in these situations to assist the family members involved to talk about past and present experiences in order to deal with the guilt and anger that have characterized their relationship, and to reach a level of understanding that will allow the necessary planning to take place. Care should be taken to prevent the encounter from becoming only an opportunity for each to blame himself or place blame on the other. We have found it helpful in such cases to encourage self-responsibility for all by focusing on the way each individual is experiencing the other and what each can do to help change the way they are relating to each other.

It is well to recognize that the prospect is not always good for resolving long-standing conflicts in relationships between parents and adult children. A major problem experienced by social workers in cases of enduring parent-child conflict is getting the children involved with the parent and the problem situation. This apparent lack of interest is a primary factor in maintaining the conflict. The following case example from our experience demonstrates resistance to involvement with a parent when conflict remains.

> Mrs. O, formerly a very successful buyer for a large department store, had for many years spent much of her time away from her family. Her misunderstandings with her two daughters apparently began during early childhood when the demands of her job prevented their spending time together. To compensate for this Mrs. O frequently bought them expensive gifts. When the daughters started to demand more of her time in pursuit of a closer relationship, she interpreted this as unreasonable and showed her irritation by threatening to discontinue the expensive gifts. At other times she would picture herself as a "poor misunderstood mother" and threaten to harm herself if her daughters "did not love her." Her husband also got his share of the blame from Mrs. O for the daughters wanting to spend more time with her. She considered Mr. O inadequate

as a husband and father whose income as a clothing store salesman was considerably less than hers. They seemed to live in constant disagreement, and their verbal battles were well known throughout the neighborhood. When the daughters graduated from high school, both chose universities outside of the state, much to the mother's dismay, as she perceived this as "running away" from her. And she never permitted them to forget this "ungrateful act."

Soon after retirement, Mrs. O began experiencing serious health problems. Mr. O, who suffered from asthma and arthritis, had retired earlier and was experiencing a great deal of difficulty himself. However, they were able to manage for a few years, but finally sought help when Mrs. O's physician recommended specialized care, and preferably a warmer climate. Both daughters were now married and lived in an ideal climate for their mother's condition. When contacted to see if they could be of assistance in planning for her, one daughter stated her mother still blamed her for "leaving home" and "ruining her health." This daughter left no doubt that she did not want her mother to move to the area where she was currently living. She expressed the belief that whatever she tried to do would be misinterpreted by her mother, and she was not willing to undergo the emotional strain of further involvement. The other daughter thought any closer involvement with her mother would destroy her marriage, as Mrs. O thought she had married "beneath herself." She said her husband and her mother "hated each other," and she saw no way of improving her own relationship with her mother. The daughters were not willing to be involved beyond making limited financial contributions, if this was needed, in providing care for their mother.

This represents a seriously damaged relationship between adult children and parent. Only minimal participation in planning can be expected from the children in such cases.

We agree with those who maintain that when the conflict is unresolved, aged parents and their children will not be able to live comfortably together. When living arrangements for a parent are involved, it would be ill-advised to consider having the parents move into the home of a child with whom there is long-standing unresolved conflict. This is not to say that all hope of improving the relationship should be abandoned. If any evidence of positive aspects of a relationship remains, the worker should try to revive and build on what is left. However, until some improvement is realized in such cases, living arrangements should be separate.

Role Reversal

In working with aging parents and their adult children, it is important to understand the role shifts that occur between them. Several authors, including Glasser and Glasser (1962), Rautman (1962), and Field (1972), have defined this shift in roles between the two generations as role reversal. In commenting on the process involved in this shifting of roles, Peterson (1974) suggests, "If middle-aged sons or daughters feel their parents are no longer capable of making decisions, the children will take over this role and become parents to their parents" (p. 225). In other words, the elder who has carried the accustomed role of protector and provider for the child at an earlier point in time now gives up this role to the adult child and becomes the receiver of these benefits.

It is necessary to point up the disagreement that exists with regard to the concept of role reversal involving adult children and their elderly parents. The literature reflects the views of some authors who do not accept role reversal as an appropriate definition of what takes place when the adult child assists, protects, and provides for the parent who is unable to plan appropriately and provide for her or his own needs. For example, Brody (1971) suggests:

> There can be no true role reversal. . . . The help and protection given by an adult child to an old parent cannot be equated with psychological relationships. In feeling, though the adult child may be old himself, he remains in the relationship of child to parent; he does not become parent to his parent. (p. 56)

She sees the adult child's activities on behalf of the parent as indicative of a mature adult's capacity to be depended on by his parent.

The aged parent does not make a complete psychological transition from the adult role to that of a child; nor does the adult child completely transfer from the role of child to that of parent to a parent. The fact that both have long experience and emotional investment in their previous roles makes a complete psychological transition of roles unlikely. Yet the adult child is frequently required to assume responsibility in relation to the aged parent that is normally associated with the parental role, and to this extent parent and child are operating in a role-reversal position, which can result in conflict for both participants. Consider the situation in which the adult child is required to make decisions that will affect the way the parent is to live for the remaining years of life. The child, especially one who has experienced a good relationship with the parent, is likely to perceive such action as causing the parent pain and will have a great deal of difficulty accepting the responsibility for making such decisions. In this context the concept of role reversal, which denotes a shift in role responsibility within the aged parent-adult child relationship, is appropriate.

Evidence of the difficulty experienced by both generations involved in role reversal is suggested throughout the literature. Rautman (1962) believes that once the individual reaches maturity and assumes the role of parent to a new generation, parents and children cannot step out of their respective roles and continue their relationship without experiencing a great deal of difficulty. Savitsky and Sharkey (1972) also see an impact on both sides of the relationship; they suggest: "When a crisis brings parents and children together, the latter's capacity to tolerate being a person depended upon by the parents is tested, as is the aged person's capacity to handle dependency feelings upon the children" (p. 5).

In our experience, role reversal frequently takes place amid a great deal of resentment on the part of parents, and much guilt is often evidenced by children. The parents are likely to view the takeover by children as another loss, which is met with a struggle to maintain as much control as possible over their own lives. On the other hand, children often perceive their actions in assuming decision-making power over their parents as degrading the persons for whom they have the greatest respect. Most children feel strongly that it is their duty to honor their parents with respect, rather than promoting within them feelings of helplessness by taking over control of their lives. The fact that this shift in roles comes at a time in the life cycle of the parents when they are less able to regain the decision-making function in their lives, and thereby may remain dependent upon the adult children, is likely to increase the burden of guilt for these children.

The child's ability to take an adult role in relation to the parent depends largely upon the degree to which separateness or individuality was established in the family at an earlier stage. When this has been realized, family members possess a differentiated self, and neither parent nor child needs to view the other as an extension of the self. As a result the adult child will be more likely to maintain objectivity in relation to the needs of the elderly parent.

Problems can occur for adult children in spite of their intellectual awareness of the parents' needs. Although children may realize that their parents are unable to function independently and a shift in roles may be necessary, they frequently need help in accepting the change on an emotional level. Parents may also need help in handling their feelings in relation to depending upon the children.

The giving up and taking on of responsibilities as inherent in the role reversal process is not limited to the two generations directly involved. The systemic properties of family functioning come into play, and family interactions at various levels are involved. Field (1972) says: "The assumption of increased responsibility for their parents' welfare may create for the children a serious dilemma, as they find themselves conflicted as to whether their responsibility to their parents interferes with the adequate discharge of their responsibility to their own children" (p. 131).

At the time added responsibility is brought on by the needs of aging parents, many adult children are still very much involved with their own nuclear families. For example, some may still have children in school or just beginning their careers who look to them for help at the same time as the elderly parents. It is also likely that many of these second-generation adults will be deeply involved in their own careers, and this too will claim a good deal of their attention. Role shifts involving aged parents under these conditions present the adult children (second generation) with quite a dilemma. In some cases they may need direct help in sorting out and establishing priorities that will allow them to continue functioning in their various roles. When there are also problems in relationships between these extended family members, the worker must understand the nature of the conflict and determine where changes are needed and can be realized.

Loss and Grief

It is important for social workers to consider grief and mourning over losses when working with aging persons and their families. Old people experience increasing difficulty in replacing losses due to diminishing inner and outer resources and may grieve over a loss that seems rather insignificant to young observers. There is little doubt that society fails to appreciate fully the dynamics of loss and, as a result, does not deal with it appropriately in many cases, especially where the aged are concerned. This is reflected in the reported perceptions children have about the experiences of their aged parents. Simos (1973) found that adult children recognized parental mourning most often when the loss involved significant others, such as spouses or children. Yet old people also may "grieve over the death of a pet, the loss of a job, a social role, self-esteem, independency, a lifetime home, or right to drive an automobile, or the failure of bodily functions or sensory activity" (p. 80).

As further evidence of children's misunderstanding of loss experienced by their aged parents, Simos (1973) reports:

> Isolation and denial as defenses against the pain of loss were seen by children as lack of feeling on the part of the parents. Feelings of helplessness and despair, normal reactions to loss, were experienced as burdensome parental traits. A desperate attempt to hold on to remaining possessions or life styles was seen as stubbornness. (p. 80)

Social workers involved in work with adult children and their aged parents need to be especially alert to the possibility of loss among older members. The likelihood that children may misunderstand the impact of such losses must also be kept in mind. When this is indicated, intervention should include helping younger family members to relate realistically to the losses of the older members.

Life-Style

Knowledge of the life-style of old people also is useful in gaining an understanding of their social adjustment. The aging individual who has spent a lifetime actively involved in various activities may find it difficult to accept the inactivity to which older people are often relegated in later years.

Those whose primary activities during their most productive years were centered around work and family may be faced with loneliness and isolation when these supports are no longer available. Simos (1973) found that many elderly persons with such life-styles had developed such a narrow range of interests, coupled with poor social skills, that they were unable to engage in social activities. Others were able to respond socially only when the opportunity was provided by the initiative of other people.

Another problem frequently encountered in work with this type of extended family unit is the conflict resulting from the extreme dependency of the aging parent on the adult child. This usually develops when a parent who has enjoyed a very close and dependent marital relationship attempts to transfer dependency needs to a child in the absence of the spouse. In such cases the smoothness of the symbiotic interactions between the parents is likely to have hidden the existence of the prevailing dependency, and the children have been presented with a picture of independent functioning. This false perception on the part of the children can contribute to a misunderstanding of the parents' behavior with regard to fulfilling dependency needs through relationships with them during the later years. In this case conflict is likely to develop between parent and child, necessitating help outside of the family to clarify the situation and provide both parent and child with a realistic basis for relating.

Social workers will find it helpful in alleviating conflict about the dependency of the aging parent on the adult child to gain some understanding of the relationship that previously existed between the parents. Awareness of the former life-style of old people is also useful in assessing their adjustment and intervening on their behalf.

Conflicts and Disagreements

Disagreements between children may be encountered in work with the multigenerational family. These disagreements may arise from misunderstanding, lack of information, rivalry between children, and so on. When failure to agree is centered around information deficits, often the situation can be corrected through improved processing and sharing of information among family members.

When rivalry between the children is involved, however, the problem is much more difficult. Not only are the principals in the rivalry situation adults, but many are also parents of adult children to whom the rivalry is likely to have been passed. When this is the case, the third generation may be involved in the problem. A tremendous amount of energy has usually been invested by the second-generation adults in relation to various forms of competition and difference over the years. As a result, their responses are influenced by a lifetime of thoughts, feelings, and experiences based on these unresolved rivalries. When these adults are seen in relation to problems involving aged parents, they are likely to have relatively fixed positions. Each child is interested primarily in working his or her own will successfully. The struggle between these adult children can easily reach the level where the parent's needs become secondary to the children's need to prevail.

In such situations each side may seek additional support and gain momentum as the struggle continues. Spouses and children frequently become involved in the conflict, and sometimes other relatives and friends lend their support to one of the sides. The following case summary reflects the difficulty that can be encountered when disagreement about planning for an elderly parent is based on rivalry between adult children.

> The patient, a frail man of 75 years, was brought to the Adult Consultation Clinic by his daughter, who explained her difficulty in continuing to maintain him in her home. As a result she was seeking help in planning for a new living situation for her father. The father did not take kindly to the possibility of residing in a special-care facility and wanted to contact a son with whom he thought he could live. The daughter was obviously distressed at the mention of her brother's involvement but gave in to her father's wishes. Soon after the father's contact with his son the son called the clinic to arrange an appointment and requested all consideration of his father entering a residential facility be discontinued.
>
> In the following weeks several members of this extended family were involved. The "tug of war" between the son and daughter was readily seen. Charges and countercharges relative to respective efforts to gain control of the patient's finances and other properties were heard from both. Each pulled in other relatives who were sympathetic to their respective views, and these relatives were as firmly fixed in their opinions as the children. Although the son could not arrange for his father to live with him and presented no alternative plan, he could see his sister "getting her way" and "maintaining an advantage with their father." He suggested the possibility of court action to protect what he perceived as his own interests, and his sister was also willing to battle with him through court proceedings. It was obvious that the aged father's needs were being ignored as the struggle intensified between the children, and the extended family's energies were now also being spent in the contest.

The social worker must keep in mind the needs of the aged parents and refrain from becoming completely consumed in the struggle between the children. This kind of struggle usually neutralizes efforts to plan for the parents, and significant change in the rivalrous relationship between the children is likely to require long-term intervention. Therefore, in the interest of the parent, it may be necessary to make clear to the children the way the worker is experiencing their struggle, which will not be dealt with specifically until an acceptable outcome has been realized on behalf of the parent. In this case the focus of intervention is removed from the children's struggle with one another to the needs of the parent and what can be done in this regard.

Role of the Spouse

It is also important to understand the role of the spouses of adult children when aging parents are included in the family group, both relationships between this adult pair and relations between the spouse and the parent. If the adult child and spouse enjoy a satisfactory relationship, work involving the aged parent will most likely proceed without representing a serious threat to the relationship of this subsystem. However, when the spouse relationship is characterized by disagreement and tension, the strain of involvement with the aging parent is likely to escalate the conflict. The resulting struggle between the spouses will interfere with the social worker's efforts to intervene on behalf of the elderly parents. If, in addition to a good relationship between the adult child and spouse, relations between the spouse and the parent-in-law are also good, the intervention process usually proceeds without major conflicts or disruptions, and outcomes are likely to be acceptable to all concerned.

When there is conflict between the spouse and the elderly parent, the work to be done will be difficult. This conflict creates the likelihood of disruption in other family relationships, especially between adult child and spouse and sometimes between the adult child and the parent, as the reciprocal aspects of relating within the family system take over.

In most situations these types of relationships are readily identified, and the strategies commonly used by social workers in dealing with relationship problems are usually sufficient. Nevertheless, the fact that problems can develop out of what appears to be satisfactory relations between adult children and spouses should not be overlooked. This outcome is not uncommon, especially in cases where one of the principals in the relationship has adapted to a deficit in the functioning of the other, and this adaptation is taxed by closer involvement with an extended family member such as an aging parent.

For example, consider the spouse who over the years has adapted to the necessity of meeting the dependency needs of the husband or wife and gives the appearance of enjoying a satisfactory relationship. When the parent is brought into the picture, the role of this spouse may be required to expand to the point of meeting the needs of not one but two dependent people. This

is especially so if the aged member needs assistance with routine maintenance or in the area of decision making. The dependent spouse will usually
have trouble carrying executive responsibility relative to these needs of the
parent as indicated by the following case summary:

> Mr. and Mrs. J had been married for 15 years without children when
> Mr. J's father came to live with them. Mrs. J was the strong member of
> this marital pair, and her authority and overall assertiveness in relation
> to family matters were accepted by Mr. J, who preferred to remain in the
> background. It soon developed that the aging father required a great deal
> of supervision with regard to his behavior and personal hygiene but was
> resistive to any effort to control his activities. The burden of responsibility
> increased considerably for the wife, as she found her husband unable to
> provide any direction for his father. In various ways he deferred decision
> making and care for the aging parent to his wife. When they were unable
> to work this out, Mrs. J asked for help. Although she was very fond of her
> father-in-law and had not objected to his moving in with them, she had
> not anticipated the problems he brought into their lives, especially her
> husband's reactions to his father's needs. In retrospect, Mrs. J could see
> that she had, in some ways, been a "mother" to Mr. J but was unwilling
> to "add a new baby" at this stage of her life.

This situation represented a real threat to the marital relationship, and
this relationship was crucial in meeting the needs of the aging father. The
social worker chose to focus on the interactions between the marital pair as
it related to roles, expectations, and so on. While alternative plans for Mr.
J's father were discussed, neither wished to have him placed outside of their
home, and Mr. J was gradually able to take on some of the responsibility
for his father.

Encounters of this type clearly indicate the importance of the role assumed by the adult child's spouse and the necessity of understanding the
spouse's relationship within the family unit. Social workers will find it very
useful in working with families in which elderly parents are members, to
pay special attention to the spouse without kinship ties to the parents. If this
individual experiences conflict in existing family relationships or is unwilling to accommodate the intervention process, the realization of desired
outcomes from such activity will be difficult.

SUMMARY

Working with the extended family concerning care for the oldest generation is becoming more widely recognized in social work practice. More and
more adult children are seeking help in planning for their elderly parents
or with conflicts in family relationships resulting from the pressures of
interacting with them. We have presented in this chapter some guidelines
for a beginning understanding of the aging process and how it affects older
people themselves, as well as those who for various reasons are involved with
them. Some problems encountered in work with families composed of adult
children and their elderly parents have been examined, and suggestions for
intervention have been offered.

Since working with the type of family unit described in this chapter is
still in the process of refinement, additional knowledge and skill will be
forthcoming and made available to practitioners in the future. In the meantime, we hope that the information presented here will enable social workers to help meet the needs of our increasing elderly population from a
family-centered perspective. Practitioners who engage in this work should
be well aware of their own perception of the aging process and their
attitudes toward old people. We believe this will help reduce subjectivity
and displacement and enhance the outcome of intervention.

REFERENCES

Bartko, J. J., Patterson, R. D., and Butler, R. N. 1971. "Biomedical and Behavioral
    Predictors of Survival among Normal Aged Men: A Multivariate Analysis." In
    Prediction of Life Span, ed. E. Palmore and F. C. Jeffers. Lexington, Mass.:
    D. C. Heath Co.
Bell, B. D. 1976. *Contemporary Social Gerontology.* Springfield, Ill.: Charles C
    Thomas, Publisher.
Botwinick, J. 1973. *Aging and Behavior.* New York: Springer Publishing Co.
Bowman, K. M. 1956. "Mental Adjustment to Physical Changes with Aging." *Geri-
    atrics* 2:139-45.
Brody, E. M. 1966. "The Aging Family." *The Gerontologist* 6:201-6.
————. 1971. "Aging." In *Encyclopedia of Social Work,* 16th Issue, Vol. I, pp.
    51-71. New York: National Association of Social Workers.
Burgess, E. W. 1954. "Social Relations, Activities, and Personal Adjustment." *Ameri-
    can Journal of Sociology* 59:352-60.
Butler, R. N. 1967. "The Destiny of Creativity in Later Life." In *Psychodynamic
    Studies on Aging,* ed. S. Levin and R. Kahana. New York: International Univer-
    sities Press.

Carp, F. M. 1973. "The Psychology of Aging." In *Foundations of Practical Gerontology,* 2nd ed., ed. R. R. Boyd and C. G. Oaks. Columbia: University of South Carolina Press.

Cummings, E., and Henry, W. E. (eds.). 1961. *Growing Old.* New York: Basic Books.

Dennis, W. 1966. "Creative Productivity between Twenty and Eighty Years." *Journal of Gerontology* 21:1-8.

Field, M. 1972. *The Aged, the Family, and the Community.* New York: Columbia University Press.

Glasser, P., and Glasser, L. 1962. "Role Reversal and Conflict Between Aged Parents and Their Children." *Marriage and Family Living* 24:46-51.

Havighurst, R. J., and Albrecht, R. 1953. *Older People.* New York: Longmans Green.

Kannel, W. B. 1971. "Habits and Heart Disease Mortality." In *Prediction of Life Span,* ed. E. Palmore and F. C. Jeffers. Lexington, Mass.: D. C. Heath Co.

Kutner, B., Fanshel, D., Togo, A., and Langner, S. W. 1956. *Five Hundred Over Sixty.* New York: Russell Sage Foundation.

Leach, J. M. 1964. "The Intergenerational Approach in Casework with the Aging." *Social Casework* 55:144-49.

Lemon, B. W., Bengston, V. L., and Peterson, J. A. 1972. "An Exploration of Activity Theory of Aging: Activity Types and Life Satisfaction among In-Movers to a Retirement Community." *Journal of Gerontology* 27:511-23.

Lowenthal, M. F., and Haven, C. 1968. "Interaction and Adoption: Intimacy as a Critical Variable." *American Sociological Review* 33:20-30.

Maddox, G. L., and Douglass, E. B. 1974. "Aging and Individual Differences: A Longitudinal Analysis of Social, Psychological, and Physiological Indicators." *Journal of Gerontology* 29:555-63.

National Center for Health Statistics. 1964–1965. *National Health Survey.* Series 10. Washington, D.C.: U. S. Government Printing Office.

Peterson, J. A. 1974. "Therapeutic Intervention in Marital and Family Problems of Aging Persons." In *Professional Obligations and Approaches to the Aged,* ed. A. Schwartz and I. Mensh. Springfield, Ill.: Charles C Thomas, Publisher.

Rautman, A. L. 1962. "Role Reversal in Geriatrics." *Mental Hygiene* 56:116-20.

Savitsky, E., and Sharkey, H. 1972. "The Geriatric Patient and His Family: A Study of Family Interaction in the Aged." *Journal of Geriatric Psychiatry* 5:3-19.

Schwartz, A. N., and Mensh, I. (eds.). 1974. *Professional Obligations and Approaches to the Aged.* Springfield, Ill.: Charles C Thomas, Publisher.

Shanas, E., Townsend, P., Wedderbrun, D., Friis, H., Milhoj, P., and Stehouwer, J. 1968. *Old People in Three Industrial Societies.* New York: Atherton Press.

Simos, B. G. 1973. "Adult Children and Their Aging Parents." *Social Work* 18:78-85.

Soddy, K. 1967. *Men in Middle Life.* Philadelphia: J. B. Lippincott Co.

Spence, D. L., Feigenbaum, E. M., Fitzgerald, F., and Roth, J. 1968. "Medical Students' Attitudes Toward the Geriatric Patient." *Journal of the American Geriatrics Society* 16:976-83.

Tallmer, M., and Kutner, B. 1969. "Disengagement and Stresses of Aging." *Journal of Gerontology* 24:70-75.

Wolk, R. L., and Wolk, R. B. 1971. "Professional Workers' Attitudes toward the Aged." *Journal of the American Geriatrics Society* 19:624-39.

CHAPTER 7

Interactions and Treatment in Child-Abusing Families

The professional literature on abusive families has been prolific. A recent annotated bibliography on child abuse from the National Clearinghouse for Mental Health Information lists over 330 items. The literature covers a wide range of concerns, including the search for causes of violence to children, the organization and delivery of social services, the role of public prosecutors and court decisions, and the incidence of unreported cases.

Information about interpersonal transactions among family members is our particular concern in this chapter. We have also sought definitions of "family" in which something more is meant than the abused child and the abusive parent, since references to the family of the abused child often turn out to mean only the abusive parent.

Several aspects of the literature are of particular relevance for these purposes. First is the attempt to identify the psychological characteristics and life history of the abuser. Often these characteristics are seen as cause, though not necessarily sole cause, of the abuse. Second, the characteristics of the abused child are identified. It is suggested that certain qualities may make the child more vulnerable to abuse by the parent. Third, there are other causal explanations that take into account the situational elements of family life, such as the family's socioeconomic and material status, size of family, circumstances of birth of the abused child, age of parents, marital conflict, family isolation from relatives and the community, and stresses such as changes in family membership or roles, illness, or loss of employment.

What we wish to emphasize, however, are the transactional elements and systemic properties of the family, which are generally neglected in the literature. While the characteristics of the child and the abusing parent are undoubtedly important, we will draw attention to the kinds of interactions that may occur between the principals. Information about these dynamics yields understanding of both the relationship and the abuse. We also broaden the understanding of "family" beyond the parent-child dyad to include other relationships within the family. The interaction of parent and child takes place, not in isolation, but within the context of the parent's relationship with a spouse (or other significant adults), or the lack of such relationships, as well as the parent's relationship to other children in the family. Beyond this, current stresses affect the relationships among all family members. This view directs attention to current relationships, transactions, and events in the life of the family, and their interactive effects as a means for understanding why the abuse occurs and to provide clues about corrective action that might be undertaken.

Rather than providing an exhaustive explanation of child abuse, or even of the functioning of abusive families and their members, this chapter synthesizes some of the existing knowledge about these families with concepts about the family as a system. Particular attention is drawn to instances in which this way of conceptualizing the family has been used and found to be helpful. The synthesis draws heavily on family systems concepts that have been developed in the family therapy field. Family therapists have not been prolific in producing studies addressed to the child-abusing family, nor have helpers of the abusive families made much use of systems understanding and treatment orientation. Our effort to draw together both of these bodies of information should be useful to social workers and other practitioners.

Barnes, Chabon, and Hertzberg (1974) suggest the importance of using the time-tested clinical and treatment information which has been at our disposal over the years.

> It is not easy to move beyond the symptom of child abuse into the dynamics which have led to it. When this process becomes possible, what

emerges is that often these families have experienced lives similar to any seriously dysfunctional family. Taking primary attention off the symptom and carefully reviewing known causal variables and present stress factors will, more often than not, yield fruitful results. (p. 609)

In support of their position, these authors draw attention to available knowledge and theory in social casework, ego psychology, and parenthood. Because their case example reveals how second- and third-generation family characteristics can influence the occurrence of abuse, their position applies to the available knowledge about family systems and family group treatment.

DEFINITION OF ABUSE

We define the child-abusing family as one in which children have been subjected to nonaccidental physical injury. Given this brief definition, we have excluded a number of kinds of maltreatment of children from discussion.

Sexual abuse, for example, is included in the legal definition of abuse in many states, but is excluded from this discussion, since the dynamics appear to be different from physical abuse situations. Incestuous relationships between siblings and between parents and children, as well as sexual relationships between children and other adults responsible for their care or involved in a social relationship with the family, are defined as sexual abuse. It is differentiated from molestation of children by persons peripherally known or totally unknown to the family. Family dynamics in cases of sexual abuse are problematic. Disclosure of its occurrence has been found to be even more problematic for the family (James, 1977).

Another excluded topic is abuse which is not physical but is administered verbally and is psychological in effect. This does not fall within most statutory definitions, however much it may concern helping professionals. Psychological abuse includes a broad range of parent-child interactions and results in a variety of outcomes for children; it may, for example, stunt physical growth to the extent of producing dwarfism (Goodwin, 1978).

Neglect also is not considered child abuse, although the separation of abuse situations from neglect situations is not always easy, since neglect readily appears to abuse the child. The issue is most clearly demonstrated in "failure to thrive" children, who may suffer physical ills due to parental neglect. While some of the family dynamics which lead to neglect may appear similar to those found in families of physically abused children, our attention will be on the physically abused child.

Within the physical abuse category there can be great variation. Physical abuse ranges in severity from surface bruises or injuries, to internal injuries, to death. In frequency it may be confirmed on the basis of a single incident or of repeated incidence over extended periods of time prior to actual reporting. Thus, both "mild," single incidents and severe, repeated incidents are reported and confirmed as physical abuse. The dynamics of specific cases may be described within this range of differences, but the same set of dynamics clearly does not apply to all cases.

Other elements complicate the effort to discuss the dynamics of abuse situations. The abuse of one child involves different conceptualizations of family processes than the abuse of several children in the same family. In some situations abuse is inflicted by a sibling rather than a parent. Parents are also involved in the dynamics of such a situation, but in a different way than when the parent inflicts the injury directly. Other forms of violence may not be unrelated to situations in which the child is abused. Sometimes children inflict bodily injury or death on a parent (Post, 1982; Sargent, 1962). Sometimes spouses abuse each other. Though there may be common family processes in all these forms of family violence, we will not attempt to account for all of them. Our discussion focuses on physical violence directed at children by parents.

A MODEL FOR UNDERSTANDING THE OCCURRENCE OF VIOLENCE TOWARD CHILDREN

A natural reaction to child abuse is to wonder how a parent could behave in such a destructive way toward a child who is helpless or at least relatively powerless in the relationship with the parent. One common theory holds that a parent who injures a child must be emotionally unbalanced or mentally disturbed. In this linear, cause-and-effect relationship, the disturbed parent's behavior is traced to internal psychological conflict due to a deprived and destructive childhood of her or his own. Typically, the abusing parent was an abused child. As we shall see, there is merit to this position, but it does not by itself explain the occurrence of abuse. Why does violence occur at some times and not at others, and why is one child in a family injured when others are not?

Other theories take a more comprehensive view of child abuse. Gelles (1973) sees the psychopathology of the parent as an insufficient explanation because it allows for only a single cause. Abuse is more complex. The sex, age, and social position of the parents and the family also must be taken into account. Though abuse occurs in all socioeconomic strata, for example, it occurs more frequently in lower-socioeconomic status (SES) families. Statistics in 1977 showed 72 percent of abusing and neglecting families to have annual incomes under $9,000 (U.S. Department of Health, Education and Welfare, 1977). This is certainly true of the abuse that is reported. It is possible that in higher SES families injured children will be seen by private physicians, who are less likely to report abuse than clinics or emergency rooms, where lower SES families are more frequently seen. Thus there may be some distortion in the reported figures, but even with correction for this discrepancy, child abuse probably occurs more frequently in lower SES families.

In this expanded model for understanding child abuse, the economic and social stresses experienced by the family are seen as contributors to the occurrence of such abuse. Like Gelles, Gil (1970) also sees the stresses on the family as a contributory factor. Beyond this he points out that the cultural view of children and prevailing child-rearing practices in some sense sanction violent behavior toward children. There is general acceptance of violence within the culture as a means of dealing with conflict. Until recently, children have not been seen as needing special protection. The right of parents to control and discipline children has not been restricted, and physical punishment, even severe punishment, has been acceptable. These aspects of the attitudinal orientation of parents also contribute to the occurrence of abuse.

In addition to the cultural, economic, and social situation of the family which impinges on family functioning, stresses that are situational and transient may also contribute to the occurrence of abuse. A classification of crises in families was introduced in Chapter 2. Some that have been found to be in evidence in studies of abusive families include unwanted or unexpected pregnancies, large family size, loss of family members through death or desertion, marital stress, illness, role changes, and other more immediate stresses such as criticism or disappointment. Yet some statistics shed doubt on family size or family composition as factors. U.S. Department of Health, Education and Welfare statistics (1977) show abusive families in 84 percent of all cases to have three or fewer children and two or fewer in 67 percent of all cases. Further, 75 percent of all substantiated cases were in two-parent families.

The characteristics of the abused child are another element in a model which seeks to account for abuse. Children who are sickly, unresponsive, aggressive, retarded, or otherwise unrewarding to the parent have been more subject to abuse than other children.

Green, Gaines, and Sandgrund (1974) define the etiology of child abuse as "based upon an interaction among three factors: the personality traits of the parents that contribute to 'abuse proneness'; the child's characteristics that enhance his scapegoating, and the increased demand for child care exerted by the environment" (p. 886). We concur that the characteristics of parent and child and the elements in their current situation interact to bring about the abuse, but we leave the more general situational elements in the background in order to focus on the nature of these interactions. In the case of child abuse, "interaction" may mean, as we understand Green et al. to mean, that the parent under situational stress responds negatively to some identifiable characteristic or behavior of the child. There is little doubt that this occurs, but we suggest further that a negative cycle of interactions proceeds from these beginnings and results in the physical violence. Violence does not occur just because these three elements are present; an ensuing interactive process is also necessary.

The following sections draw on the existing literature to identify data and events that are needed for understanding the various elements and the interactions among them. We offer our conceptualization of the process that occurs and identify treatment methodology that has been developed to disrupt the negative processes and to promote the well-being of the abused child, siblings, and parents.

CHARACTERISTICS OF THE ABUSED CHILD

A whole array of characteristics of abused children has been reported. Children of both sexes and all ages are abused. According to a recent report of the National Institutes of Mental Health (1977), male and female children are abused in about equal numbers. Some studies report that more younger children than older children are abused, but it is not clear that this is generally true, since many investigations have focused on younger children. Gil (1970) reports that almost half of the children were over six years of age. The American Humane Association's summary of national statistics

(1982) show 43 percent of abused children to be five years or under with decreasing percentages in succeeding five-year age brackets. Thus, sex and age as characteristics of the child do not appear to be factors in vulnerability to abuse. Birth order or sibling position may be a factor. Only child, oldest child, or youngest child have all been identified in various studies as more subject to abuse (Janzen, 1978; NIMH, 1977).

Physical illness appears to make children more subject to abuse. Lynch (1975) compared abused children with nonabused siblings and found statistically significant differences in the amount of illness (including illnesses which require hospital admission) experienced by abused children and their unabused siblings during the first year of life. Fomufod, Sinkford, and Lowy (1975) and Pasamanick (1975) report similar findings and concerns. These troubles appear to antedate the neonatal period, since Lynch also reports that the period of pregnancy with the later-abused child was often characterized by complications requiring investigation or hospitalization, or by denial of the pregnancy or refusal of prenatal care. During the prenatal period, also, there were significant differences between the abused child and the normal sibling group.

Other studies have reported that the abused child may have a physical defect or be retarded, may be colicky or irritable, or may manifest poor impulse control (Green et al., 1974). Johnson and Morse (1968) report that the children failed to respond to care, to thrive, and to show normal growth and development. Children under five were described as whiny, fussy, listless, demanding, stubborn, unresponsive. Children over five were hyperactive or listless, boisterous or silent, immature, and overly dependent for their ages. Ounsted, Oppenheimer, and Lindsay (1974) describe a condition of "frozen watchfulness" which appears to be unresponsiveness to contact.

Other characteristics of the abused child appear to be important only because they produce certain images in the minds of the parents. The child may represent to the parent a hated parent, spouse, paramour, or sibling because of certain physical features, sibling position, or circumstances of conception and birth. These characteristics are of the order of those Vogel and Bell (1968) have reported as important in the selection of the family scapegoat and may thus help to account further for the selection of the child to be abused.

Kadushin and Martin (1981) provide an extensive review of characteristics of abused children. They conclude that certain patterns of child behavior are apt to be at high risk for abuse. The irritable child, the negativistic child, the demanding, overdependent child, the hyperactive child, and the unresponsive child impose greater demands on and offer fewer satisfactions to the parent (p. 67).

Steele and Pollock (1972) conclude that in the possession of these characteristics the child contributes unwittingly to the abuse. It is not clear from any studies to date, however, that the characteristics were always existent prior to the abuse. Possibly they appeared after the abuse occurred. Lynch's (1975) data on physical illness during early months would suggest the illness as a precursor, but she also produces data about the condition and attitudes of the mother during pregnancy which complicates the picture. Premature birth has also been mentioned as a characteristic of the abused child. However, one study (Hunter, Kilstron, Kraybill, and Loda, 1978), which compared abused and nonabused children who were born prematurely, found differences in their families and not in the children themselves. Corey, Miller, and Widlak (1975), in a study of two years of hospital admissions, compared children admitted because of battering and those admitted for other reasons. They also found more differences in the families than in the children themselves. Such reports suggest that some child characteristics, including physical illness, may be responsive to parental behavior. The inability to determine which comes first, the child's characteristics or the parents' responses, implies that parental perceptions and the interactive process may be more important than the characteristics of the child by themselves.

We would also note that it should be clear from the brief survey that child characteristics do not by themselves account for the occurrence of abuse and certainly do not in all instances evoke a negative response. We do nevertheless conclude, as does Smith (1984, p. 342), that "most research studies which measure the abusive parents' perception of the abused child indicate that most abused children are seen as more difficult by their parents."

CHARACTERISTICS OF THE ABUSER

The catalog of characteristics of the parents who abuse their children is lengthy. Social class is one of these characteristics. The National Institutes of Mental Health (1977) found that "Among reported cases, low-income, low-skill, and low-education families are over-represented" (p. 132). Smith and Hanson (1975) found that many of the personal characteristics and attitudes attributed to abusers are confounded by social class, but they do not appear to differentiate abusers from nonabusers when controls for social class are instituted. One characteristic they do identify as differentiating abusive parents, when social class is controlled, is their tendency to use physical punishment, which suggests that "they are under-controlled rather than over-controlled aggressors." Since social class may be viewed as a characteristic of both the parent and the social situation, it may be that social situational stresses, rather than personality characteristics, are the significant aspect of class which contributes to the perpetration of abuse. Thus any emphasis on the personality characteristic of the parents needs to be tempered by awareness of social class characteristics.

Green et al. (1974) characterize abusive mothers as relying on their children to gratify their dependency needs, having poor impulse control, feeling worthless, suffering from shifting self-identifications, using projection and externalization to defend their self-esteem, and projecting their own negative attributes onto their children. Ounsted et al. (1974) found various mental disturbances were present, but they do not elaborate statistically, since that would be more "likely to mislead than to clarify." We agree that it is not particularly helpful to identify categories of mental illness as a characteristic. Ounsted et al. describe the mothers as feeling "trapped, unwanted, unloved and unequal to their roles as children, as spouses and as parents." Johnson and Morse (1968) describe both parents as anxious, hostile, depressed, and untrusting. The parents studied responded inappropriately, impulsively, and excessively to events and sought love, gratification, and fulfillment in their children. Physical deficiencies (Blumberg, 1974) and low frustration tolerance (Gayford, 1975) have also been observed in abusive parents.

There is almost universal agreement that parents who abuse their children were themselves as children deprived and subject to parental violence (Steele and Pollock, 1974), though USDHEW statistics reported that only 12 percent of substantiated abusers were abused as children. Nevertheless, they suffer from an intense need for love, acceptance, and self-affirmation. Picket and Maton (1977) say that they are alienated from their parents historically and currently and that they yearn for love and affection. There is also general agreement that abusive parents lack parenting skills and clear images of what can reasonably be expected from their children (Tracy and Clarke, 1974). Their own childhood histories suggest that their family models prepared them inadequately for their roles and behavior as parents and contribute to their maltreatment of their children. Since most abusing parents give evidence of such a childhood history, there is reason to be concerned that the presently abused child will become an abusive adult. There are, however, no firm data from longitudinal studies that support the contention that all abused children will become abusive parents (Jayaratne, 1977), and several recent reports suggest that only 20 to 30 percent of them do (Hyman, 1978).

Many of these characteristics are attributed to both parents of the abused child, not only to the overt perpetrator of the abuse. Mothers do not abuse children significantly more often than fathers (NIMH, 1977, p. 135). In a given situation one parent may be the overt abuser while the other is an accomplice who accepts, condones, and sometimes abets it (Steele and Pollock, 1972). The fact that a disproportionate share of abuse occurs at the hands of females would be logically explained by the fact they they are more frequently the child's caretaker.

FAMILY INTERACTIONS

Dyadic Interaction

The particular characteristics of parent and child in child abuse situations set up conditions for a relationship which is likely to be unsatisfying to either of them. For example, a small child who is sickly and in need of a great deal of care and attention is likely not only to be unsatisfying to the parents but also to place additional demands on them. Parents who in their own development lacked both needed nurturance and a clear understanding of their needs may find the neediness of the child overwhelming, and this may result in unresponsive neglect or an aggressive response. In either case the child may respond with more of the same crying and parent-requiring behavior, rather than less of it, resulting in more of the same response from the parent. In other instances, the infant may not possess any particular physical or mental characteristics, but the circumstances of birth or some other element that prompts a negative image of the infant in the mind of the parents may prompt the negative parental response.

Kadushin and Martin (1981) offer further insight into the parent/child interaction. In an extensive and detailed review they document the bidirectionality of parent/child interaction. Their own research on abuse incidents showed that behavior on the part of the child had precipitated the abusive incident, prior to which the parent had tried to deal with the behavior in other ways. "Parents were described as reacting to crying, disobedience, hostility or some other behavior of the child in nine out of ten of the incidents" (p. 114). In their view children respond selectively, sometimes positively, sometimes negatively, to parent behavior. Parent behavior is contingent upon child behavior as well as the other way around. "The feedback from each party in the interaction has consequences for each, which, over a period of time, establishes the patterns of behavior which characterize the relationship" (p. 149). This is not to say that the child "causes" the abuse, because this is only one of many factors operative, but it does suggest that new interaction patterns could be helpful in precluding further abuse.

For an infant, the behavior cannot in any sense be thought of as premeditated, but only as an expression of the needs of the child and thus an "unwitting" contribution to the situation. Older children have their own ways of expressing their need for a positive parental response. Both their withdrawn and unresponsive and their aggressive behaviors may be means of seeking such response, but neither is likely to be perceived by the parents as rewarding their own need for a positive response from others. When they respond negatively to the child's behavior and thereby fail to meet the child's need for positive response, they also do not dispose the child to friendly behavior in return. The negative response of each to the other becomes more extreme until violence to the child results or something else happens to interrupt this sequence. Such sequences are defined as symmetrical escalations by Watzlawick, Beavin, and Jackson (1967). In older children violence toward the parent may also in some instances be a consequence.

Family Triads

The dyadic interaction of parent and child does not take place in isolation from other forces and events. A number of factors contribute to its occurrence and perhaps, occasionally, to its interruption. Among the more significant of these situational factors is the relationship between the parents.

The studies of abusive families are rich with data about the problems in these relationships. Blumberg (1974) says that:

> The hostility that one parent feels toward the other but cannot express because of fear can be displaced onto the child. A similar mechanism can play a role concerning one parent's child by a previous partner. . . . In the

case of an unmarried mother, or when the husband or paramour deserts the home, the mother with a poor ego structure and a vulnerable personality may resort to battering her child when she is faced with a stressful situation. (p. 25)

Steinhausen (1972) also sees the child as a substitute for the partner who, in a dominant-submissive marital relationship, cannot be attacked. In a study of battered wives, Gayford (1975) found that the women in many instances discharged their frustration on their children. In a study of the battered child syndrome, Bennie and Sclare (1969) found that in the weeks prior to abuse of a child the marriage of the abuser had been in a turbulent state. One form of filicide is done deliberately to bring suffering to the marital partner, according to Resnick (1969). Moore (1974) describes abused children as "pawns in marital wars" who are injured in trying to defend one parent in a battle with the other. Jealousy by one parent of the other parent's feelings toward a child is seen as a factor in abuse by Ounsted et al. (1974). In one of their cases the father tore the baby from his wife's breast and threw it across the room, saying, "Those breasts are mine." Situations in which the abused child is seen by the mother as competition for the father's love are also reported by Lansky and Erickson (1974).

Some of the subtleties of these interactions are described by Steele and Pollock (1972). A spouse who very much needs to please may be instigated to abuse a child by the other parent's comment that the child is spoiled or needs more discipline or by critical comments about the spouse's handling of the child. Alternately, an overwrought parent may instigate the other parent's violent response with a "You do something" attitude (Kempe and Kempe, 1976). In other instances a nonabusing parent may attempt to compensate the child for negative treatment by the other parent, giving rise to jealousy and further hostility on the part of the abusive parent. In an instance in our experience, the father insisted that the adolescent child needed a firm hand and discipline to compensate for the mother's tendency to overlook the child's negative behavior. The mother felt she needed to be kind and loving to compensate for the father's abusing, rejecting behavior. A reduction in the abusive behavior of one parent also has consequences for the other parent; Steele and Pollock (1972) report that the nonabusing parent may become abusive when the previously abusing parent becomes more tender. Again, the jealousy of the other parent is evident. Vogel and Bell (1968) report that the marital relationship becomes more stormy when the attacks on the child subside.

In family triads, therefore, three different dynamics are likely. The first is that the child is a scapegoat for the hostilities which the parents do not direct at each other for fear of disrupting their relationship with each other. Second, love and attention given to the child are seen as being subtracted from what one parent has to offer the other, which gives rise to jealousy and a consequent attack on the child. The child is seen as depriving the spouse of desired and needed affection. Finally, the attack on the child is also a means of pleasing the spouse in response to a critical comment. In a stable husband-wife relationship, according to Blumberg (1974), "both parents share the responsibilities of child rearing in one way or another. Frustrations can be communicated and solutions or advice can be forthcoming." This is obviously not the situation in the relationships between an abusive parent and a spouse. Their relationship with each other does not meet their needs for love and affirmation, and is not seen as doing so. They are in no position to be supportive of each other as spouses and thus do not offer a base for effective parenting. Smith and Hanson (1975) found that abusive mothers reacted more negatively to difficulties with their husband than to difficulties with their child, that the behavior toward the child "is based not on a rejection of the child as such, but on a rejection of their unsatisfactory social, marital, and parental roles" (p. 522). According to Newberger (1973), "We are coming to see that the essential element in child abuse is not the intention to destroy the child, but rather the inability of the parent to nurture his offspring, a failing which can stem directly from ascertainable environmental conditions." (p. 327)

The third member of the triad need not necessarily be a legal spouse, nor even a spouse. The dynamics of triads would certainly apply to common-law or live-in situations as well. The third person may also be an extended family member, living in the home or not, most likely a parent, but not necessarily. Anyone who has some significance in the life of the parent might serve as the third member of the triad and could evoke the feelings of criticism, blame, loss, jealousy, and anger that lead to the abusive behavior. Single-parent families are thus not exempt from the possibilities of negative triadic interaction, and workers are well advised to obtain information about the participation of seemingly irrelevant or distant persons.

Siblings

There is amazingly little documentation of the position of siblings of the abused child in the occurrence of violence. In some instances siblings are also abused (Johnson and Morse, 1968), sometimes worse than the child whose abuse was first reported. If the abused child is removed from the home, another child is sometimes scapegoated by being singled out for abuse. In other cases, a sibling may ally himself or herself with the parent in attacking a child or even become the means of the parent's attack on the child, similar to the way a spouse can be provoked to attack a child. And a sibling who is neither victim nor perpetrator may live in fear that what happened to the abused child may also happen to him and may doubt the parents' love. In some instances siblings feel they are somehow responsible for the abuse, and they should have protected the abused child (Beezley, Martin, and Alexander (1976). Whatever their role, their participation in the family will be affected. Treatment also should attend to these various aspects of the siblings' experience, both to enable their own growth and to improve the functioning of the family group.

OTHER SITUATIONAL ELEMENTS

Illness in the parents, like illness in the abused child, can be a factor in abuse. Parents who are ill are limited in ability to meet the child's need and may be frustrated because they are deprived of meaningful roles, either within the family or outside it. Galdston (1965) notes that illness or disability sometimes deprives parents of a meaningful role outside the home as a breadwinner and thrusts them into a more direct but unaccustomed child-caring role when the spouse goes to work. Their inability to adapt to the illness or disability, plus the thrust into the undesired role, both serve to upset whatever balance in relationships existed prior to the illness. Underlying or together with all of these factors may be the frustrations in some families brought about by poor housing and limited resources.

Losses of relationship also appear to be a significant situational element. Losses may be barely discernible, as when the nonabusing parent leaves the house or is unavailable when needed or desired by the child-caring parent. Other losses may be more obvious. The withdrawal of a boyfriend from a relationship or the separation of a spouse can serve to undermine the parent's ability to respond positively to a child. Baldwin and Oliver (1975) report "frequent changes of adults in charge of the children as spouses, cohabitees and relatives came and went" (p. 212). Family change and instability both appear as situational elements contributing to abuse.

Illness and losses might be manageable if the family had other supports. But Holland (1973) reports that abusive families are isolated, including isolation from social agencies to which they had in the past gone to seek to have their needs met. Bennie and Sclare (1969) found "lack of support of parents and parents in-law was often evident, sometimes because of religious conflict, more frequently because of psychopathic attitudes. The management of the deprived home devolved upon one individual, usually the assailant." There is in such situations little relief from child-caring responsibility, or any support when other stresses such as illness, change of housing, loss of employment, or intrafamily conflicts occur. Smith's (1984) recent review confirms the impact of current life stress in abuse families.

The combination of limited parental coping capacity, the care-requiring characteristics of the child, the tenuously balanced relationships between pairs or triads of family members, and situational stress appear to set the stage for abuse of the child. In some instances material means may discourage violence by allowing relief through the hire of child-care services or making the parent feel rewarded with treats or purchases. Such relief is not available to the economically deprived family. Newberger (1973) points out that welfare programs offer inadequate help in such stressful circumstances. Nor does such relief always serve to avoid violence, as is evident in more affluent families in which abuse occurs. In other instances a responsive environment in the form of an empathetic circle of friends or a caring extended family might be helpful. But where these are not available or helpful, other means of treatment are necessary.

TREATMENT EFFORTS

While interdisciplinary treatment teams and concrete services are both useful and necessary in work with abusive families, our discussion of treatment will draw on the three elements of the model proposed above for understanding the occurrence of violence toward children and the interactions between these elements: characteristics of the child, characteristics of the parents, and the situational effects of the environment in which the interactions take place. We also will not consider the authoritative aspects of involvement, though we recognize that in these cases the use of authority and questions about who uses it and how it is used are extremely important and difficult, particularly in the initial stages of contact with abusing families.

The characteristics of the parents and of the child in child-abuse situations, as described above, are vulnerabilities that they bring to the interaction. Some of the treatment efforts considered here serve to help parents and children deal with these vulnerabilities, and thus to interrupt the negative cycle of interaction that takes place between them and to set their relationship on a course likely to be more satisfying to both. Insofar as the relationship between the parents—assuming two-parent families, or the parent and significant other adults in one-parent families—is a factor in the situation, treatment efforts should be designed to enable parents to find other ways of coping with their difficulties. Some treatment efforts to be described are directed to this end. Other efforts are directed to other elements of situational stress, necessitating both hard and soft services.

Interventions with Parents

Meeting Parents' Needs. The worker with abusive parents needs first of all to convey that he or she is there to understand, care, and help rather than to threaten or criticize. A nonjudgmental attitude is essential (Roth, 1975). The worker responds to the parents' strong dependency needs and to their need for a parenting, caring person in their lives. Consistency in this accepting and caring position is important because the parents' own feelings of guilt and their previous life experience may lead them to find such an attitude unbelievable and perhaps even frightening. Ounsted et al. (1974), who work in a residential setting with mothers and children, observed a "second day packing" phenomenon—a wish to flee—that results from these feelings. Most workers have found that concern about the parents' own needs and feelings should be emphasized with the parents, rather than concern about the child, and this concern should be for the needs of both parents. By this approach, the worker avoids arousing the same feelings of jealousy and neglect that have characterized the family's internal interactions. The applicable principle from conjoint family treatment is the worker's ability to identify with each member present and to avoid siding with one family member against another.

The worker's ability to identify with both parents is not only critical in conjoint sessions; it is also necessary in separate individual sessions. For some workers this may be particularly difficult, at least initially, in relation to the overt perpetrator of the abuse. Blumberg (1974) notes that some spouses are not able to share the worker and that conjoint sessions should come later in the work with the family. Individual sessions may be necessary, especially early in the case. Separate workers from the interdisciplinary treatment team appear in these instances to be particularly useful.

The giving, nurturant approach is manifest first of all through the workers' attitudinal orientation, but giving comes in more concrete forms also. The residential program described by Ounsted and Lynch (1976) provides complete care for mothers and children. Tuszynski and Dowd (1978) describe a day-care program which children attend five days a week and in which parents participate two days. In neither of these programs is the child separated completely from the family, but the parents are given relief from child care and the opportunity to observe how others care for children. Observing a child worker's tender care for their children in some instances stirs negative feeling in the parent (Bentovim, 1977), requiring attentive response to that parent by the worker. This again confirms family systems theory that the entry of the worker into the system alters the system. In other programs parent aides offer assistance to the parents in their own homes, working with the parents and providing support, companionship, and relief from child care. In still other programs, children may be left for short periods of time with child-care staff, so that the parent has relief from this responsibility. Services which meet family needs for income maintenance, housing, employment, and medical care are also provided.

The NIMH review (1977) notes that some programs consider nurturance to the parents sufficient in itself, since it meets deep needs of the parents which have in the past been unmet and thereby enables them to be more giving to their children. In our view, as in that of the NIMH study of programs, no program can be effective without this base; other elements of treatment may not begin until parents experience an alliance with the worker. However, meeting the needs of the parents by itself is not sufficient. Jones (1977) concludes that "although parents can and do make considerable personal gains through intensive, supportive treatment, this does not automatically improve the quality of life and relationships for their children" (p. 116). Specifically, parenting skills must be developed, the parents' denial and guilt need to be dealt with, and the social isolation of the family should be ended.

Teaching Parenting. Many activities fall under this broad rubric. The work just described in meeting the parent's needs for nurturance serves to strengthen them as individuals and puts them in better position to function as members of the parental hierarchy. Their task for the family is to give leadership and structure to the organization. With the nurturance they have been offered, energies are freed for them to individualize each other, to be more assertive in setting expectations, to set rules and develop behavioral guidelines for the children, to communicate verbally more frequently and effectively, and to see and respond to each child as a separate person. The following interventions contribute in one way or another to these ends.

Providing parents with the opportunity to observe how others care for their children offers them the chance to learn new skills in child care and to overcome the deficits in their own parental role models. Seeing how others approach a colicky, unresponsive, stubborn, insistent, or otherwise difficult child enables them to learn other, more useful responses. These can be substituted for their own aggressive responses in order to arouse a positive reaction in the child. These opportunities are provided in residential and day-care programs but also constitute an aspect of parent-aide activity. Opportunities of this nature may also be provided by social workers during parental visits with children who are temporarily separated from the family.

In addition to modeling parenting skills, some programs teach specific aspects of child care and offer parents instruction about what can reasonably be expected of children of a given age. Their own experience and models have not provided this knowledge, which is particularly crucial.[1] Instruction is sometimes given individually to parents, sometimes in classes. It may be given by social workers or by other members of a treatment team.

Attempts have also been made to teach specific modes of interaction with children. Beezley et al. (1976) have found Parent Effectiveness Training to be useful but in need of modification because in its original mode it seems too advanced for abusive parents. Other approaches which modify the behaviors of both parent and child have been found to be effective. Jeffrey (1976) shows parents how to give positive reinforcement and teaches them to communicate, to play, to give positive attention, and to adapt the house to the child. She also helps parents draw up behavioral contracts with children and demonstrates how to deflect both their own and their children's aggressive responses.

---

[1]This lack of parental knowledge and experience may help to account for the fact that in some studies "only" children or "oldest" children, no matter what age, appear to be more frequent victims of abuse. Some learning of child care may have taken place by the time the second and later children appear.

We emphasize the importance of conjoint work with the parent or parents and the child in several of the projects cited. While didactic instruction for parents has its uses, the conjoint effort provides immediate opportunity for the parent to try new behaviors suggested by the worker, and for the worker to observe the interactional process and to give further guidance to both parent and child in response to what she sees.

Work with a mother who had held her seventeen-year-old child's hand over a fire revealed that she was giving intermittent reinforcement to the child's negative behavior (Palakow and Peabody, 1975). She was taught to identify the child's positive behaviors and reinforce them instead through the provision of allowances or attention. Tracy and Clark (1974) suggest that parents should try to "catch the child being good" and then offer rewards for the behavior. Treatment for a mother who had tried to suffocate and drown her child, but who had subsequently withdrawn from interaction to avoid further violence, involved incremental steps toward reengagement which were likely to be rewarding to both child and parent (Gilbert, 1976). The husband was involved in rewarding the wife for positive steps between the treatment sessions. Gilbert proceeds on the assumption that behavior change can precede changes in feeling but will lead to changes in interaction and in the feelings of the participants toward each other. By these means mothers in a program conducted by Tracy, Ballard, and Clark (1975) "improved their techniques for controlling the children, using less physical punishment. In addition, by increasing the parents' sense of competence as parents and adults, consistent improvement was shown in other areas of family functioning."

Modeling, teaching parenting skills, providing knowledge about the expectable behaviors of children are all useful in giving parents models and skills they can use to alter parent-child interaction. The negative cycle can be changed to a cycle of interactions that is more rewarding to both. The effort to alter parents' responses to their children, however, can take place only in the context of a relationship in which the parents can clearly experience concern for themselves as persons, and not only as instruments to meet their children's needs. Thus, their learning occurs in the context of being given to and nurtured. The modeling of care-giving behavior has teaching value because it provides parental relief from child care. Learning can occur when teaching is experienced not as a criticism but as a means of achieving a more rewarding relationship with a child.

Parent skills training serves to develop more realistic and consistent responses of parent to child and a clearer expression of parental expectations. This makes the child more clear about the rules and less likely to deviate from parental expectations, so that less demand is placed on the parent for direction and supervision. It also makes the child feel more comfortable, positive, and responsive to the parent. A changed interaction pattern should follow. In giving attention to the dyadic interactive process, the worker needs to bear in mind the balance of relationships throughout the family. This avoids rearousal of jealousy between parents and children and prevents its appearance between family members and the worker or workers on the treatment team.

Teaching Communication. Wells (1981) draws attention to deficits of verbal communication in abusive families. Noting the earlier work by Polansky, Borgman, and DeSaix (1972) on "verbal inaccessibility" in neglect families, she says that abusive families manifest similar inaccessibility. Communication rates are lower. Behavior occurs as a substitute and elicits minimal comment. The need is for talk and verbal exchange of observations, thoughts, feelings, and reactions instead of nonverbal communication. Worker effort promotes conversation, no matter what the topic. Conversation between parent and child conveys interest and caring. The worker stops nonverbal interaction to label actions and talk about them. Explanations by the parent to the child which are often lacking are encouraged and serve to provide instruction and structure. Expressing feelings and being listened to offer relief and provide understanding. Since feelings of futility, depreciation, and powerlessness lie behind the noncommunicativeness, the opening of communication stimulates hope and frees energy. Increased conversation between spouses can have similar effects. Listening as well as talking may be difficult, and worker effort may be needed to enable other family members to be attentive, to take seriously what has been said, and to respond with relevant verbalization of their own. Clarity of messages can be facilitated by worker suggestions for rephrasing when needed or by proffering verbalizations when the individual is having difficulty in finding appropriate words. These need to be confirmed by asking the individual whether the worker's words convey accurately what he or she intended to say.

Communication problems other than verbal inaccessibility may be present. Interruptions, simultaneous talking, irrelevant remarks, or a general escalation of noise require worker regulation of verbal behavior so that family members listen to each other and convey respect and affirmation through their listening behavior. When noise levels are high it may also be necessary to be clear about who is talking to whom and to require members to talk *to* each other rather than *about* each other.

We have placed this discussion of communications in the context of parent/child relationship treatment where it is clearly needed and useful. Regulation of communication may also be necessary with other family pairs and, in some aspects, more applicable when more family members are in conjoint sessions.

Encouraging Parental Acceptance of Responsibility. Parents also can be helped to move from a defensive denial of responsibility for the child's injury to ownership of responsibility, to concern for the child's welfare and recognition of their own wish to be better parents. In the context of a giving and nonjudgmental relationship, it becomes possible for them to do so. They are often relieved to reveal the assault and to talk about their emotions at the time and how they felt afterward. These sessions, timed rightly, can be individual with one parent or conjoint with both. Ounsted et al. (1974) found that parents can set for themselves the task of breaking the cycle of violence that has been characteristic of their families for generations. The worker's questions about their own childhood family experiences help them become aware of this cycle and make it more possible for them to break the hostile identification with their own parents. Increasing the individuation of the parents and their separateness from their own parents helps to establish a separate identity and increases confidence and competence. In instances in which the child is scapegoated because in a parent's eyes he or she is representative of some other hated person in the life of the parent, the displacement has to be recognized and the original feelings about those persons need to be resolved.

These interventions, which are of a psychotherapeutic nature, may occur in individual or conjoint sessions with parents. Group treatment has also been found to serve this purpose productively (Oppenheimer, 1978). But they may also occur when time is allowed in visits to day-care centers, in sessions in which plans are made for visiting a child who is separated from the home, or interspersed in parent skills training sessions.

The mix of the various interventions with parents—nurturance, parent skills training, and psychotherapy—will be different for different parents. The readiness of the parents to engage in parent training or emotional abreaction will come at various stages of contact, depending on their ability to trust the worker's acceptance and caring for them. The mix of interventions depends also on the family's material status and needs and the agency's ability to provide services such as day care, parent aides, and other needed services in support of the parents and their parenting efforts. Worker assessment and reassessment of needs and readiness must be continuous.

Treatment of the Abused Child

The NIMH (1977) study of treatment programs notes with approval the great amount of effort devoted to nurturing abusive parents as family leaders, which enables them to fulfill themselves and their functions as parents. It also notes, with some sadness, the widespread neglect of treatment for the children who are abused. These children also need help, of course, and for some of the same reasons as the parents. Beyond immediate physical care, their emotional needs must be met, and their interaction with their parents needs to be changed.

The child's need to be given to and attended to can take many forms. At a minimum, physical injuries and health problems must be cared for. When the child feels physically well, the demands on parents for care are reduced, and child and parents can feel more friendly to one another. Caring attention can release the child from "frozen watchfulness," unresponsiveness, or withdrawal, and from the opposite behaviors of hyperactivity and unregulated or hostile responses. New behaviors appear first with substitute caretakers while the child is receiving residential or day care, and only tentatively in contacts with the child's own parents. But as parents learn to respond to the child's changed responsiveness, the child's responsiveness to parents continues to improve. The changed interaction between parents and child is made possible initially through meeting each party's individual needs, and then through the more reasonable and explicit structure provided by the parents. Jeffrey's (1976) effort to teach children how to respond shows promise of promoting positive interactions between parent and child.

Beyond these efforts, play therapy or psychotherapy may enable abused children to cope with their feelings about injuries and illnesses, and about their parents and siblings. The hurts and rejection they have experienced will no doubt be alleviated by the changed behavior of the parents and the new interaction pattern which will result. But play therapy or psychotherapy can remove further blocks to children's growth and development and make it possible for them to behave in relationship-seeking ways which are rewarding to them and to the parents.

Marital Treatment

The treatment of the parents and the abused child described thus far is designed to help them as individuals and to change their interactions. However, the dyadic interaction between parent and child occurs in the context of other relationships, some of which do not involve the child's participation but which nevertheless result in child abuse. These relationships also need correction and alteration. As Blumberg (1974) says, treatment should meet the needs of parents as persons before it focuses on marital problems. The NIMH (1977) report suggests this sequence of treatment activity for the family.

While we agree that a focus on marital problems in general may be out of place in the early stages of treatment, we suggest that marital relationships as they affect behavior toward the child can be considered early in the contact. Once the parents have acknowledged their violence to the child, the relationship between spouses may be considered as a situational element in the *specific* act of abuse—what was going on at the time, how the spouse behaved, and how the abuser felt about these events. The parents can be encouraged to express not only feelings of anger and rejection, but also their views of what was wanted from spouses and others and what would have been helpful. These feelings and the responses of the spouse to the abusing parent can be elicited in conjoint sessions. The worker is in a position to acknowledge the needs of each, to note the expectancies of the other that give rise to disappointment, jealousy, and scapegoating behavior. The spouse's ability or inability to respond, his or her wish or unwillingness to do so can be made explicit and can then be taken into account in the further development of the child care plan and of the marital relationship.

The problem to be solved at this stage of treatment is the occurrence or avoidance of further abuse. The task of the family adults is to find a way, if they can, of helping each other to achieve avoidance of further abuse. At this stage of the treatment the parents can learn what each needs from the other to achieve this goal.

These efforts may move them, over time, to deal with many aspects of their relationship, so that in the long run they can depend on each other rather than on their child for positive responsiveness and affirmation. Alternatively, they may have to accept the knowledge that the dependability they seek will not be forthcoming, and they can learn to avoid further disappointment by looking to their own strengths or elsewhere for the support they need.

In addition to the clarification of roles and expectations, couples can benefit from help in learning how to communicate in ways that promote positive relationships. Communications that are vague or ambiguous, and sequences of communications that do not result in clarity, can be corrected by means we have suggested elsewhere (see especially Chapter 5 on problem poverty families). Work on communications not only facilitates the clarification of roles and expectations; it can also help to resolve differences and disagreements so that they do not build into reservoirs of ill will which might eventually spill onto spouse or child.

For many parents, work in couples groups offers an added advantage in that they can often respond better to other parents than to professionals. The group can bolster both the parental and marital roles. McNeil and McBride (1979) have reported success with couples groups that covered such subject matter as parenting, discipline, finances, sex, communication, sensitivity, and decision making. The group offered support for both partners, especially the overtly abusive parent. A male-female therapist team was seen as particularly useful as a model for working together.

Our underlying assumption is that solid relationships between the parents or between a single parent and other supportive adults or agencies reduce parental dependence on positive responses from the child as a means for affirming parental identity and self-worth. These adult relationships, therefore, ought to be fostered and enhanced. The relationships of one or both adults to external systems may also need to be encouraged, changed, or enlarged, so that these systems can be supportive of the nuclear family group.

Treatment for the Family, Including Siblings

The literature on child abuse is almost totally silent on family therapy, except to note that it is strange in a field in "which the focus is on the family, that so little family therapy is offered" (NIMH, 1977). The net result of all the previously described aspects of treatment should be improved family relationships and functioning. While work on any part of the system can and should help the family as a whole, work with the whole system is still important and offers added advantages.

Work with the family as a whole has been undertaken in all-day programs for groups of families (Alexander, McQuiston, and Rodeheffer, 1976), on a full-time residential basis (Bentovim, 1977), and in regular sessions in the home (Cautley, 1980). Other formats of varying duration and intensity may be developed. Such extended and more intensive contact with the entire family around a variety of activities and circumstances allows workers to observe interactions between all family members, including siblings of the abused child, and to focus attention on interactive processes as they occur. In the residential and all-day programs multiple-family participation promotes interaction around work, food, and play as well as talk, and work in split groupings of children, couples, mothers, and fathers as well as whole-family meetings. In these situations, action is live and attention can be directed to changing interpersonal transactions, using many of the procedures described above for changing parent-child or spousal relationships, such as learning to respond to good behavior, improving communications, and sharing feelings.

Cohesiveness can be fostered by whole-family participation. Family structure can become more firm and clear. Individual isolation and blame is minimized. Children and their parents may be helped to negotiate behavior changes and the rewards that follow. Boundaries between parental and child generations may be strengthened through worker support of the parental subsystem. Multiple-family groups in all-day, residential, or outpatient programs allow families to see how other families work and to learn from each other.

Work with the Extended Family

In some cases it is useful to help an abusive mother work on her relationship with her own mother, to resolve the disappointment, fear, and ambivalence that characterize the relationship (Steele and Pollock, 1972). We see the need for both parents to achieve greater separateness and detachment from their families of origin and to define an identity of their own. This work on differentiation of self is characteristic of the family therapy field. It may be accomplished by direct work on these relationships in contacts with members of the extended family (Bowen, 1971), or by asking individuals or couples to describe relationships in their families of origin. In these ways they may become aware of the origins of their expectations for current relationships, and this awareness can relieve them of the need to continue these relationships and enable them to negotiate new kinds of interaction.

In instances in which the parents' relationships with their own parents and with siblings are characterized less by hostility, ambivalence, and lack of differentiation and more by simple lack of contact, it may be possible for the worker to enable the extended family to be more of a resource for the parents. This can provide the parents with avenues of social contact or, in some instances, emotional or tangible support.

Coping with Situational Stress

While relationships with spouses, paramours, and the extended family are one form of situational stress, other crises may also require intervention. These stress situations include pregnancy or birth of another child, loss of employment or other change in financial situation, illness of an adult or child, or loss of an immediate or extended family member. Any of these stresses can disrupt whatever balance has existed in the give-and-take of family relationships. They may overwhelm a child-caring parent or thrust the parent into an undesired role. New expectations can arise for all family members.

Workers should be available at such times to family members, either individually or as a group, to help them deal with feelings and find ways of coping. Tasks must be defined and agreement reached as to how they are to be accomplished and by whom. Where external resources are needed, the worker needs either to make arrangements for them, with family members' consent, or to serve in a broker or advocate role for the family. The worker's availability at times of crisis seems particularly important in this group of families, where the balance of relationships and personal and social resources is often precarious.

The social isolation of the family is another aspect of situational stress, or, more specifically, a factor in the lack of relief from situational stress. Inputs from the extended family are, of course, one way of reducing the isolation. Initially, however, the treatment agency is the chief avenue for reducing social isolation. The agency provides the family with new feedback about its operations and supplies it with specific means of support and help. Treatment in groups, in residential settings, or even in weekend camps (Oppenheimer, 1978) can open up new personal contacts for the family. These new experiences can provide them with the skills needed in interactions with individuals outside the immediate family group and offer them a bridge to relationships in the larger community. Referral to Parents Anonymous, a self-help group of abusive parents, can serve to reduce isolation and provide support.

A NOTE ABOUT THE ORGANIZATION OF SERVICES

The kind of connectedness of the agency to the family that we have described requires considerable outreach, substantial time in contact, and a variety of modes of helping and giving. These are not always available. Certainly, it is not enough to assign a single worker to a huge caseload of families. The literature refers repeatedly to the necessity for interdisciplinary teamwork, both for diagnosis and treatment. This provides a variety of modes of helping and meets the need to work with all members of the family, not only with the person who has physically inflicted the abuse.

There is a great need to broaden and strengthen the range and availability of services to include all of these elements, if families in which abuse has occurred are to be successfully helped. Treating agencies will increase their effectiveness to the degree that they are organized toward these ends.

SUMMARY

In this chapter we have taken note of some specific characteristics of abusing parents and abused children and have observed how these characteristics give rise to negative patterns of interaction. We have noted that the interaction of abusive parent and abused child does not take place in isolation but is affected by other interactions in the family and events in the family's situation. The relationship between the parents is seen as particularly crucial, perhaps as crucial as the relationship between parent and child. There has been relative neglect in the field of the experiences of siblings of the abused child, and the family as a whole is seen as likely to be isolated from external supports, or in difficult relationships with extended family. Unlike other writing on child abuse, which focuses primarily on the abused child and the overt perpetrators of the abuse, we have emphasized the transactions between family members and with the larger family system.

The treatments described are designed to strengthen individual identity and competence, to improve interpersonal transactions, and to alter relationships within and beyond the immediate family. The efforts include nurturance of the parents, imparting skills and knowledge for parenting, help in dealing with feelings, and recognition of reactions to members' own behavior and that of others. These activities are useful in interrupting old patterns and initiating new behaviors, and thereby altering interactional patterns. Enabling the parents to alter their relationships so that they can support each other in child-caring and parenting activities is an important means of helping the child, as well as providing greater satisfaction for the parents themselves. Where other situational stresses affect the balance of family relationships, agency action is needed to provide relief and support.

The range of services encompassed requires comprehensive care which cannot be provided by a single worker assigned to a huge caseload. Thus, the interdisciplinary teams which are widely noted in the literature, and services to the entire family, are valued and needed in effective programming for families in which abuse of the child occurs.

REFERENCES

Alexander, H., McQuiston, M., and Rodeheffer, M. 1976. "Residential Family Therapy," in *The Abused Child,* ed. H. P. Marten. Cambridge, Mass.: Ballinger Publishing Co.

American Humane Association. 1982. *Annual Statistical Report: National Analysis of Official Child Neglect and Abuse Reporting.* Englewood, Colo.

Baldwin, J., and Oliver, J. 1975. "Epidemiology and Family Characteristics of Severely Abused Children." *British Journal of Preventive and Social Medicine* 29:205-21.

Barnes, G., Chabon, R., and Hertzberg, L. 1974. "Team Treatment for Abusive Families." *Social Casework* 55:600-11.

Beezley, P., Martin, H., and Alexander, H. 1976. "Comprehensive Family Oriented Therapy." In *Child Abuse and Neglect,* eds. R. Helfer and C. Kempe. Cambridge, Mass.: Ballinger Publishing Co.

Bennie, E. H., and Sclare, A. B. 1969. "The Battered Child Syndrome." *American Journal of Psychiatry* 125:975-79.

Bentovim, A. 1977. "Therapeutic Systems and Settings in the Treatment of Child Abuse." In *The Challenge of Child Abuse,* ed. A. W. Franklin. New York: Grune and Stratton.

Blumberg, M. L. 1974. "Psychopathology of the Abusing Parent." *American Journal of Psychotherapy* 28:21-29.

Bowen, M. 1971. "Family Therapy and Family Group Therapy." In *Comprehensive Group Psychotherapy,* ed. H. Kaplan and B. Sadock. Baltimore: Williams and Wilkins Co.

Cautley, P. 1980. "Treating Dysfunctional Families at Home." *Social Work* 25 (5): 380-86.

Corey, E., Miller, C., and Widlak, F. 1975. "Factors Contributing to Child Abuse." *Nursing Research* 24:293-95.

Fomufod, A., Sinkford, S., and Lowy, V. 1975. "Mother Child Separation at Birth: A Contributing Factor to Child Abuse." *Lancet* 2:549-50.

Galdston, R. 1965. "Observation on Children Who Have Been Physically Abused and Their Parents." *American Journal of Psychiatry* 122:440-43.

Gayford, J. 1975. "Wife Battering: A Preliminary Survey of 100 Cases." *British Medical Journal* 5951:194-97.

Gelles, R. 1973. "Child Abuse as Psychopathology: A Sociological Critique and Reformulation." *American Journal of Orthopsychiatry* 43:611-21.

Gil, D. 1970. *Violence Against Children: Physical Child Abuse in the United States.* Cambridge, Mass.: Harvard University Press.

Gilbert, M. 1976. "Behavioral Approach to the Treatment of Child Abuse." *Nursing Times* 72:140-43.

Goodwin, D. 1978. "Dwarfism: The Victim Child's Response to Abuse." *Baltimore Sun* September 24.

Green, A., Gaines, R., and Sandgrund, A. 1974. "Child Abuse: Pathological Syndrome of Family Interaction." *American Journal of Psychiatry* 131:882-86.

Holland. C. 1973. "An Examination of Social Isolation and Availability to Treatment in the Phenomenon of Child Abuse." *Smith College Studies in Social Work* 44:74-75.

Hunter, R., Kilstron, N., Kraybill, E., and Loda, F. 1978. "Antecedents of Child Abuse and Neglect in Premature Infants: A Prospective Study in a Newborn Intensive Care Unit." *Pediatrics* 61:629-35.

Hyman, C. 1978. "Some Characteristics of Abusing Families Referred to NSPCC." *British Journal of Social Work* 8:171-79.

James, K. 1977. "Incest: The Teenager's Perspective." *Psychotherapy: Theory, Research and Practice* 14:146-55.

Janzen, C. 1978. *Child Abuse Families in Baltimore County.* Report to the Inter-Agency Child Abuse and Neglect Committee of Baltimore County.

Jayaratne, S. 1977. "Child Abusers as Parents and as Children: A Review." *Social Work* 22:5-9.

Jeffrey, M. 1976. "Practical Ways to Change Parent/Child Interaction in Families of Children at Risk." In *Child Abuse and Neglect*, ed. R. Helfer and C. Kempe. Cambridge, Mass.: Ballinger Publishing Co.

Johnson, B., and Morse, H. 1968. "Injured Children and Their Parents." *Children* 15:147-52.

Jones, C. 1977. "A Critical Evaluation of the NPSCC's Battered Child Research Department." *Child Abuse and Neglect* 1:111-18.

Kadushin, A., and Martin, J. 1981. *Child Abuse: An Interactional Event.* New York: Columbia University Press.

Kempe, R., and Kempe, H. 1976. "Assessing Family Pathology." In *Child Abuse and Neglect*, ed. R. Helfer and C. Kempe. Cambridge, Mass.: Ballinger Publishing Co.

Lansky, S., and Erickson, H. J. 1974. "Prevention of Child Murder: A Case Report." *Journal of the American Academy of Child Psychiatry* 13:691-98.

Lehigh University Center for Social Research. 1976. "Treatment of Families Exhibiting Violence Toward Children." Mimeo report.

204 / FAMILY TREATMENT IN SOCIAL WORK PRACTICE

Lynch, M. 1975. "Ill Health and Child Abuse." *Lancet* 2:317-19.

McNeil, J., and McBride, M. 1979. "Group Therapy with Abusive Parents." *Social Casework* 60(1):36-42.

Moore, J. 1974. "YoYo Children." *Nursing Times* 70:1888-89.

National Institutes of Mental Health. 1977. *Child Abuse and Neglect Programs: Practice and Theory.* Washington, D.C.

Newberger, E. H. 1973. "The Myth of the Battered Child Syndrome." *Current Medical Dialogue* 40:327-34.

Oppenheimer, A. 1978. "Triumph over Trauma in the Treatment of Child Abuse." *Social Casework* 59:352-58.

Ounsted, C., and Lynch, M. 1976. "Residential Therapy: A Place of Safety." In *Child Abuse and Neglect,* ed. R. Helfer and C. Kempe. Cambridge, Mass.: Ballinger Publishing Co.

Ounsted, C., Oppenheimer, R., and Lindsay, J. 1974. "Aspects of Bonding Failure: The Psychopathology and Psychotherapeutic Treatment of Families of Battered Children." *Developmental Medicine and Child Neurology* 16:447-56.

Palakow, R., and Peabody, D. 1975. "Behavioral Treatment of Child Abuse." *International Journal of Offender Therapy and Comparative Criminology* 19:100-103.

Pasamanick, B. 1975. "Ill Health and Child Abuse." *Lancet* 2:550.

Pickett, J., and Maton, A. 1977. "Protective Casework and Child Abuse." In *The Challenge of Child Abuse,* ed. A. W. Franklin. New York: Grune and Stratton.

Polansky, N., Borgman, R., and DeSaix, C. 1972. *Roots of Futility,* San Francisco: Jossey-Bass.

Post, S. 1982. "Adolescent Parricide in Abusive Families." *Child Welfare* 61(7):445-55.

Resnick, P. J. 1969. "Child Murder by Parents: A Psychiatric View of Filicide." *American Journal of Psychiatry* 126:325-34.

Roth, F. 1975. "A Practice Regimen for Diagnosis and Treatment of Child Abuse." *Child Welfare* 54:268-73.

Sargent, D. 1962. "Children Who Kill." *Social Work* 7(1):35-42.

Smith, S. 1984. "Significant Research Findings in the Etiology of Child Abuse." *Social Casework* 65(6):337-46.

————, and Hanson, R. 1975. "Interpersonal Relationships and Child Rearing Practices in 214 Parents of Battered Children." *British Journal of Psychiatry* 127:513-25.

Steele, B., and Pollock, C. 1972. "A Psychiatric Study of Parents Who Abuse Infants and Small Children." In *Helping the Battered Child and His Family,* ed. C. Kempe and R. Helfer. Philadelphia: J. B. Lippincott Co.

Steinhausen, H. 1972. Sozialmedizinische Aspekte der Korperlichin Kindes-mishandlung [Social-Medical Aspects of Physical Maltreatment of Children]. *Monatschrift fuer Kinderheilkunde,* 120:314-18.

Tracy, J., Ballard, C., and Clark, E. 1975. "Child Abuse Project: A Followup." *Social Work* 20:398-99.

Tracy, J., and Clark, E. 1974. "Treatment for Child Abusers." *Social Work* 19:338-42.

Tuszinski, A., and Dowd, J. 1978. "An Alternative Approach to the Treatment of Protective Service Families." *Social Casework* 59:175-79.

Vogel, E., and Bell, W. 1968. "The Emotionally Disturbed Child as the Family Scapegoat." In *A Modern Introduction to the Family*, ed. N. Bell and E. Vogel. New York: Free Press.

Watzlawick, P., Beavin, J., and Jackson, D. 1967. *Pragmatics of Human Communication*. New York: W. W. Norton & Co.

Wells, S. 1981. "A Model for Therapy with Abusive and Neglectful Families." *Social Work* 26(2):113-18.

U.S. Department of Health, Education and Welfare. 1977. *National Analysis of Official Child Abuse and Neglect Reporting*. Washington, D.C.: Government Printing Office.

CHAPTER 8

Family Treatment With Black Families

Extensive study of the black family is reflected in the literature. However, there has been little investigation of this group in relation to treatment. There are probably many reasons for the limited publication of information in this area. Nathan Ackerman suggests (in Sager, Brayboy, and Waxenberg, 1970) that one of the most significant factors is a lack of knowledge of the behavior and outcomes of the black family in treatment.

We suspect another reason for this dearth of information about treating the black family is the possibility that work with this group has been included in the reports of intervention with other groups, such as hard-to-reach families, multiproblem families, low-income families, and problem poverty families. Another likely reason is that black families, other than those from the low socioeconomic group, have not been extensively involved in family therapy. And, of course, it is also possible that the clinicians who have written about their work are not aware of a significant difference between work with black and other minority families and work with white families. In this case there would be no compelling reason to address either group specifically in discussing family treatment.

Be this as it may, there is a dearth of information on treating black families. We share the opinion of those who believe that the similarity of all families as a social system is much greater than the differences among them. Yet we suggest that what is different about the black family is of sufficient significance that it should be considered in making an assessment of the family upon which to base effective intervention efforts.

Therefore, we will consider these differences and the meaning they have for the functioning of black families and offer some ideas about intervention. While we will address factors relevant to work with low-income families, the main thrust of this chapter is toward the black middle-class family. Our decision to take this approach is the result of existing literature, which provides a good deal of information about low-income families, both minority and nonminority. On the other side of the black middle class is the upper-class black family, which is not likely to use a social work agency for treatment. This further supports our decision to focus on the middle-class family and agency-based practice, which is the primary context within which social workers' therapeutic activity takes place.

The assessment of any family must include gathering sufficient information about family transactions to enable the therapist to put the problem to be worked on into proper perspective, while helping the family to see and relate to the problem appropriately. As in preceding chapters, the focus of intervention with families is on the interactions among family members. The primary objective of the therapeutic encounter is to alter dysfunctional interactional patterns in such a way as to improve family functioning. While this process applies to work with black families, some variations in emphasis and strategy are necessary.

To assist those who work with black families, we will discuss some of these necessary variations later in this chapter. However, we begin by identifying the black middle class in contemporary society, presenting its family structure, and discussing some aspects of family functioning.

THE BLACK MIDDLE CLASS

The foundation of the black middle class can be traced to the rural South and the institution of slavery. The conditions of servitude to which blacks were subjected under the system of slavery and its impact on family life have been documented. Historically, the black man was denied the opportunity of being the responsible head of his family, while the black woman was allowed to surface in this role. For various reasons, this continued to be the dominant perception of black family structure long after slavery was abolished. It has served to perpetuate a myth prominently presented in much of the literature.

There is evidence of a large increase in the number of blacks who have achieved middle-class status within the past decade. There is also evidence that the black middle class of today does not fit the description of a group struggling to imitate the white middle class, as suggested by Frazier (1962) and others. A more recent study by Kronus (1971) presents the black middle class as a group with its own identity. This class is highly family oriented, and the families are usually small. Family orientation indicates a kind of togetherness, with members spending time and engaging in activities together as a functioning unit, which was not often recognized by earlier researchers.

The black middle class of today does not stand in awe of its white counterpart and in many cases welcomes the opportunity for competition. Self-determination appears to be the dominant theme among the black middle class, as indicated by increasing demands for input in the areas of education, employment, politics, and so on. As a group, they are no longer focused only on issues pertaining to the middle class but assume a strong posture relative to improving the position of blacks in general. This seems to reflect greater security for this group, although the degree of status security may vary within the group. It is composed of well-educated persons who are interested in the welfare of family members. The majority of families include both parents. There is little desire for what might be considered the superficial aspects of life, including expensive and flashy automobiles or clothes. Education is seen as an important means of access to the economic opportunity structure. As a group members of the black middle class tend to live within their means and to accept responsibilities to their families, their employers, and to their communities. In sum, the black middle class is a self-determined, responsible group which participates in a pluralistic society.

FAMILY STRUCTURE AND FUNCTIONING

When using a social systems approach to provide an appropriate framework within which to assess family functioning, it is necessary to consider the totality of interactions and interdependencies that influence the family's behavior. In keeping with this approach, this chapter views the middle-class black family as a system composed of subsystems. The family itself is seen as a subsystem within the broader network of the black community and wider society.

The typical black middle-class family of today consists of two parents and two or three children sharing the same household. The husband-father carries the primary provider role for the family, although it is likely that the wife-mother also is employed. The father is very much involved in the rearing of children, and the household usually does not include extended-family members.

As a social system, the black family interacts with and is influenced by both the black community and the wider society. These two systems have different expectations and different behaviors are required in order to succeed and earn status. The reference group in the wider society is the conjugal white family, usually of middle- to upper-middle-class status, and this status is determined by employment, education, and income. In the black community status is based more on consumption patterns and other visible achievements than on employment, education, and income. As a result, different life-styles emerge in each situation. This difference in life-style between the black community, in which black families are rooted psychologically, regardless of where they reside physically, and the wider society, in which they must also participate, places an extremely heavy demand on the black family in its effort to adapt to both systems. The situation also has tremendous impact on the socialization of black children, whose parents must try to prepare them to deal successfully with both experiences. It is necessary for the black family to incorporate the values of two different reference groups with two distinct life-styles if its members are to participate successfully in the American dream and compete for the rewards available through this process. White families need not engage in this type of socialization process to prepare their children to function in society.

In the attempts of black families to meet the requirements of the wider society while satisfying the needs of family members, an interchange of customary roles is not uncommon. The widely accepted rule that the husband-father performs the instrumental functions while the wife-mother carries out the expressive function is, as suggested by Billingsley (1968), "far too simplistic a framework for examining the functioning of black families" (p. 25). It is well established that the black wife-mother frequently plays a major role in the execution of instrumental functions, but it is not so well known that the black husband-father performs many expressive functions.

This pattern of functioning within the black family is tied to a history in which the black female had greater access to the economic opportunity structure of society than the black male did. Both husband and wife generally accept this way of contributing to the well-being of the family. We are not suggesting that instrumental and expressive functions are necessarily mutually exclusive in any case, but the black husband-father is likely to be much more involved in performing expressive functions and the wife-mother in performing instrumental functions than their white counterparts are.

This departure from the widely accepted norm of family functioning should not be interpreted as deviant behavior or an automatic source of conflict in family relationships, however. Social workers should take into account the life-styles which have emerged from the experience of black people in America. Attempts to assess black family functioning by using only the norms of the white family may result in something less than accurate measurement.

Spouse Relationship

One of the keys to understanding family interactional patterns is knowledge of family relationships, such as those between husband and wife. In the wider society, Scanzoni (1971) suggests:

> The relationship between husband and wife in modern society can be thought of in terms of a reciprocal exchange of role duties and rights. The more fully the husband fulfills his chief role obligation as provider, the more fully the wife is motivated to fulfill her chief obligations as "expressive agent," or "socio-emotional hub" of the conjugal family. (pp. 199-200)

This suggests that the relationship between husband and wife is significantly influenced by the rewards provided by the husband. Occupational status, education, and income are primary factors in the husband's ability to provide these rewards. Scanzoni found that among white families, the greater the husband's claim on these three status symbols, the more rewards he provided to his wife, and the more positively both husband and wife considered their primary relations. This was not the case with black families. An increase in these indicators of social position and the provision of greater rewards to the black wife did not bring a corresponding increase in her positive perception of her relationship with her husband.

Scanzoni contends that the concept of relative deprivation as suggested by Pettigrew (1964) may be responsible for this difference between the two groups. This concept is based on the fact that even though the black family now has greater access to the opportunity structure and claims more rewards from it than ever before, the rewards are not equal to those received by white families of similar educational levels. At the same time that black family rewards are increasing, the expectations of black families are increasingly based on the opportunity structure's standard of rewards to their white counterparts. As a result, there is an inevitable comparison between the lesser rewards they receive and the greater rewards received by whites, which produces a feeling of deprivation on the part of blacks.

In connection with the idea of relative deprivation, we suggest the black wife's failure to show an increase in positive feeling for her husband as a result of his provision of increased rewards is in no way an attempt on her part to punish him. Neither does it reflect a lack of appreciation for the increased rewards. Instead, the black wife's expression is a reflection of her dissatisfaction with the opportunity structure's double standard of distributing rewards. In addition, there is an awareness on her part that the opportunity structure is controlled by whites, which is a strong reminder that the black family is not in complete control of its middle-class status. Therefore, a certain tentativeness is associated with the increased rewards the black husband provides, and the wife with a history filled with uncertainties does not allow herself to experience fully rewards that can be denied by powers beyond her control.

The black wife is also supportive of her husband and ascribes to him the role of primary provider for the family. Her failure to increase or decrease expressive responses in direct proportion to the provision of status rewards is likely to be reassuring to her husband, who does not completely control the rewards he is able to provide. This also frees the husband from fluctuation in his wife's affections toward him. It follows, then, that the quality of the black husband-wife relationship is not dependent on the amount of status rewards he can provide. Therefore, social workers might find it useful in the intervention process to gain knowledge of the extent of mutuality in the perception of roles between the black husband and wife, as well as the extent of satisfaction experienced in relation to their role performances.

Another consideration in viewing the black husband-wife relationship is the often-implied interference resulting from the wife's employment. Contrary to the notion that the white wife is "allowed to work" by her husband, the black wife's employment is generally considered normal and is usually accepted by her and her husband. This is probably helped along by the black wife's history of greater accessibility to the economic opportunity structure, while the husband has been denied an equal opportunity to participate. However, it is customary for the black wife to keep a low profile in relation to her working and performing instrumental functions within the family. It is probably fair to assume that both the wife's history of participation in the labor market and her de-emphasis of the role of her employment in family functioning are largely responsible for the absence of threat to the husband's provider role. Hence her employment offers little threat to their relationship. While the possibility of conflict arising from the wife's employment should not be ignored in working with the black family, it is not likely to be the primary source of disruption.

We also support the position of Hines and Boyd-Franklin (1982), who advise caution in assessing the black wife's attitude toward the shortcomings of her husband. For example, the wife's vacillation with regard to her husband exercising responsible behavior is not usually a reflection of her inability to be realistic and objective in matters pertaining to his performance. Instead, this failure to hold him strictly accountable most often indicates her identification with her husband's frustrations with society's denial of opportunities and rewards accorded his white counterpart. As a result she may not always be firm in holding him to what might be viewed by the larger society as responsible behavior.

The distribution of power between the black husband and wife is another key to understanding their relationship. The social worker intervening with the black family can no longer approach the task with the traditional view of the family as a matriarchy. Neither can the worker apply the popular conceptualizations relative to the distribution of power and authority that have been found to exist within the white family. For example, Scanzoni (1971) found that the black wife did not attribute more power and authority to the husband out of deference for increased status rewards he could provide (p. 205), but the white wife tended to respond in proportion to the rewards received. In fact, the black family operates in an egalitarian power structure, which is to say that power and decision making are shared equally by husband and wife.

It is important that the relationship between the black husband and wife be viewed within the context of the black family experience. Workers working with black families should have some knowledge of the cultural heritage of black people. We also suggest caution in drawing conclusions about black husband-wife relationships; they should not be based solely on variables known to influence the relationship of white husbands and wives. An exploration and differential evaluation of the specific attitudes of each black husband and wife toward their own roles and the roles of the other party will enhance workers' understanding of the conflict.

Socialization of Children

One of the primary functions of any family is the socialization of the children. Usually we think of this process as teaching the child values and expectations in keeping with the dominant society. Billingsley (1968) concludes that the socialization process in the black family has a dual purpose, in that children must be taught "not only to be human, but how to be black in a white society" (p. 28). This is applicable to both the low- and high-income black family. It involves preparing black children for successes and disappointments. The latter, particularly, may be more closely related to race than to competence.

Black parents also seem to be aware of the particular vicissitudes that may arise in their children's transactions across family boundaries, as a result of their being black and relatively disadvantaged. Consequently, they try to communicate to them the values and specific role obligations that will enable them to cope with the greater stresses that inevitably face the members of black families (Scanzoni, 1971, p. 82).

McAdoo (1974), who seems in general agreement with Billingsley and Scanzoni, suggests that the socialization of black children requires them to become a part of the dominant culture while also internalizing the values of the black community. This socialization process, which prepares the child to function successfully in two different social systems, places a heavy burden on the child. It should be taken into consideration by workers and others seeking to understand the child's behavior.

Black parents also expect their children to earn greater rewards from the opportunity structure than they themselves were able to achieve. This requires, among other things, holding on to middle-class status and taking advantage of opportunities to move up the socioeconomic ladder. One of the proven ways of socioeconomic advancement is education, which makes access to the opportunity structure less difficult. Black parents therefore emphasize the need for their children to obtain educations which prepare them for participation in the dominant culture with middle-class status. In many cases the parents select the best schools for their children, sometimes at great personal sacrifice, in the hope of enhancing their opportunities for success. Scanzoni also found that many black middle-class parents warned their children of the consequences of associating with people who might interfere with their social and economic advancement.

This kind of intensity of purpose may result in parent-child conflict in some situations, with the child struggling to differentiate from a family that is seen as far too controlling. In this case the worker needs to examine family boundaries and other systemic aspects of family functioning. As in the case of any other family, adjustments to allow for greater individuation among family members must be considered.

There is a likelihood, however, that a congruence exists between the perceptions of the black parent and child with regard to these socialization activities. There may be a mutual understanding and acceptance of roles and behaviors. This can be a result of the parent's communicating to the child her or his difference as it relates to the majority population and teaching the child how to cope with the consequences of being different. When this understanding is present, it minimizes the likelihood of confrontation and conflict centered around socialization activities. Cooke (1974) offers support for this conclusion in her reference to the socialization of the black male, in particular. She suggests the lesson usually learned by the black male child is that "the often ambivalent role of polarities projected by his parents, especially his mother, when rearing him is preparation for his later subordinate role in a white society" (p. 81).

Therefore, behavior which in a different set of circumstances might be perceived as a likely conflict-producing situation, involving an overactive parent and a rebellious child, should not be so viewed in black parent-child interactions. Social workers should proceed cautiously in reaching a decision relative to the implications of this behavior. It will be useful to determine the extent to which a congruence of perceptions exists in the parent-child relationship before planning specific intervention strategies.

Support Systems

In the American population as a whole, demographic factors of age, occupation, and education account for much of the difference in mobility among individuals. As blacks have made some progress in closing the gap between themselves and whites in terms of education and occupation, it is likely they will have greater geographical mobility. Such mobility often places individuals and families in unfamiliar surroundings that result in a disruption of opportunities for feedback about themselves and validations of their expectations of others (Caplan, 1974). In other words, geographical mobility often severs the family's connection with its support systems.

While this is applicable to any family, black families are likely to find the loss of social support systems more disruptive than white families do. The black family uses the white family as a reference group in relation to the achievement of rewards from the dominant society, but it also has expectations which are framed in terms of the black community and the family's own previous experiences. This means the black family requires feedback and validation from the black community as well as from the wider society. White families are not faced with this duality, since as a rule they seek validation only from sources within the dominant culture. Therefore, they experience less difficulty than blacks in moving from one location to another and maintaining or establishing the pattern of ties necessary for preserving their psychological and physical integrity.

Cassel (1973) also suggests that there are differences among the reactions of people to incomprehensible feedback (support disruption). The risk involved is not shared equally by all who experience breakdown in feedback regarding expectations and evaluations of behavior which serve to support and guide actions. For example, Cassel posits the existence of a dominant-subordinate factor in which a position of dominance tends to minimize the effect of experiencing loss of support, while a subordinate position tends to increase the effect. When we consider that the black family occupies a subordinate position to that of the white family in the dominant society, we believe it agrees with Cassel's finding to assume that the black family will experience greater difficulty when their support systems are disrupted.

The role of black culture as a source of support for the black family must not be overlooked. Chestang (1976) states that the function of black culture is to deal with environmental threats in such a way as to guarantee the survival, security, and self-esteem of black people (pp. 99-100). We agree, and suggest further that black culture is tied to the institutions of the black community which serve as a resource for the survival and security of the black family. It is within the context of this culture that black people get a sense of what Billingsley describes as we-ness, or peoplehood.

When feedback through familiar cultural channels is limited or disrupted for any reason, the black family's perception of itself as a viable unit is likely to suffer. For example, a breakdown in the supportive network of the black family may occur when it moves from one geographical location to another, leaving behind friends, relatives, familiar institutions, and accustomed ways of relating. The effect of the breakdown is most likely to surface when the family experiences a threat to its integrity. Such a threat may be brought on by conflict among family members, or it may result from transactions with systems outside family boundaries which necessitate the use of resources beyond those customarily used by the family for support and assistance in performing tasks. In the absence of familiar sources upon which to draw for help, the family may find itself, as Caplan suggests, unfamiliar with the communication signals that enable it to perceive the expectations, friendliness, or hostility in their immediate surroundings. As a result, family members, unable to feel safe and valued, are more likely to become susceptible to a crisis in functioning.

The black family has traditionally maintained an extensive extended-family network of blood-related and nonrelated individuals upon whom it depends for various kinds of assistance. Most social workers can readily envision the structure of an extended family that is connected by biological ties and the likelihood that role sharing might occur under certain conditions. However, an extended family that includes nonrelatives may be somewhat more difficult to visualize. Yet, this type of extended family is not unusual among black families, especially those from less affluent backgrounds. The inclusion of nonrelatives in this way is sometimes born of necessity, and a very close relationship is likely to develop that includes the sharing of responsibilities, in the same manner as would be experienced in an extended family network based on biological ties. When nonrelatives are involved in the extended family network, social workers should view this as an integral part of the family support network and bring them into treatment as a part of the family when necessary.

GUIDELINES FOR TREATMENT

Theoretical Perspective

From a theoretical point of view, a systems perspective is necessary in work with black families, as it is with all families. We find symbolic interaction theory especially useful in viewing the functioning of the black family. This frame of reference addresses not only the concepts of status (or position) and role but also questions of socialization and personality. While status and role are important considerations in work with black families, socialization and personality are essential in understanding their behavior. In our view, socialization refers to "the process by which the human organism acquires the characteristic ways of behaving, the values, norms, and attitudes of the social units of which he is a part," and personality is "the development of persistent behavior patterns" (Stryker, 1964, p. 133). These patterns of behavior are the result of experiences over time and should be viewed in this context when working with black families.

In the final analysis, Blumer (1969, p. 2) suggests symbolic interactionism rests on three basic premises:

1. Human beings act toward things on the basis of the meanings that the things have for them.
2. Meanings are derived from, or arise out of, the social interactions that one has with one's fellows.
3. These meanings are handled in, and modified through, an interpretive process used by the person in dealing with the things he encounters.

In applying these guiding principles of symbolic interactionism to work with black families, we favor a sociological-psychological approach to the explanation of meanings attached to experiences. We do not overlook the importance of the meaning of things toward which the members of black families act. However, we suggest that the meanings they attach to these things are influenced by a history of experiences common to black people. For this reason the meaning given to an experience in the context of social interaction is not only an expression of what black family members derive from the experience itself, it also reflects the disappointments, successes, happiness, and fear of earlier times. For example, when the black mother expresses dissatisfaction with her child's poor grades in school, the meaning she attaches to this experience comes from her own observation of the difficulty she and her people have had in earning rewards from the opportunity structure of the wider society. She also realizes that education is at least one way of making access to this structure less difficult, and poor grades mean a greater struggle for success.

Consider also the black husband who adapts to his wife's working by accepting increased responsibility for child care and housekeeping chores, and who shows little concern over the equal distribution of power that exists between himself and his wife. The meaning this has for him is shaped by his awareness of the difficulty long associated with the black males' access to employment and the greater opportunity for black females. Therefore he reacts not only to what is encountered physically—that is, his wife's working—but also to this experience as modified through an interpretative process which is influenced by his previous experiences. The husband responds to a symbolic environment created in part by his own internal processes.

A symbolic-interactionist conceptualization of human behavior lends itself to exploration and understanding of the uniqueness of the black family experience. It suggests the likelihood and significance of individual reactions to a symbolic environment that is derived from the meaning the person attaches to what is experienced. We suggest that the experience of black people in American society shapes the meaning they give to what they encounter in various transactions with their environment. And their response to other persons and situations, based on this meaning, will influence the way others respond to them. We believe that viewing black family interactions within a systems-interactionist framework allows for the most complete understanding of the family's transactions, member with member, and members with the world outside of family boundaries.

Specific Treatment Considerations

The primary objective of family treatment is to alter dysfunctional interactional patterns between family members. Many family therapists believe this can be accomplished while obtaining only a minimum of history information from the family. We agree with this approach for the most part, but we believe an exception is necessary when working with black families. Among the reasons for this shift in emphasis is the cultural heritage of black people in general, which is distinctly different from other racial or ethnic groups. The circumstances surrounding the development and maintenance of the black family in America have also resulted in a variation of life-styles among these families. Therefore, in order to make a differential assessment of family functioning and to plan for effective intervention, the worker needs to examine selected aspects of the family's history, depending on the difficulty experienced.

Not only is history information important in understanding the functioning of black families, but certain kinds of history information are essential. Our concern is for experiential information rather than strictly chronological-developmental data. The experiences of the parents as children growing up in their families of origin; their coming together as a couple; their ideas about raising their own family; and the impact social, economic, and political forces have had on their lives are all important experiences which usually prove to be profitable areas for exploration. However, social workers must keep in mind the specific problem being presented by the family and develop the necessary information around this difficulty, instead of routinely developing generalized information about the family.

For example, if the problem is presented as the parents' frustration over the child's apparent lack of interest in school, it would hardly be necessary or profitable to explore in detail how the parents became interested in each other and what each wanted from the marriage. Instead, it would likely be most productive to examine what they want for their child and how they arrived at these expectations. A better understanding of the situation might also be realized by obtaining some idea of what their own parents had expected of them as children and their vision of possible obstacles to the child's future participation in the economic opportunity structure. It is likely that the parents' frustration in such cases is rooted in a desire to see the child prepared for a better life than they have experienced, and failure to take advantage of educational opportunities is for them a painful disappointment.

When the parent-child relationship is the target of intervention, it will be helpful to explore socialization patterns, including the parents' own experiences with the socialization process in their families of origin. While this information is useful in work with nonminority families as well, it has special significance in intervening with black families. The black child undergoes a unique and demanding socialization process which incorporates the values and expectations of two different cultures, as we have noted. Socioeconomic success is also an important family value that is imparted to the black child as he is taught to participate successfully in the economic opportunity structure of the wider society. Although the socialization experience of black children does not automatically produce a pathological situation, it does have the potential for problem development and should be fully explored when parents and children are experiencing difficulty in communicating and relating to each other.

With many families, especially those who come for help after a recent change in geographical location, we suggest an examination of the family's support systems. Hansell (1976) has suggested a number of attachments to various resources as instrumental in helping people cope with the kind of distress that is usually experienced in the loss of social supports. Although he was concerned primarily with the individual, some of his ideas are also applicable to families and can provide direction for social workers intervening with black families, especially where a breakdown in sources of support has been established. The following points are extrapolated from Hansell's suggestions (p. 33):

1. The family must be attached to appropriate sources of information. The family in unfamiliar surroundings may not have sufficient access to sources of information; in this case the worker can connect the family with individuals, groups, or organizations with which they can communicate and from which they can receive necessary information.

2. There should be attachment to resources that will enable the family to realize its identity as a functioning unit. If the family has lost its connection with familiar resources that have customarily fed back to them what is expected and how well they are meeting these expectations, the worker must provide for new sources of validation. This can often be realized by helping the family establish interdependent connections with other families, or other persons outside its boundaries, with whom members can share mutual interests and activities and can develop trust. This attachment will allow the exchange of suitable information and increase feedback to the family about its operations.

3. It is essential that the family be attached to groups of people who regard it as belonging. These might include religious groups, political groups, and so on, which have the capability of assisting the family with various tasks.

When support systems are disrupted, the worker should examine the family's attachment to these resources and plan to effect connections where indicated. The primary objective is to connect the family with others who will be able to "speak their language" and with whom family members can feel comfortable, build trust, and gain a sense of self and a feeling of security.

In the case of the less affluent black family there is usually a reluctance to seek help for family problems from organizations that provide mental health services. In the first place there is a tendency to think of those who receive these services as being of unsound mind. Furthermore, help with problems is usually sought from more familiar sources such as the extended family, clergy, and trusted friends. Turning to a social service or mental health agency is often a last resort and usually comes as a result of referral from agencies such as the schools or courts. In such cases the social worker should expect and be ready to deal with resistance to taking help and realize that long-term treatment is not likely to succeed. Therefore, therapeutic efforts should be focused on helping the family experience some desired change as soon as possible, regardless of how small it might be.

When viewed as a social system, the similarities between the black middle-class family and the white middle-class family are far greater than the differences. However, if we are to understand the black family, we must examine its functioning within a framework that allows us to view what is different and determine what, if any, impact this difference has on family transactions. Billingsley (1968, pp. 150-51) has suggested a set of guidelines for understanding the black family which we believe are essential. First, he suggests that the black family should be viewed as a social system interacting with a number of other systems. Second, a historical perspective of the black family is necessary in order to understand its structure and functioning best. Third, it must be realized that black people operate with a differentiated set of social structures which should be considered in viewing their behavior. In other words, differences exist between black families in the same way as differences exist between white families, and differential assessments and intervention strategies are necessary in work with different families. Fourth, black family structure should be perceived as an adaptation to a set of conditions existing in the family's wider social environment which is related to its efforts to meet the needs of its members and the demands of society.

It is also well to remember that self-determination is very important to black families. This determination is likely to be reflected in the family's transactions with other systems, and social workers must be prepared to deal with this. In addition, we suggest that workers take into consideration the local and national sociopolitical climate at the time of the therapeutic encounter, as the struggles of the black middle-class family may be related to these phenomena.

SUMMARY

Working with black families is not a completely different experience from working with other families. The similarities are greater than the differences. Nevertheless, there are a few differences which are significant, and social workers should take them into consideration when planning change with black families.

It is important to recognize the cultural heritage of the black family in America, society's perception of the family, and the family's perception of itself. The basis of relating between husband and wife, the socialization of children, the importance of support systems, and the impact of the prevailing sociopolitical climate are important areas for consideration in work with this group.

A systems-symbolic interactionist approach is a useful framework within which to view black family functioning. Social workers must also remember that there are differences between black families, and a differential use of treatment techniques and strategies is necessary.

REFERENCES

Acosta, Frank X., Yamamoto, Joe, and Evans, Leonard A. 1982. *Effective Psychotherapy for Low-Income and Minority Clients*. New York: Plenum Press.

Billingsley, A. 1968. *Black Families in White America*. Englewood Cliffs, N.J.: Prentice-Hall.

Blumer, H. 1969. *Symbolic Interactionism: Perspective and Method*. Englewood Cliffs, N.J.: Prentice-Hall.

Caplan, G. 1974. *Support Systems and Community Mental Health*. New York: Behavioral Publications.

Cassel, J. C. 1973. "Psychiatric Epidemiology." In *American Handbook of Psychiatry*, vol. 2, ed. G. Caplan. New York: Basic Books.

Chestang, L. 1976. "The Black Family and Black Culture: A Study of Coping." In *Cross Cultural Perspectives in Social Work Practice and Education*, ed. M. Sotomayor. Houston: University of Houston, Graduate School of Social Work.

Cooke, G. 1974. "Socialization of the Black Male: Research Implications." In *Social Research and the Black Community: Selected Issues and Priorities*, ed. L. Gary. Washington, D.C.: Institute for Urban Affairs and Research, Howard University.

Frazier, E. F. 1962. *Black Bourgeoisie*. New York: Collier Books.

Hansell, Norris 1976. *The Person in Distress*. New York: Human Sciences Press, Inc. 72 Fifth Avenue, New York, N.Y. 10011.

Hines, P. M., and Boyd-Franklin, N. 1982. "Black Families." In *Ethnicity and Family Therapy*, ed. M. McGoldrick, J. Pearce, and J. Biordano. New York: Guilford Press.

Kronus, S. 1971. *The Black Middle Class.* Columbus, Ohio: Charles E. Merrill Publishing Co.

McAdoo, H. P. 1974. "The Socialization of Black Children: Priorities for Research." In *Social Research and the Black Community: Selected Issues and Priorities,* ed. L. Gary. Washington, D.C.: Institute for Urban Affairs and Research, Howard University.

Minuchin, S., Montalvo, B., Guerney, B., Rosman, L., and Shumer, F. 1967. *Families of the Slums.* New York: Basic Books.

Pettigrew, T. F. 1964. *A Profile of the Negro American.* Princeton, N.J.: D. Van Nostrand Co.

Sager, C. J., Bayboy, T. L., and Waxenberg, B. R. 1970. *Black Ghetto Family in Therapy.* New York: Grove Press.

Scanzoni, J.H. 1971. *The Black Family in Modern Society.* Boston: Allyn & Bacon.

Stryker, S. 1964. "The Interactional and Situational Approaches." In *Handbook on Marriage and the Family,* ed. H. T. Christensen. Chicago: Rand McNally & Co.

CHAPTER **9**

Helping the Family with Alcoholic Members

Family members are increasingly involved in the treatment of alcoholics. They come to the agency for help with or without the alcoholic. The help provided may do much for the family and may or may not resolve the drinking problem. We are concerned to help the family whether or not the drinking problem is resolved. From our systems orientation we expect that resolving family problems and reducing the drinking problem go hand in hand.

There is no doubt that alcoholism is a family problem whether the family is seen as victim of the alcoholic or the alcoholic is seen as victim. Given that one or more additional members of the family may feel the consequences of the drinking problem, help for the family seems justified whether the alcoholic changes or not. Some treatment programs do not seem to be as strongly committed to the family as that implies and retain their focus on the alcoholic alone. The evidence suggests, however, that help to the family is also help to the alcoholic (Janzen, 1977), and that helping the alcoholic to change is clearly also help to the family.

Our position about alcoholism and the family is thus a systems position. Change in one part of the family system necessitates response or adaptation of some kind in other parts of the system. The drinking member's behavior, whether the drinking is increased or reduced, has family impact. Members are affected and adjust their behavior one way or another. Their new behavior is experienced by the alcoholic who responds with either more of the old behavior or some new behavior. The family's response to the drinking may neither have been helpful in reducing the drinking nor in alleviating the family's distress about it. The alcoholic's response to family behavior may have done little to alter the behavior of other family members. They seem locked in a repetitive cycle that results in no satisfaction for either party. There is no way of establishing where this cycle starts, and it seems fruitless, for treatment purposes, to seek first causes. The concern in treatment is to find ways of interrupting the destructive cycle. It seems evident that both the family and the alcoholic are, by their behavior, seeking to relieve distress and that the means they use to do so serve to increase rather than decrease it for both parties. If either the family or the alcoholic can find other means to relieve their distress, this serves to elicit new ways of coping on the part of the alcoholic or the family. Helping family and alcoholic to find new ways of coping in response to the distress they experience is the essence of our treatment approach.

Our definition of family treatment, given this point of view, is an intervention in any part of the interactive system. It is not contingent upon seeing the family members together. The essence of family treatment is that the social worker thinks of the family as a system and keeps in mind, whatever part of the family is being seen in a given treatment session, that changes occurring as a result of treatment will have impact on other parts of the system. Such impact needs to be anticipated and forecast, helping the members present to prepare for possible responses. Our interest in treatment is in changing the interactive process. Though we are saying here that it is not necessary to have all family members present to understand and change the interactive process, we do note that there may be advantages to having them present, both for the purpose of understanding how the interaction works in the here and now of behavior and also for promoting a change in it.

Our discussion will proceed initially in relation to the adult male family member's alcoholism. Practice and experience have focused on him as the identified alcoholic. We will devote some discussion later in the chapter to the situation in which the wife/mother or an adolescent is the identified alcoholic, though there is less available knowledge and experience in family treatment in these situations. We will direct our attention first to the interaction between spouses and the relationship between the marital interaction and the alcoholism and then to the functioning of children in the system.

MARITAL RELATIONSHIPS AND ALCOHOLISM

Several different views have been held about the relationship between the wife and her husband's alcoholism. In earlier writings the wife was seen as disturbed, struggling with strong feelings of inadequacy and dependency, which prompted her to relate to the alcoholic in a controlling and aggressive manner. These behaviors would be intended to perpetuate the relationship in a way that would be sure to meet her needs but instead had the opposite effect of burdening the alcoholic and thus promoting the drinking or at least giving him an excuse for drinking, a view which he might himself be prone to take.

Several studies (Fox, 1968; Krimmel, 1971; Rae, 1972) refute such a position about the wife's disturbance. In their view, the wife may indeed have behaved this way, but the behavior was seen as a consequence rather than the cause of the drinking. Other studies (Bailey, 1968; Cohen and Krause, 1971; Kogan and Jackson, 1965) show that such behavior on the part of wives subsides as the alcoholic's drinking is reduced. Edwards, Harvey, and Whitehead (1973) in a summary review of research pertaining to wives doubt that such behavior is characteristic of all wives, since they vary in personality type. Long-term functioning was not shown to be deteriorating, but rather fluctuating, depending on the status of the husband's drinking. It seems evident from these studies that even though the wife's behavior may affect the alcoholic, the direction of effects is not just one way.

Such an understanding of the relationship between the alcoholism and the persons involved focuses on personality, though it clearly conveys consequences for the interaction between persons. Other positions are more specifically attentive to the interaction between spouses. Some writers note that the conflict between alcoholic and spouse is independent of the alcoholism. Ballard (1959) has shown that marital conflict was more likely in alcoholism couples than in control couples, all aside from the alcoholism. Orford, Oppenheimer, Egert, Hensman, and Guthrie (1976) note the lack of cohesion in alcoholic marriages. Spouses are likely to refer to each other in derogatory terms. There is little giving or receiving of affection and minimal participation by the alcoholic in family activity. Increased participation and expressions of affection are needed as is a change in the negative picture each holds of the other.

Esser (1968, 1971) also advances this view. Spouses in alcoholic relationships have difficulty admitting marital problems, and drinking serves to avoid facing them. If marital problems are mentioned in a treatment session, drinking episodes often follow, and subsequent sessions revert to focus on the drinking.

Al-Anon Family Group (1967) also notes that alcoholics and their wives have trouble seeing their difficulties as marital, whether the alcoholic is still drinking or is sober. Al-Anon asserts that alcoholism does not create all their problems, nor does sobriety cure them.

Even though the case for the complete independence of marital problems and alcoholism may be made, it is still possible that there is a functional relationship between them. The possibility of a functional relationship between the alcoholism and family interaction has been demonstrated in yet another way. Steinglass (1976) observed families while drinking and also during nondrinking times. He notes,

> A family that claimed drinking by their "identified alcoholic" caused depression, fighting and estrangement, was observed to show increased warmth toward each other, increased caretaking, and greater animation when the alcoholic was permitted to drink. (p. 105)

Cadogan (1979) writes that in some instances drinking can strengthen family bonds and provide a sense of purpose, that of helping sick members, and gives the family a sense of meaning and importance which is otherwise lacking. The behavior serves a function for the system in such cases but is obviously dysfunctional for the alcoholic and also in a larger sense for the family. Carter (1977) makes similar points. These observations may not be generalizable to all families with alcoholics, but they do support the idea of a functional relationship between family interaction and the alcoholism. They also suggest that discontinuance of the drinking would still leave the family with other interactional problems and that treatment would need to be attentive to them.

Our understanding of the relationship between the alcoholic and the spouse is furthered by attention to the role-taking of the two actors, to their struggle for power and position, and to the payoffs for both which result from the interaction. The role-taking of each is seen as being driven more by the behavior of the other than by personality. Role-taking changes over time as the participants' views of each other's behavior and of their own predicament changes.

From this standpoint, alcoholic and spouse are reciprocal roles. (See Strausner, Weinstein, and Hernandez, 1979; Black, 1980; Wegscheider, 1981.) In beginning phases of the drinking problem both alcoholic and spouse collude in denial of a drinking problem. Typically the spouse excuses the drinking as a response to stress, as something occasional or temporary. When the drinking reaches more problematic proportion and becomes harder to deny, it may still be disguised in an effort to avoid embarrassment, save the alcoholic's job, or avoid family conflict and potential breakup. The spouse thus serves a supporting role in the alcoholic's denial. Still later, when the problems caused by the drinking can no longer be overlooked or excused, she may seek to control the drinking in various ways such as by drinking with, by limiting money supply, by disposing of alcohol on hand, or by limiting affection, attention, or care. The alcoholic resists such resistance to his behavior. He denies his wife such control. He asserts his independence by not changing in the way she desires. The more she tries to control, the more he defies. Whether the wife is denying or controlling, she is, unintentionally, an actor in a self-perpetuating exchange. Both are stuck in the pattern.

Gorad's (1971) investigation, in which he compared alcoholic and nonalcoholic spouse pairs, supports this view. He says that spouses in alcoholic marriages compete with each other more than those in nonalcoholic marriages. Sharing and self-revelation which are suggestive of more openness and less manipulation of others are less frequently exhibited.

Wiseman's (1976) study of Finnish couples shows that the wives used persuasion, crying, pleading, and threats in response to the drinking. These behaviors, which may be seen as an effort to control, had no durable effect on the drinking.

The irresponsible behavior or dependency of the alcoholic may not seem controlling, but they do require action and response on the part of the spouse, and they imply resistance to doing the spouse's bidding, manifesting his part in the struggle for control of the relationship. Thus, neither spouse dominates more than the other. The control struggle continues with the only variations being variations in intensity. Thus, whether the spouse's participation occurs by collusion in denial or by efforts to control, the drinking persists.

The control struggle we have outlined implies that the spouses in alcoholic marriages view each other as instruments of their own bidding, as extensions of self, and not as separate persons. Al-Anon notes this conception and goes on to point out that it is destructive to believe that "being married to a man puts us in charge of him. We are so deeply involved that we treat those closest to us as though they were part of ourselves" (Al-Anon Family Group, 1967). Bowen (1974) talks of failure of differentiation to refer to that same condition. Individuals are not individuals in the sense of having a clear sense of being a separate self. If one partner is less responsible, the other becomes more responsible. If one (the alcoholic) underfunctions, the other compensates by overfunctioning, and the underfunctioning spouse becomes even less functional. Independence and autonomy are clearly lacking. Bowen sees the overfunctioning spouse as more capable of change, that is, of assuming less responsibility and becoming more autonomous, and works with that spouse for change in the relationship.

It seems evident that there is some advantage to the spouses of the role reciprocity we have described. Steiner (1969) makes a definite point of this. There are "certain interpersonal payoffs" that motivate the behavior of each. A clear example can be seen in Ward and Faillace (1970, p. 686):

> If the wife is forgiving, the husband has learned that forgiveness for being drunk can be obtained, provided he is appropriately remorseful and very sick. If she punishes him for his behavior by criticizing him, his guilt and shame are relieved and he feels considerably less anxious. In either case the pattern cannot be understood except in terms of the total sequence.

And in either case the sequence recurs because it is reinforcing to both spouses.

Problems in communication go hand in hand with these relationship problems. Cadogan (1979) notes that communication between spouses is one-directional, going from spouse to alcoholic, who responds with silence or by leaving. Conversations are filled with blaming statements; defensive and counterblaming statements are the response. Old conflicts and resentments surface repeatedly and are left unresolved. Family members, particularly children, hesitate to share interests, bring concerns, raise issues, or to voice doubts, questions, or differences for fear of being responded to with impatience, hostility, or retaliation. Capacity to listen and respond empathically to another's description or point of view is minimal. Maintaining a conversation which leads to understanding, resolution of conflicts, or problem solving has become next to impossible. Assistance in engaging in constructive communication is sorely needed.

The conceptions discussed in this section clearly apply to the relationships between male alcoholics and their wives. A later section on female alcoholics will suggest that these conceptions hold when the sexes of the participants are reversed. Role reciprocity and communication problems exist as well between alcoholics and other members of the family, including children.

CHILDREN IN ALCOHOLIC FAMILIES

Children are affected by and may affect relationships in alcoholic families. Cork (1969), Auger et al. (1973), Chafetz, Blane, and Hill (1971), Cohen and Krause (1971), and many others have documented a variety of effects on the children. Bosma (1972) has noted their tendency to become alcoholic themselves or to marry alcoholics. Different problems may occur at different age levels including stuttering, fears, bed-wetting, tantrums, fighting, and school problems. After reviewing many studies El-Guebaly and Offord (1977) conclude that difficulties in the research efforts result in inability to conclude that these children have more problems than children in other kinds of problem families, but there is no doubt that they do suffer. They also say that the problems these children have may not be solely attributable to alcoholism, since other problems such as poverty or family disorganization were also present in the families studied. And it is not clear exactly how these problems interact with the alcoholism.

Children are affected by the general atmosphere of unhappiness, by parental quarreling and fighting, and by lack of their parents' interest in them. These factors, more than the drinking itself, serve to create their problems. Even when parents do concern themselves with the children, they are inconsistent, sometimes spoiling, sometimes punishing. Uncertainty and unreliability undermine their growth and confidence. Denial of the alcoholism confuses them and mars their reality testing. The nonalcoholic parent is often no more helpful than the alcoholic because of her own confusion and unmet needs (Clinebell, 1968) and is unable to provide structure and nurturance. If both parents are alcoholic, children have to assume complete responsibility for themselves and often for their parents as well.

Children in alcoholic families are often caught in triangular relations with their parents (Krimmel, 1971; Press, 1975). The mother may seek the child's support and understanding in her difficulties with her husband, forming an alliance against him. Or she may involve the child in her attempts to control the drinking. Likewise, the alcoholic may air his complaints to the child about being misunderstood and abused by his wife. The child, caught in the tug-of-war, is put in the position of having to decide between the parents or take the role of peacemaker. Taking sides loses the support of the other parent. All three get locked into their respective roles, and nothing happens to diminish either the conflict or the alcoholism. In addition to the psychological suffering, the child may even be physically hurt in attempts to interfere when conflicts between the parents become physical. Efforts to mediate parental conflict require more maturity than the parents themselves possess and puts the child in a parental role with them. The phenomenon of an overfunctioning member compensating for underfunctioning members is thus evident in this even more inappropriate manner. In taking any of these roles in the family interaction, the child is not only experiencing the effects of parental behavior but unwittingly serving to perpetuate the problematic interaction as well.

Different children take different roles in these family situations, depending on age, sex, and sibling rank as well as on other factors. The specific influence of each of these factors has not been identified and has received only limited comment, except in the review by El-Guebaly and Offord (1977). Our foregoing discussion has inferred victim, peacemaking, and parental role-taking. Black (1980) identified additional roles such as responsible one, placator, or adjustor. Strausner, Weinstein, and Hernandez (1979) and Wegscheider (1981), in addition to the role of primary enabler, who is usually the spouse, identify still other roles taken by children such as hero, scapegoat, lost child, and mascot. These roles are also seen as enabling of the alcoholism, since each in a unique way contributes to its perpetuation. The consequences for the role-player are different in each case but similar for the alcoholic in that they serve an enabling function. Sex, age, or sibling rank of the various roles is not to be inferred from the following sequence description.

The hero child takes a great deal of responsibility for himself, stays out of trouble, and achieves in school. He is good, is successful, and parents his parents. He may have a favored position with one or both parents. He gives no clue that anything is wrong and thereby serves to perpetuate the denial of the alcoholism along with his parents. His behavior has a positive function for him as well in setting a lifelong pattern of doing well, but carried to the extreme and accompanied by compulsion to achieve and by denial of any dependency, can result in serious adjustment problems. Black (1980) comments that this responsible and self-denying role sometimes sets the individual up to become alcoholic in later life.

The scapegoat child performs in a negative, acting-out manner, seeking attention by negative behavior, since outdoing the hero child by good behavior seems impossible. Parental attention is of necessity turned to him, distracting them from the alcoholism and their problems with each other and defining him as the problem instead. It perpetuates their denial and interferes with their attention to resolution of their problems. The child can feel more certain that the home will not be broken, but at the same time faces increasing difficulty in life if his behavior becomes entrenched in a delinquent pattern.

The lost child is shy, a loner, stays out of the way. He or she is unnoticed, the neglected child in the family. Since she causes no trouble for the family, the parents' denial of the alcoholism and their difficulties with each other is maintained. The danger in this role for the child is the extent of retreat into isolation and fantasy. Black's (1980) "placating" child may be similar— a child who is totally adaptive to anything that happens. Such flexibility and attentiveness are assets for the family but do deprive the child of an adequate sense of a self whose needs and wishes are worthy of attention.

The mascot takes the role of family clown, relieving tension for self and family by humor, antics, and distraction. Here too the parents can feel that all is well and the child herself can bask in the approval of others. Yet, though these qualities seem useful in this situation, and may even be so in some gainful occupations, the disguising of their pain may in the long run create difficulty for them.

These roles may not be taken only by children in alcoholic families but are often present in them. They are illustrative of the systemic properties of the family in that the role serves a function for the family as well as for the person taking the role. It is adaptive for the individual and serves to stabilize the system. As long as this is the case, the system is locked in, with no change either in relationships or in the alcoholism.

BEYOND THE NUCLEAR FAMILY

Where alcoholic families do not live in isolation from extended family, parents or siblings of the alcoholic and/or the spouse may become participant in the alcoholic family interaction in ways similar to those described for immediate family members. They may assume an enabling role similar to the spouse. They may be drawn into a triangular relationship with the marital pair either as a peacemaker or ally. They may divert attention to themselves by argumentativeness, dependency, or demandingness. The parent of an alcoholic may seek to defend him by efforts to excuse, explain, or harbor him at critical times, and then blame and criticize the spouse. Similarly, the parent of the nonalcoholic spouse may join her in blaming or criticizing the alcoholic, or shelter her or encourage her to separate. Members of the extended family thus do not separate themselves and stand apart from the problems of the nuclear family's interaction.

In Bowen's (1974) terms, such extended family participation represents the failure of the couple to achieve a sufficient degree of differentiation from each other and from their family of origin. When tensions between the spouses is high, they may seek parents or sibs as allies, asserting their disdain and independence of one another, and returning to each other when the tension subsides or when tension with family of origin increases. Family interaction problems persist, as does the drinking.

TREATMENT

The systems view of the nuclear and extended family and its relation to the alcoholism which we have outlined leads clearly to the importance of the family's participation in treatment. Participation may be seen as benefiting the family in any event, especially in those cases in which the alcoholic is not initially motivated for help or change. Change which begins with them will affect the alcoholic and may lead to change on his part. Conversely, if change begins with the alcoholic, it will affect the family and necessitate adjustments on the part of other members. In the paragraphs that follow we will focus on work with the family and its consequences for the alcoholic, and also demonstrate how the family needs to change if and when the alcoholic changes.

Our view of family treatment is not characterized by a particular method of working with the family such as conjoint family interviews, but rather by the conception that change in one part of the family system affects the rest of the system. The worker therefore may work with various members as parts of the system but is always watchful of the consequences of change in those members for the interaction between members.

A review of literature pertaining to the treatment of families of alcoholics reveals that some programs have not served the alcoholic member directly or have served him only secondarily (Cohen and Krause, 1971; McDowell, 1972). Family members have been involved in outpatient treatment programs for the alcoholic (Woggon, 1972) as well as during inpatient stays, some of which required the residential stay of family members (Corder and Laidlaw, 1972; Catanzaro et al., 1973; Laundergan and Williams, 1979; Cameron, 1979). Some treatment programs have been for the entire family at the home rather than the office (Esser, 1968, 1971; Pattison, 1965).

Spouses are the most frequently involved family member and are seen individually and separately or in groups for spouses (Smith, 1969; Gallant et al., 1970). Couples are seen alone or in groups of couples (Berman, 1968; Burton and Kaplan, 1968). Children are included in sessions for the whole family (Esser, 1971; Meeks and Kelly, 1970) and sometimes in groups for children or for families (Janzen, in press). In all these reports, positive gains for the family and for the alcoholic are identified (see the review by Janzen, 1977), supporting our contention that method of work with the family is not the crucial variable.

The fact of and the extent of family participation appear to be a more crucial variable for the alcoholic's improvement. Attendance of a family member at even one session of a treatment program has been associated with the alcoholic's continuance in treatment (Gerard and Saenger, 1966). His continuance in treatment is lengthened by lengthening family participation (Wright and Scott, 1978; Berger, 1981; Edwards, 1982).

The many literature references to family involvement convey a great enthusiasm for family treatment. Regan, Connors, O'Farrel, and Jones (1983) have shown, however, that services to the family are often limited in scope and follow-through, especially for children. The needs of the family are viewed as secondary to the help that the family can offer to the alcoholic. Janzen's (in press) survey confirms that finding and notes frequent lack of understanding of the needs of the family and lack of clarity in conception of the relation of the family's operations to the alcoholism. Nevertheless, many programs did describe themselves as having a family systems view of these situations and viewed help to the family as help to the alcoholic as well.

Some treatment programs for families of alcoholics can be clearly identified as using specific theories of family treatment. Bowen (1974) used the same theoretical orientation with these families as he does with other problem families. Berenson (1976) and Carter (1977) also employ Bowen theory, though Carter also makes use of structural family therapy techniques in early stages of treatment. Esser (1968, 1971) implicitly and Wegscheider (1981) explicitly use Satir's (1967) communications approach to treatment. Transactional analysis conceptions have been used by Ward and Faillace (1970) to understand the interpersonal transactions within these families. Each of these theories appears to be productive in achieving understanding of the relationship of the alcoholism and family interaction and in planning treatment.

Our approach to treatment draws on several theoretical orientations as the earlier part of the chapter suggests and on multiple possibilities for ways to involve the family. Our discussion has not meant to imply that the family causes the alcoholism, only that family interaction may be a factor in its perpetuation. In this conception it becomes important to interrupt the interaction which enables the continuance of drinking and which defeats the family in solving its problems. As a first step, it is necessary to deal with the denial of alcoholic and family of the drinking problem. Then the family's efforts to regulate and control the drinking need to be interdicted. In these steps there can be relief for them and possibility of change for the alcoholic member.

The first step has already been taken when alcoholic and/or family seek treatment. Next steps may be accomplished in several ways. One way is to teach the spouse that alcoholism is a disease over which she has no control and therefore cannot cure. She can therewith be relieved of her guilt for causing it and the burden of being responsible for helping her husband with it. This method has been used in numerous instances and has been found to be helpful. Cohen and Krause (1971) have shown that spouses treated by workers using the disease concept were able to help the spouse to change and to function more effectively in the family and that this often served to draw the alcoholic into treatment. Workers not using the disease concept, however, were also able to produce the same effect using their general treatment theory of individualizing and valuing clients as persons, supporting them in the idea that they could only be responsible for their own well-being, and demonstrating that they did not really have the power to regulate the behavior of others. Thomas and Santa (1982) also demonstrate that unilateral work with the spouse can be helpful to the spouse, to the alcoholic, and to the relationship between them. Mueller (1972) describes how this works. He says that the wife needs to recognize that she did not cause the illness and that she is not capable of or responsible for curing it. Once freed of that burden, she can drop her ineffective coping and rescue operations. She can learn to stop nagging, making threats without carrying them out, and protecting her husband from the consequences of his drinking. . . . Her consequent lack of action should not emanate from anger and retaliation but rather, so far as possible, from a sense of objectivity and detachment . . . surrender and release. (p. 82)

Thus, she makes herself to be a separate person from her husband (Bowen's differentiation-of-self concept) and becomes a stronger person within the family (Minuchin's concept of strengthening subsystems).

The wife and other significant adults are also well served by a referral to Al-Anon, which provides a peer-group experience as a complement to the help provided by professionals (Gorman and Rooney, 1979). Davis (1980) sees such referral as not only helpful but necessary. These groups share with family therapists the idea that family members suffer if they only react to the behavior of the alcoholic. Al-Anon members learn in their groups, as they do in family treatment, that being only reactive does not alleviate the drinking but may indeed serve to perpetuate it as we have described above. They also learn that they can only be responsible for themselves, that they are not only "justified" for such "selfish" behavior but that it can have a positive effect on the alcoholic. Continuity and long-term membership in these groups can provide a long view which may not be available in therapy groups and which will help new members persevere in the initial stages of change.

The concern in our method is for the well-being of the spouse and for that of the alcoholic, though we have described only work with the wife which, we note, may be done on a one-to-one or group basis. The alcoholic may see the wife's new behavior as a loss of interest and caring and may respond by increased drinking, greater dependency, or belligerence. The wife must be helped to see this as a phase. Since the alcoholic can no longer accuse his spouse of running his life, he must begin to assume responsibility for his own behavior. He can begin to see himself as someone free from the direction of others and as more of a person over whom he may come to develop some control. Such positive results from the family's unilateral action may be more likely if the family seeks help early in the alcoholism career. However, if the situation is of long duration or severely deteriorated, more drastic action on the part of the family may be needed before the alcoholic will change or enter treatment.

When the family no longer denies the problem, family members may be prepared for more direct approach to the alcoholic (see Wegscheider, 1981). They are encouraged to recall their many instances of disappointment, the money shortages caused by the drinking, the lack of love and relationship, the abuse they have experienced, the shame they have endured, the isolation of the family and alienation from friends. When they are ready for confrontation, a meeting with the alcoholic is arranged as is admission to a treatment program for the alcoholic should he decide to seek it as a result of the confrontation.

Success of this method in getting the alcoholic to change is not guaranteed. Though willingness to confront is clearly based on a wish to restore a positive relationship, this step may need to be undertaken with the recognition that the further step of threatening to end the relationship through separation or divorce may be necessary. The spouse's willingness to consider such a possibility depends on her confidence in herself and her ability to survive, both psychologically and materially. If financial or employment resources are lacking, worker support in obtaining these as well as the psychological support must necessarily be a part of the treatment offered.

The alcoholic may respond positively to these drastic actions if his relationship with his family is still meaningful to him. Here again it is evident that earlier action on the family's part, before relationships deteriorate beyond the possibility of restoration, seems more likely to produce positive response than delay. Where relationships are still valued and the change in the drinking behavior occurs, both the alcoholic and the family gain.

If the alcoholic stops drinking or enters treatment as a result of the family's effort, family interaction has to change to adapt to his new behavior (see Jackson, 1956). The recovery phase has its own tasks. If he now seeks to assume a more responsible role, family members will need both to learn to trust that he will actually do so and to relinquish some of the role responsibilities they had undertaken in his place. Children may need to learn to count him into their activities. The wife may need to relearn to consult him about discipline or other family decisions. Everyone's hypersensitivity will likely show in verbal exchanges. Meeks and Kelly (1970) and Esser (1968) have demonstrated the usefulness of conjoint sessions at this phase to promote constructive family communication, problem solving, and conflict resolution. Additional work during the recovery phase should address the communication and marital difficulties we noted above.

CHILDREN IN THE TREATMENT PROCESS

As we have described them, children are both victims of the alcoholism and unwitting participants in its continuance. As victims they need treatment for their own sake to help them with their fears of abandonment, neglect, or violence, their sense of shame, and their feelings of guilt about having contributed to the family difficulties. They need also to be freed from the side-taking alliances into which they may have been drawn and from age-inappropriate role behavior such as their sense of responsibility for comforting or parenting their parents. Some of this may come as a result of their mother's change and her ability to assume stronger parental responsibility, unless she too is alcoholic. In that instance extra supportive measures will be needed, and if the parents are not responsive to treatment, removal from the home may be warranted.

Children may also be helped in the same manner we have outlined for the spouse by education in disease concepts and by the concept that they can and need be responsible only for themselves. By freeing them in these ways, they may be freed of the roles we have described and thereby from their unwitting functions as secondary enablers in the family. Some of this learning may come as a result of separate treatment for the children. Individual treatment may be appropriate for some. Richards (1979) says that group treatment is preferable for most children. Conjoint family sessions are certainly valuable for all the purposes just mentioned. Participation in family sessions can enable them to join in family communication processes in a new way, helping them to learn that it is again safe to ask questions, give observations, and express feelings. They can come to contribute in a positive way to family problem solving. Beyond this they will also benefit from referral to Alateen, which operates by principles similar to Al-Anon and which is organized especially for children of alcoholics. This is especially important if treatment programs which include children are limited in scope.

More recently there has been an expanding movement to services for adult children of alcoholics. Professionals providing therapy for adults have long known that the problems of children of alcoholics continue into adulthood. There is now an expanding self-help movement within this population which is becoming more accessible with expansion in numbers of groups and which is providing an extremely useful service. Referral to such groups in addition to therapy can add to their therapy.

HELP WITH SOCIAL ASPECTS OF ALCOHOLISM

Many consequences for the family's social situation arise as a result of the alcoholism. Money spent on alcohol can leave the family without essential food, clothing, and sometimes shelter. Physical assault and abuse sometimes occur along with the alcoholism. Concern for safety as well as needs for food, clothing, and shelter are often what prompt the family to request help (see Flanzer, 1978). Simple withdrawal or escape from abusive behavior and denial of the neglect the family experiences no longer suffice. The spouse may need support of family, friends, and eventually social agencies in the form of material assistance or alternative shelter. Her (and the children's) needs must be met while she is also given the psychological encouragement to protect and care for herself and the children. She has taken a long time in coming to the conclusion that she needs or will accept outside help. It is obvious that she is no longer relying on the alcoholic to be responsible. Our support of her during this is again based on the position that she can only be responsible for herself and that he must be responsible for himself. If he also can recognize this as a result of her focus on her own needs, this is all to the good, but she is supported in proceeding to meet her own needs whether he recognizes the change or not.

ALCOHOLIC WOMEN AND THEIR FAMILIES

While an increasing number of writings are appearing about female alcoholism, the research and reporting on family treatment for their situation is sparse. In the limited publications that do appear, contradictory views about these women's relationships to their spouses and children are reported, as was the case for the male alcoholic. On the one hand, it has been reported that the spouse of the female alcoholic is less likely to attempt control of her drinking and more likely to be either passively receptive of it or to separate himself from her. Corrigan and Anderson (1978) and Dahlgren (1979) have presented data that sheds doubt on that view. Corrigan (1980), relying on the reports of women alcoholics, reports that most of the husbands of the women she studied had considered separation, but few of the women reported that their husbands had actually threatened it.

The issue of the husband's personality type has also been raised as it was with the wives of alcoholic husbands. According to Fox (1972) some are long-suffering and controlling; some alternate ambivalently between leaving and begging to return; others are dependent or hostile and sadistic. Wolin (1980) notes that many have psychiatric problems, and Corrigan (1980) reports that many of the husbands are also alcoholic. At a minimum, it seems possible to conclude that there is no single personality-type husband of the female alcoholic. Clemmons (1979) draws attention to the fact that men leave their wives after they have stopped drinking because "she's changed . . . boring," (p. 141), an observation which suggests that her drinking serves some function for the man.

Wolin's (1980) research also shows that the marriages are characterized by a higher frequency of unsettled arguments, of disturbed communication patterns, and of a poorer match of self-perceptions of the spouses than in nonalcoholic marriages. Similar points have been made, as shown above, about the marriages of male alcoholics. Wilson (1980) asserts that marital problems of women alcoholics are more common and more severe. Ewing and Fox (1968) report that these marriages are highly resistant to change. Babcock and Connor (1981) view them as more stressful for the woman than for the man, since the basic cultural expectation is for the woman to adapt to her husband's role and position. There is in this position the suggestion of a power differential in favor of men generally. In these marriages, the struggle for control may be even more severe, and the female alcoholic may need more specific support in treatment.

Babcock and Connor advocate marital treatment for alcoholic women who are still in marriage because the marital role is so stressful. Page (1980) supports this position.

> Success (for her) should need to be not only related to drinking consumption but also to personal, family and mental health. For women it is clear that this definition of success is inevitably intertwined with their own cure. They are more inclined than men to be influenced by and dependent upon their husband's view of their health and progress. (p. 170)

In her view, marital treatment is more likely than individual treatment to result in rapid improvement. The sharing and participation of the spouse diminish guilt and rage and serve to open channels of communication. These factors seem similar to those noted earlier when the wife participates in the husband's treatment. However, Dinaburg, Gleck, and Feigenbaum (1980) caution that research demonstrating support for marital treatment of women alcoholics suggests that marital treatment by itself is insufficient to assure successful outcome. They advocate additional referrals to A.A., Al-Anon, and Alateen, and so do we.

Data on the situation of children of alcoholic mothers are also limited in availability. As many as three-fourths of women alcoholics live with and care for their children in some way. The impact on them would likely vary according to their age, sex, and sibling rank, as was the case with children of male alcoholics, and with the time of onset of her drinking. The male spouse's ability to nurture and protect them from the consequences of her behavior is also likely to vary. Wilson (1980) suggests that the problems for the children may be due more to the marital conflict than to the mother's drinking. She also contrasts the situations of children of alcoholic fathers and mothers in reference to family coalitions. Whereas children of alcoholic fathers have been observed to coalesce with mothers against the fathers, "no equivalent coalition exists between fathers and children (of alcoholic mothers) and that the woman's isolation ends when she sobers up" (p. 109). Beyond this, Wilson's discussion cites family dynamics and problems for the children that are similar to those described here for families of male alcoholics. Clemmons (1979) also describes problems and adjustments for children in the same way. Morehouse (1984), working with alcohol-abusing children of alcoholic mothers and fathers, also does not differentiate problems for children of alcoholic mothers from those of children of alcoholic fathers. She does point out that when parents stop drinking and resume more responsible, limit-setting roles in the family, children often complain.

Corrigan's (1980) research found that the women themselves acknowledged giving too little attention and too much responsibility to their children. Their husbands agreed with this evaluation. Richards (1979) cautions that therapists must resist the tendency to supplement the alcoholic mother in her child-rearing tasks, since this will alienate her, but should instead work to strengthen her in her parenting role. She also suggests that in separate work with the children care be taken not to overidentify with the children against the mother. Page (1980) says that a family systems orientation is needed for effective treatment of the woman alcoholic. Treatment should include the family and be goal specific in changing the system. Just "seeing the family" and "being supportive" are not adequate orientations to the tasks of treatment. Family participation in problem solving in conjoint interviews will serve to lift the woman's self-esteem. Page says that centered and highly structured work will likely lead to positive results in a short term of treatment.

Davis and Hagood (1979) describe a program of homemaking and child-care assistance to help in situations where the female alcoholic's ability to care for her children is extremely limited. When her limited capacity is coupled with that of a spouse who is also impaired by alcoholism or personality limitations, protective services intervention on behalf of the children may be needed.

FAMILY TREATMENT FOR ADOLESCENT ALCOHOLICS

What is known about the treatment of adolescent alcoholics suggests that their alcoholism is a behavior problem which can be viewed as similar to other adolescent behavior problems. The family dynamics, too, appear to be similar. Denial by the family of the adolescent's drinking is common (Unger, 1978), as in the case of the alcoholic parent, particularly if the parents are also alcoholic, a situation that is often reported. It has been noted that children of alcoholics often come to be alcoholics. According to Lee (1984) the adolescent alcoholic of the alcoholic parents is the acting-out, rebellious child. For treatment to be effective it is necessary, as in the case of the alcoholic adult, to break through the denial, or treatment will be sabotaged (Wynne, 1984). Family failure to cooperate reinforces the adolescent's problem. Since parental alcoholism is common to cases of adolescent alcoholism, it will be necessary to enable the parents to deal with their feelings about their own drinking (Morehouse, 1984).

Lee (1984) notes that the adolescent's drinking serves to distract attention from his or her parents' marital problems. In that sense, it is functional for the family, serving to contain and minimize anxiety. It also serves to diminish the adolescent's anxiety about the pain in the family, though it is destructive to him as well. Shifting alliances are observable in the family triangle. A parent may ally himself or herself with the drinking adolescent, thereby meeting a need of the parent and protecting the adolescent from the other parent's knowledge of his difficulty. Ultimately, parents may ally themselves against the adolescent, blaming him for all family problems. These shifts may be abetted by the alcoholism of one or the other or both parents.

An adolescent whose drinking creates problems for him in the community draws parental attention and engagement, leaving him more dependent and family-involved. The problems of separation and independence typical of adolescence are exacerbated and make it more difficult for both adolescent and parent to achieve a satisfactory degree of separateness.

This brief review reinforces the impression given at the outset of this section that family dynamics of adolescent alcoholics are very similar to those found with any child behavior problem. Parental failure to provide nurture, structure, direction, and discipline are evident. The possibility, however, that the parents may also have problems with alcohol complicates matters, increasing the strength of denial of family problems and the magnitude of the therapeutic task in dealing with denial. Research and reporting on family treatment for alcoholic adolescents is limited and needs to be undertaken in a more systematic fashion than has heretofore been reported.

SUMMARY

We have defined alcoholism as a family systems problem in that there is a functional relationship between alcoholism and the problems of the family. While family problems may not be viewed as the sole cause of alcoholism, they may exacerbate the alcoholism and alcoholism exacerbate family problems. Our effort was not to determine causality but to focus on the interactive characteristics of the system. All family members, including children, may be unwitting contributors to both the alcoholism and the family problems, and all members are obviously affected by both. While the primary focus of the chapter has been on the alcoholic male and his spouse, many of the interactions are seen to be similar in the case of the female alcoholic, or even of the adolescent alcoholic. A key issue in the interaction is the struggle between spouses to control and assume responsibility for each other. Consequently, a key issue in treatment is to enable family members to relinquish the effort to control the behavior of others and to accept responsibility only for themselves. This is facilitated in treatment by viewing alcoholism as a disease over which others have no control and by individualizing family members and encouraging them to be attentive to the meeting of their own needs.

The approach described in this chapter emphasizes that family treatment is any form of treatment that meets the needs of the family whether it does or does not solve the problem of the alcoholism. At the same time, treatment that serves the family is seen as contributing to reduction of alcoholism or at least as a means of promoting the alcoholic's participation in treatment. Once the alcoholic does begin to change, continuing work on family communications and problem solving is required to deal with problems in family relationships, since the drinking is not the only problem the family has to solve.

244 / FAMILY TREATMENT IN SOCIAL WORK PRACTICE

The limited attention given in these pages to the situation in which the adult woman or an adolescent child in the family is the alcoholic suggests that family dynamics are not so dissimilar in these cases as to warrant substantially different family treatment approaches for them.

REFERENCES

Al-Anon Family Group. 1967. *The Dilemma of the Alcoholic Marriage.* New York: Al Anon Family Group Headquarters.

Auger, R., Bragg, R., Corn, D., and Milner, M. 1973. "Preliminary Assessment and Prognostic Indicators in a Newly Developed Alcohol Treatment Program." *Newsletter for Research in Mental Health and Behavioral Sciences* 15:21-24.

Babcock, M., and Connor, B. 1981. "Sexism and the Treatment of the Female Alcoholic." *Social Work* 26(3):233-38.

Bailey, M. 1968. "Alcoholism and Marriage: A Review." *Quarterly Journal of Studies on Alcohol* 22:81-97.

Ballard, R. 1959. "The Interaction Between Marital Conflict and Alcoholism as Seen Through MMPI's of Marriage Partners." *American Journal of Orthopsychiatry* 29:528-46.

Berenson, D. 1976. "Alcohol and the Family System." In *Family Therapy Theory and Practice*, ed. P. Guerin. New York: Gardner Press.

Berger, A. 1981. "Family Involvement and Alcoholics' Completion of a Multiphase Treatment Program." *Journal of Studies on Alcohol* 42:517-21.

Berman, K. 1966. "Multiple Family Therapy: Its Possibilities in Preventing Readmission." *Mental Hygiene* 50:367-70.

_____. 1968. "Multiple Conjoint Family Groups in the Treatment of Alcoholism." *Journal of Medical Society of New Jersey* 65:6-8.

Binder, S. 1971. "Newer Therapeutic Procedures for Alcoholics." *Zeitschrift für Psychotherapie und Medizinische Psychologie* 21:239-47.

Black, C. 1980. "Children of Alcoholics." *Alcohol, Health and Research World* 4(1):23-27.

Bosma, W. 1972. "Children of Alcoholics: A Hidden Tragedy." *Maryland State Medical Journal* 21:34-36.

Bowen, M. 1974. "Alcoholism as Viewed Through Family Systems Theory and Family Psychotherapy." *Annals of the New York Academy of Sciences* 233:115-22.

Brown-Mayers, A., Seelye, E., and Brown, D. 1973. "Reorganized Alcoholism Service." *Journal of the American Medical Association* 224:233-35.

Burton, G., and Kaplan, H. 1968. "Group Counseling in Conflicted Marriage Where Alcoholism is Present: Client's Evaluation of Effectiveness." *Journal of Marriage and the Family* 30:74-79.

Cadogan, D. 1979. "Marital Group Therapy in Alcoholism Treatment." In *Family Therapy of Drug and Alcohol Abuse*, ed. E. Kaufman and P. Kaufman. New York: Gardner Press.

Cameron, L. 1979. "St. Croix: An Outpatient Family Treatment Approach." *Alcoholism, Health Research World* 3(4):16-17.

Carter, E. 1977. "Generation After Generation." In *Family Therapy: Theory and Practice*, ed P. Papp. New York: Gardner Press.

Catanzaro, R., Pisani, V., Fox, R., and Kennedy, E. 1973. "Familization Therapy." *Diseases of the Nervous System* 34:212-18.

Chafetz, M., Blane, H., and Hill, M. 1971. "Children of Alcoholics." *Quarterly Journal of Studies on Alcohol* 32:687-98.

Clemmons, P. 1979. "Issues in Marriage, Family and Child Counseling in Alcoholism." In *Women Who Drink*, ed. V. Burtle. Springfield, Ill.: Charles C Thomas, Publisher.

Clinebell, H. 1968. "Pastoral Counseling of the Alcoholic and His Family." In *Alcoholism: The Total Treatment Approach*, ed. R. Catanzaro. Springfield, Ill.: Charles C Thomas, Publisher.

Cohen, P., and Krause, M. 1971. *Casework with Wives of Alcoholics*. New York: Family Service Association of America.

Corder, R., and Laidlaw, N. 1972. "An Intensive Treatment Program for Alcoholics and Their Wives." *Quarterly Journal of Studies on Alcohol* 33:1144-46.

Cork, M. 1969. *The Forgotten Children*. Toronto: Addiction Research Foundation.

Corrigan, E. 1980. *Alcoholic Women in Treatment*. New York: Oxford University Press.

————, and Anderson, S. 1978. "Training for Treatment of Alcoholism in Women." *Social Casework* 59(1):42-50.

Dahlgren, L. 1979. "Female Alcoholics IV: Marital Situation and Husbands." *Acta Psychiatrica Scandinavica* 59:59-69.

Davis, D. I. 1980. "Alcoholics Anonymous and Family Therapy," *Journal of Marital and Family Therapy* 6(1):65-73.

Davis, T., and Hagood, L. 1979. "In-Home Support for Recovering Alcoholic Mothers and Their Families: The Family Rehabilitation Coordinator Project." *Journal of Studies on Alcohol* 40(3):313-17.

Dinaburg, D., Gleck, I., and Feigenbaum, E. 1980. "Marital Therapy of Women Alcoholics." In *Alcoholism in Women*, ed. C. Eddy and J. Ford. Dubuque, Iowa: Kendall/Hunt Publishing Co.

Edwards, D. 1982. "Spouse Participation in the Treatment of Alcoholism." *Social Work With Groups* 5(1):41-48.

Edwards, P., Harvey, C., and Whitehead, P. 1973. "Wives of Alcoholics: A Critical Review and Analysis." *Quarterly Journal of Studies on Alcohol* 34:112-32.

El-Guebaly, N., and Offord, D. R. 1977. "On Being an Offspring of an Alcoholic: An Update." *Alcoholism Clinical and Experimental Research* 3:148-57.

Esser, P. H., 1968. "Conjoint Family Therapy with Alcoholics." *British Journal of Addiction* 63:177-82.

————. 1971. "Evaluation of Family Therapy with Alcoholics." *British Journal of Addiction* 66:86-91.

Ewing, J., and Fox, R. 1968. "Family Therapy of Alcoholism." *Current Psychiatric Therapies* 8:86-91.

Finlay, D. 1966. "Effect of Role Network Pressure on an Alcoholic's Approach to Treatment." *Social Work* 11:71-77.

————. 1974. "Alcoholism: Illness or Problem in Interaction." *Social Work* 19:390-405.

Flanzer, J. 1978. "Family Management in the Treatment of Alcoholism." *British Journal on Alcohol and Alcoholism* 13:45-59.

Fox, R. 1968. "Treating the Alcoholic's Family." In *Alcoholism: The Total Treatment Approach*, ed. R. Catanzaro. Springfield, Ill.: Charles C Thomas, Publisher.

————. 1972. "Children in the Alcoholic Family." In *Problems in Addiction: Alcoholism and Narcotics*, ed. W. C. Bier. New York: Fordham University Press.

Gallant, D. M., Rich, A., Bey, E., and Terranova, L. 1970. "Group Psychotherapy with Married Couples: Successful Techniques in New Orleans Alcoholism Clinic Patients." *Louisiana State Medical Society Journal* 122:41-44.

Gerard, D., and Saenger, G. 1966. *Outpatient Treatment of Alcoholism: A Study of Outcome and Its Determination*. Toronto: University of Toronto Press.

Gorad, S. 1971. "Communicational Style of Alcoholics and Their Wives." *Family Process* 10:475-89.

Gorman, J. M., and Rooney, J. F. 1979. "The Influence of Al-Anon on the Coping Behavior of Wives of Alcoholics." *Journal of Studies on Alcohol* 40:1030-38.

Jackson, J. 1956. "The Adjustment of the Family to Alcoholism." *Marriage and Family Living* 18:361-69.

Janzen, C. 1977. "Families in the Treatment of Alcoholism." *Journal of Studies on Alcohol* 38(1):114-30.

Janzen, Curtis. In press. "Use of Family Treatment Methods by Alcoholism Treatment Services." *Alcohol Health and Research World*.

Kogan, K., and Jackson, J. 1965. "Stress, Personality, and Emotional Disturbance in Wives of Alcoholics." *Quarterly Journal of Studies on Alcohol* 26:486-95.

Krimmel, H. (ed.). 1971. *Alcoholism: Challenge for Social Work Education*. New York: Council on Social Work Education.

Laundergan, J. C., and Williams, T. 1979. "Hazeldon: Evaluation of a Residential Family Program." *Alcohol, Health and Research World* 3(4):13-17.

Lee, J. 1984. "Adolescent Alcohol Abuse." *Focus on Family and Chemical Dependency* 7(3):22-25.

McDowell, F. 1972. "The Pastor's Natural Ally Against Alcoholism." *Journal of Pastoral Care* 26:26-32.

Meeks, D., and Kelly, C. 1970. "Family Therapy with the Families of Recovering Alcoholics." *Quarterly Journal of Studies on Alcohol* 31:399-413.

Minuchin, S. 1974. *Families and Family Therapy*. Cambridge, Mass.: Harvard University Press.

Morehouse, E. 1984. "Working with Alcohol Abusing Children of Alcoholics." *Alcohol, Health and Research World* 8:14-19.

Mueller, J. 1972. "Casework with the Family of the Alcoholic." *Social Work* 17:79-84.

Orford, J., Oppenheimer, E., Egert, S., Hensmen, C., and Guthrie, S. 1976. "The Cohesiveness of Alcoholism: Complicated Marriages and Its Influence on Treatment Outcome." *British Journal of Psychiatry* 128:318-39.

Page, A. 1980. "Counseling." In *Women and Alcohol,* ed. Camberwell Council on Alcoholism. London: Tavistock Publications.

Pattison, E. 1965. "Treatment of Alcoholic Families with Nurse Home Visits," *Family Process* 4:74-94.

Press, L. 1975. "Treating the Family." *Maryland State Medical Journal* 24:32-35.

Preston, F. 1960. "Combined Individual, Joint, and Group Therapy in Treatment of Alcoholism." *Mental Hygiene* 44:522-28.

Rae, John, 1972. "The Influence of Wives on the Treatment Outcome of Alcoholics." *British Journal of Psychiatry* 120:601-613.

Regan, J., Connors, G., O'Farrel, T., and Jones, W. 1983. "Services for Families of Alcoholics." *Journal of Studies on Alcohol* 44(6):1072-82.

Richards, T. 1979. "Working with Children of an Alcoholic Mother." *Alcohol, Health and Research World* 3(3):22-25.

Satir, V. 1967. *Conjoint Family Therapy.* Palo Alto, Calif.: Science and Behavior Books.

Smith, C. 1969. "Alcoholics: Their Treatment and Their Wives." *British Journal of Psychiatry* 115:1039-42.

Steiner, C. 1969. "The Alcoholic Game." *Quarterly Journal of Studies on Alcohol* 30:920-38.

Steinglass, P. 1976. "Experimenting with Family Treatment Approaches to Alcoholism, 1950-1975: A Review." *Family Process* 15:97-123.

Straussner, S. L., Weinstein, D. L., and Hernandez, R. 1979. "Effects of Alcoholism on the Family System." *Health and Social Work* 4(4):111-27.

Thomas, E., and Santa, C. 1982. "Unilateral Family Therapy for Alcohol Abuse." *American Journal of Family Therapy* 10(3):49-59.

Unger, R. A. 1978. "The Treatment of Adolescent Alcoholism." *Social Casework* 59(1):27-35.

Ward, R., and Faillace, L. 1970. "The Alcoholic and His Helpers." *Quarterly Journal of Studies on Alcohol* 31:684-91.

Wegscheider, S. 1981. *Another Change: Hope and Health for the Alcoholic Family.* Palo Alto, Calif.: Science and Behavior Books.

Wilson, C. 1980. "The Family." In *Women and Alcohol,* ed. Camberwell Council on Alcoholism. London: Tavistock Publications.

Wiseman, J. P. 1976. "The Wives of Alcoholics: Diagnosis of Alcoholism and Treatment Strategy Involving the Family." *Alkoholipolitiikka* 41:62.

Woggon, H. 1972. "The Alcoholic Unit at Broughton Hospital." *Inventory* 22(2):18-19.

Wolin, S. 1980. "Introduction: Psychosocial Consequences." In *Alcohol and Women: Research Monograph No. 1.* Rockville, Md.: National Institute on Alcohol Abuse and Alcoholism.

Wright, M. D., and Scott, T. B. 1978. "The Relationship of Wives' Treatment to the Drinking Status of Alcoholics." *Journal of Studies on Alcohol* 39(9):1577-81.

Wynne, M. 1984. "Teenage Chemical Dependency Treatment." *Focus on Family and Chemical Dependency* 7(3):20-21.

CHAPTER **10**

Treatment During Family Dissolution

Disruption of marital relationships and separation of one or other of the partners and children to different residences are increasingly facts of everyday life. The divorce rate doubled from 1965 to 1975, and 3 million people were affected by divorces in 1975 (*Journal of Divorce*, 1977). In 1982, 22 percent of all children under eighteen lived with only one of their natural parents (Lyon, Silverman, Howe, Bishop, and Armstrong, 1985). Weed (1980) projects that of all marriages contracted in 1976, 49.6 percent will end in divorce—that is 47.8 percent of all first marriages and 55.4 percent of all remarriages. Of first marriages 16.4 percent will have ended within five years. Of all remarriages, 24.3 percent will have ended in five years. The average expected duration of first marriages is 25.8 years, which is a lowered expectancy, given the high percentage not expected to endure. At the time of marriage, the projected expectancy of life together for remarried couples is 15.9 years, a figure also reduced by the high rate of breakup. Very few professionals remain unaware of the phenomena among their clientele or within their social circles.

Marital separation and the consequent disruption of family life are stressful and painful, no matter how stressful and painful the family's life together had been or whether the separation had been earnestly sought or strenuously resisted. Both partners suffer as do the children. Although there may be relief for the partners, and in some instances for the children too, breakdown of family relations to the point of separation of family members is still seen and experienced as deviant because of the pain, loss, increased difficulty in relationships, and the new and unknown complexity of the ensuing years. Yet, because of its frequency and the fact that so many lives are affected, it must also be seen as a family life experience that needs to be understood, so that it can be normalized, perhaps even ritualized in order to give people the ways and means to cope when they come face to face with such a major transition in their lives. A massive amount of experience, research, and publication has been devoted to understanding the formation of families, giving guidance for that life transition. By comparison, relatively little guidance, and consequently little support, has been available for the transition out of the nuclear family group. People have been left to suffer and cope alone and on their own as best they can. Professionals have similarly been at a loss for knowledge and the best ways to help.

Nevertheless, as the rate of marital dissolution continues unabated, there has been an increasing tendency to recognize serial monogamous relationships as a common form of the family life cycle. Hunter and Schuman (1980, p. 447) note that the fact that families dissolve and reconstitute shows "the low level of commitment by parental members of the household group to maintain any particular household as a stable unit over an extended period of time." This has come to be an increasingly accepted standard. A period of life with one partner ends. It may or may not have brought with it the arrival of children. It is followed by a period of singlehood and/or single parenthood which ends by remarriage and the constituting of a new household, which may include children from one or both previous marriages as well as births to the current marriage. The family in the phase of dissolution, or of single parenthood, and of remarriage is a different kind of organization from the first family. Each family stage needs to develop its own rules, relationships, and place in the community.

This chapter will be devoted only to the family in the dissolution phase. The subsequent chapter will look at the family formed out of two prior families. We see the dissolution phase as a transitional crisis for the family in which psychological and social stresses place severe demands on individual adjustment and interpersonal relationships, and for the meeting of which personal and social resources may be lacking. Within the dissolution phase there are smaller identifiable phases. We will describe these phases in terms of their impact on family members. We will also suggest goals for treatment. Without doubt, research on what helps most, for what kinds of situations, and for which phase or dissolving family type is still in short supply. At the same time, popular books on the topic are increasingly available as is professional literature.[1] Books on marital and family treatment now generally include chapters on divorce therapy. A quarterly interdisciplinary *Journal of Divorce* began publication in 1977. Another publication, the *Journal of Mediation*, new in 1983, devotes the majority of its content to mediation of family disputes, particularly of issues that arise during the divorce phase of family experience. The bibliography attached to this chapter attests to the growing body of literature.

UNDERSTANDING FAMILY DISSOLUTION

Our overall objectives in working with dissolving family units are to help the couple achieve a successful psychic separation and to enable them to continue a positive parental role and relationship with their children. Achieving an understanding of how the relationship failed and of the kind of relationship it was that had been dissatisfying to the partners can facilitate the detachment and also forestall the possibility that the ex-spouses will repeat a bad relationship with a new partner. In initial stages of treatment, reasons for breakup are put forth in justification for it and need to be put in perspective.

Reasons for Divorce

Causes of difficulty in marriage are many, but they do not always lead to complete breakdown of marital relationships and divorce. The combination of factors leading to a decision on the part of one or both partners to separate is not clear for marriages in general or often even for a particular marriage. Some of the specific reasons for seeking divorce have been identified in various studies. Levinger (1966) noted that husbands and wives do not give the same reasons. In his study, wives cited, in order of frequency, physical abuse, financial problems, mental cruelty, and neglect of home and

---

[1]See, for example, M. Krantzler, *Creative Divorce*, 1973; M. and R. Hunt, *The Divorce Experience*, 1977; and C. Napolitane and N. Pelligreno, *Living and Loving after Divorce*, 1977, all by Signet Books.

children. Husbands most frequently cited sexual incompatability, followed by neglect of home and children, infidelity, in-law troubles, and mental cruelty. For both husbands and wives there were variations due to social class.

Little (1982) suggests the possibility that the actual behavior of the partners may be less of a factor than the fact that there is a disparity between an ideal image of other as partner and parent and the actuality of the partner's performance. What might be reason for divorce in one relationship may not be sufficient reason in another relationship. Little identifies clusters of role images that seem to be important. Closeness, companionship, and intimacy were ranked high as characteristics of ideal husbands and wives by both husbands and wives; yet, both saw themselves and their spouses as failing to meet these expectations. A second cluster pertaining to caring for and modeling behavior for the children was not ranked quite as high. Both husbands and wives rated themselves as well as their spouses better than on the previous cluster. They were more satisfied with their own than their spouse's performance. The third cluster, income production and family management items, ranked lower in overall importance to the marriage. Both spouses scored themselves and their spouses higher in meeting expectations on these items. In this study, then, men and women put highest priority on companionship, sharing of feelings, and listening and caring. It is in this area that they are most disappointed, and for deficits in this area that they are most likely to divorce. Of interest also in Little's study is her report that 65 percent of the women and 70 percent of the men identified the wife's going to work as a factor leading to separation. Husbands being too involved with work was also frequently cited.

Lyon, Silverman, Howe, Bishop, and Armstrong (1985) identified additional specifics such as extramarital relationships, drug or alcohol abuse, poor communication, money problems, and the spouse's failure to accept personal change in the partner. In their study 57 percent of the respondents blamed the spouse for failure of the marriage. In this and other studies it is interesting to note that substantial numbers of respondents thought that their own behavior as well as their spouse's contributed to the failure of the marriage. They did not put sole responsibility on the partner.

Levinger (1965) in a speculative review posits that a change in the combination of bonds and bars leads to a shift from cohesiveness in marriage to its dissolution. Cohesiveness in the marriage is "a direct function of the attractions within and barriers around a marriage and an inverse function of such attractions from other relationships" (p. 20). When the cohesiveness is due more to barriers to dissolution than to bonds between the partners, the marriage may be seen as an empty shell but still hold together. Attraction may be for intrinsic reasons such as genuine affection, esteem, and companionship, or for extrinsic reasons such as financial or social status. Barriers to dissolution may consist of feelings of obligation, moral proscriptions, community pressures, or legal bars. Promoting dissolution are such things as alternate affections (toward lovers or kin loyalties), differing religions, or alternate sources of income. Levinger cites research which has demonstrated the importance of all these factors, but the relationship between them and the exact combination of them which would lead to dissolution are left to be determined.

Some of these factors suggest the impact of broad social forces such as the changing place of women in society as factors in marital dissolution. Their entry into the work force, whether for reasons of financial necessity or personal gratification, as a factor draws attention to this larger picture. Another such broad social factor is our society's emphasis on individual freedom and satisfaction. Whitaker and Keith (1984) draw attention to this when they say, "In our 'do your own thing,' 'preserve your freedom' culture a person has to be crazy to get married' " (p. 53). Achieving individuality is often emphasized in seeking separation and divorce. There is the pervasive concern that individual identity will be lost in commitment to the family. Making interpersonal relationships work and endure always involves struggle, negotiation, and effort. The part of each individual that does not want to make the effort is reenforced by the cultural norm to which Whitaker and Keith draw attention. We have noted at other places in this book that the balance between separateness and connectedness, between individual goals and the goals of the family group is constantly shifting. It may be that in the emphasis on "doing one's own thing" one may lose sight of the possibility that in struggling for relatedness one's individuality may also be enhanced.

However intense the struggle for individuality has been, attachment has also come to be of great importance. It is the remaining attachment that makes for part of the difficulty in separation. Furthermore, one is never left unchanged by a relationship. In Whitaker and Keith's words "It is impossible to go back to being single. Marriage is like a stew that has irreversible characteristics that the parts cannot be rid of. Divorce is leaving part of the self behind," and that adds to the difficulty and stress of separation and divorce.

We do not suppose that we have in the foregoing material exhausted the discussion of reasons for divorce. The specific impact of each differing cause on the way the divorce proceeds remains to be understood for each situation. However, awareness of at least some of the reasons can give the social worker an idea of the issues the partners will bring to the help-seeking effort. Conceptually framing the specifics as role-image disparities and as a balancing of bonds of cohesiveness and bars to dissolution also provides the worker with a way of looking at the specifics. In some instances the specific reasons will also influence the ease or difficulty with which the divorcing process flows.

Divorcing Types

Several relationship typologies of divorcing couples have been identified. While the studies from which these typologies are drawn have not firmly established that they were also the type of the marriage, there is the suggestion that type is related to the way in which the disengagement of the partners proceeds as well as to the subsequent adjustment of family members. Knowing these should help the worker know what to anticipate. Understanding the relationship the couple has had may also make it more possible for the partners to let go of the relationship and to avoid entry into another similar and unsatisfying relationship.

Little (1982) identifies six types of dissolving relationships in which the nature of the relationship was in itself reason for the divorce. She also sees the character of the relationship as a determinant of the postdivorce adjustment of the couple and of the kinds of decisions made about custody for the children. In the fragile-bond marriage the spouses replayed without question the patterns in their families of origin. They did not communicate feelings, lived in separate worlds, and never struggled to create a common world. They eventually withdrew from each other and parted company completely. In the fractured family the couple also initially played out patterns from families of origin. However, in addition to withdrawing, they began to appeal to, attack, or try to coerce each other into new behavior. Conflict and competition developed and led finally to dissolution.

In the doll's-house marriage, the husband initially controlled a very submissive wife who later became more assertive. Both partners then resorted to posturing, rewarding, persuading, depreciating, and inflating tactics, which finally led to moves to end the relationship. A stalemate-marriage type was devoid of emotional expressiveness, particularly on the part of the man, who never invited or demanded expressiveness from his wife. The woman, however, demanded it from her husband and was seen as more striving and achieving.

The perfect-model marriage is so labeled because the relationship started as the picture of success with outside careers of both partners, healthy children, and a relatively egalitarian relationship. However, the man expected deference, discounting his wife and making her needs secondary. A sixth marriage type was unformed families, in which adequate bonding had never occurred and in which the partners lacked self-awareness. Little asserts that these ways of relating continued through divorcing and divorce periods and profoundly influenced the adjustment of the children. As in the classification which follows, degree of individuation and levels of communication, conflict and investment in the relationship are important variables.

Kressel, Jaffee, Tuchman, Watson, and Deutsch (1980) offer a typology of divorcing couples based on the degree of ambivalence manifested by the participants, the level and overtness of the conflict, and the frequency and openness of their communication. They were interested in determining whether type was associated with readiness to accept or benefit from divorce mediation efforts. They found all four types among couples who had and couples who had not sought mediation.

An enmeshed type of couple showed high levels of conflict, communication, and ambivalence. They stated explicitly their wish to divorce, but manifested in many ways their inability to let go by continually taking opposing points of view and sometimes reversing their positions in doing so. Turmoil continued even after the divorce was finalized.

Autistic-pattern couples showed a low level of communication and overt conflict. The spouses avoided each other physically and emotionally. Expressed ambivalence was at a low level. There was a low level of communication of doubt and uncertainty about the divorce. A disengaged-pattern group similarly showed a low level of ambivalence but had had a much lower level of intimacy in their earlier relationship, so that the conflict at the time of divorce was much less. They showed a strong wish to avoid conflict, and the danger in working with them was excessive cordiality.

A direct-conflict pattern group of couples manifested high levels of conflict and open communication about the possibilities of divorce. Initially high ambivalence was resolved over the space of a year. This was the only group which the authors identified as having a good experience with mediation and as achieving a successful postdivorce adjustment.

Another classification of divorces is based on the characteristics of surprise and mutuality. Divorces that are sought by one partner and resisted by the other are characteristically more difficult than those in which both partners have concluded that divorce should be sought. Sprenkle and Cyrus (1983) see the divorce that is sudden and unexpected for one of the partners as a crisis situation. The initiating partner has often pondered leaving for a long time (ten years in one of our cases) before announcing intention and sometimes even before voicing dissatisfaction. The abandoned partner must recover from shock as well as other feelings attendant upon divorce. The surprise factor is indeed an added stress for the person being abandoned and creates greater difficulty at least initially than the situation in which thoughts of separation have been openly discussed by both spouses as the marital difficulties increased.

DIVORCE AS PHASES OF CRISIS

The time span from awareness of hardly bearable dissatisfaction with the marriage to the completion of parting into separate households, legalization of the divorce, and a more or less stable pattern of singlehood or single-parenthood may be divided into distinguishable phases, each of which has its own set of stresses, feelings, and tasks. Each may be considered to be a crisis which requires successful resolution before the tasks of the subsequent phase can be fruitfully engaged. The work and use of treatment are tailored as much as possible to the needs of the phase. Though some things are more at issue in some phases, many will have residuals in subsequent phases and some work on them will likely have been done in phases prior to our placement of them.

Some features are applicable to all phases (Hunter and Schuman, 1980). Role ambiguity and role confusion abound. "How am I supposed to behave? What is expected of me? How do I want to be? What can I or should I say?" There are no guidelines for what to do and likely no one else who can give the benefit of their experience. And even if there were someone, resistance to seek out such a person is great because of the accompanying feelings of failure. In all phases there are also boundary problems for the family system. What can be taken outside the family system? Whom can we tell? To what extent are problems and feelings shared across generational boundaries, or how much should they be? How much can parent and child confide and rely on each other for solace and support? Conflicting loyalties also arise.

How much do I owe myself? How much to my spouse? To my children? And for the children there is the question of siding or not siding with one or the other of the sparring parents.

Feelings of loss and grief are ever present for the spouse who seeks the separation as well as for the one who resists it. Mutual suspicion is strong, as is wariness that the other will take some advantage and be unfair. Self-blame, lack of self-worth, and uncertainty about who one really is add to difficulties in adjustment and coping over the entire span of the divorcing process.

Many factors contribute to the level of stress experienced at this time and to the ability to cope with it. The spouse who is opposed initially to separation and divorce will experience greater stress. Suddenness and unexpectedness of the action add to stress. Length of the marriage and the degree of intimacy once achieved in the marriage may make separation more difficult. Numbers of children in the family and any problems they have can make a difference. Loss of friends, changes in residence, and limited finances all add their burden.

Level of coping depends on personality strengths and social resources. Persons may be limited in coping by residual effects of past losses and separation (see Counts and Sachs, 1985). Another loss is even more devastating when grief over past relationships is unresolved and the capacity for new attachments has not been developed. Remaining overclose attachments to family of origin indicate a limited capacity to detach and achieve independence and will result in ambivalent holding on and letting go during the separation period. These characteristics suggest a limited degree of individuation and separation and a limited capacity for independent living.

Social resources can complement personal coping resources. Friends and family may be supportive both psychologically and with material resources and advice. Availability of material resources may also enhance coping capacity.

Predivorce Phase

Disillusionment with the marriage evolves eventually into a decision to separate and divorce. In Spanier and Thompson's (1984) research it took less than six months for over half of the women and almost two-thirds of the men studied for that evolution to end with filing for divorce. But it took as long as two years for a third of the men and 43 percent of the women.

Kressel and associates (1980) say that the "leavers" had been considering leaving for eleven months, on the average, before seeking mediation. The "abandoned" spouse may have had only a month. Disappointment becomes disillusionment when one partner recognizes that the other is not what had been hoped for. Love erodes, and the tenderness of earlier attachment disappears (Kessler, 1975). In the midst of this come efforts to restore the relationship, and the assistance of marriage counselors is sometimes sought. When efforts to restore fail, the public facade of marital bliss is shattered and energies shift to consideration of separation and divorce (Kressel and Deutsch, 1977). Decisions are made and unmade. Most permanent separations are preceded by at least one trial or temporary separation.

Actual consideration of divorce is devastating for both partners. Intensity and difficulty vary. The "initiator" may have handled many feelings and developed a fairly clear picture of what it was all going to be like before announcing intent, but for the "abandoned spouse" the announcement comes as a shock. "I am being rejected, I am a failure, You are being unfair. I am hurt. I am angry. You can't, you shouldn't do this to me." Or "What have I done? What do you want me to do? Please stay! I'll do anything. Don't leave me alone." Sprenkle and Cyrus (1983) suggest that in the offer of the "abandoned one" to change is the implicit recognition that he or she has in some way previously been the abandoning one. In any event, ambivalence runs high. Fighting alternates with clinging when the anxiety level engendered by the prospects of the future is raised or when self-confidence flags and doubts occur about whether this is really the best course to take.

Grief is strong. Loss of the love relationship is no doubt central. An important someone no longer cares. And separation also means loss of familiar routines, familiar environment, and familiar associations outside the family with friends and kin. The experience is emptiness, with no prospect of filling it or the confidence that one would even know how to go about it and loss of prospects, disruption of hopes and plans.

It seems initially strange to consider that the "initiator" would also grieve. That is an emotion one tends to attribute only to the "abandoned one." It is nevertheless a loss. It is the loss of investment in the relationship. It is leaving a part of oneself. It is loss of an image of what might have been and of what one had waited for, the end of hope that what was desired will ever be attained.

There is also the loss of outside relationships for both spouses. Friends have often been friends of the couple, rather than of one or the other, and are uncertain how to relate, whether with sympathy or congratulations. They too feel a loss and tend to withdraw. Further, they are unwilling to be caught in taking sides. The latter may be less true for kin than for friends. It is not unknown for kin to side with their in-law rather than with blood relatives. Research by Kitson, Moir, and Mason (1982) concludes that even relatives are not inclined to be helpful if they disapprove of the divorce. All these losses serve to leave the parting couple with minimal sources of support at a time when support is most needed and could be most helpful.

For both partners, loss engenders anger, blame, and fighting. Elkin (1977) calls it "angerism—a deep-seated unresolved anger, dependency, anxiety, fear, and at times a degree of irrationality and an inability to set aside the anger long enough to do what is necessary for all concerned, especially the children" (p. 56). It can continue five or ten years. It needs to be resolved.

Evaluations of the helpfulness of treatment are not always definite about the phase at which treatment occurred or the reasons for seeking it. In some instances the search for treatment during this phase has the objective, at least on the part of one of the partners, of seeking to restore the marriage. Sometimes the other spouse comes along to make a last effort to save the marriage, though it is sometimes also evident that coming along is only for show when in reality they have made up their minds to separate. Spanier and Thompson (1984) said that 70 percent of their research sample had sought help at some point during the process, though it was not clear whether the purpose was to save the marriage or to ease the process of divorce. About a third of these couples had sought help from clergy persons and another third from marriage and family counselors. Of the sample, 30 percent found their counseling to be extremely helpful, and another 51 percent thought it was somewhat helpful.

Earlier studies (Beck, 1975; Cookerly, 1973) had concluded that individual interviews were more helpful than conjoint interviews for dissolving relationships. Storm and Sprenkle (1982) suggest that this may be doubted, since marriage counseling and divorce counseling cases may have been grouped together. They suggest that during the predivorce or decision-making stage and the next restructuring stage of divorce therapy, conjoint interviews can be very useful. Our experience tends to confirm this view.

Couple type may be a factor in the ability to benefit from either individual or conjoint treatment during this phase. The types we have mentioned have been only briefly sketched by their developers, and diagnosis is most certainly difficult. However difficult, a relationship diagnosis is helpful. The couple with low rates of communication, such as Little's "fragile-bond" type, may particularly benefit from an increased flow of information and exchange of feeling that is possible in conjoint sessions. A couple diagnosis of the enmeshed pattern (Kressel et al., 1980) may suggest limiting the expression of feeling and an emphasis on cognitive grasp of the situation or a focus on the difficulties of letting go. Couples of the enmeshed type achieve neither harmony nor separation until one of them is strengthened for greater assertiveness and independence. On the other hand, their "direct-conflict" type would seem likely to benefit from conjoint treatment at this stage as well as from mediation at a later stage.

Goals of treatment in the decision-making phase are to help the partners become clear about the nature of their relationship and whether there is any possibility that either partner could or would make the changes needed for the relationship to become satisfying. If one of the spouses has already decided to separate, the contact can demonstrate whether the decision can be reversed and/or help the other spouse to make a case for reversal or to accept the inevitable. Communication can be promoted in conjoint sessions which identifies the issues and the capacity of the partners to respond to them. Each can evaluate the importance of the issues and the possibilities of change. Clients differ in their wishes for the conduct of the treatment sessions. Some simply want to hear what their spouses have to say or to have their spouses listen to what they have to say. Others seek more active help in resolving as well as in clarifying issues.

Each spouse also begins at this stage to deal with feelings of badness and failure, with their sense of loss, and with what lies ahead. They also begin to develop ways to present themselves to the outside world and to anticipate how friends and kin will respond to them. They begin to hear how the other is thinking about who will move, who will have the children, what their financial situation will be. All of these considerations enter the basic decision to be made at this stage—whether to stay together or to part.

Negotiating and Restructuring

Once the decision to separate and divorce has been made, the central task is to restructure the family. This means achieving an end to the marriage that is as constructive as possible and at the same time recognizing that a family continues to exist if children are involved and making workable plans for that family. Ahrons (1980) points out that divorce creates new households of single parents, but it results in a single-parent family only when one of the spouses is or becomes unavailable. A parental coalition must be preserved, or created, while the marital coalition is dissolved (Goldman and Coane, 1983). For constructive resolution for the children, and for themselves as well, the former spouses must achieve an ability to cooperate in responsible care for the children and in continuing their own separate relationships to them. Housing, financial support, property settlement, child custody, and visiting arrangements must all be negotiated. Lyon and associates (1985) call this the litigation phase. It is indeed litigious, even if it does not come to legal litigation. The issues are highly charged emotionally.

Restructuring has an emotional and a rational practical component. For the crisis of divorce to be resolved successfully, both components must be addressed. Rational planning and handling of reality matters cannot be completed if the emotional issues are unresolved. And unless reasonable plans are made, emotional tension will remain at a high level. Skill for assisting the couple with both aspects should be part of the social worker's repertoire, though, as we suggest later, referrals to mediators for financial and custody mediation may be useful.

Emotional Issues. Work on emotional issues will have begun in the initial phase. The couple's efforts to arrive at a decision about dissolution of the marriage exposes feelings of rejection, pain of loss, anxiety about the future, guilt over past behavior, feelings of inadequacy, and the hostility and anger directed at the other for being incompetent, irresponsible, or unfair. Tension and anger levels may still be high. The "abandoned one" may still be defending against "narcissistic injury" (Rice, 1977) by projecting all blame and attempting to instill guilt in the leaving spouse. In some instances attacks, retaliatory behavior, and even suicide threats are made in efforts to keep the other bound to the relationship. These may be based on a concept of self as unlovable and unworthwhile and a conviction that "no one else will ever want me." Limits on such behavior need to be set. Drawing attention to the incendiary results of threatening and "get-even" behavior may help. Interventions need to be designed to build confidence in self and one's ability to survive. Praise for small achievements and reassurances of one's worthwhileness conveyed through worker interest and caring contribute to that end. Teaching practical skills needed for survival such as cooking or banking or organizing will not only aid survival but build confidence and hope as well.

Separate individual as well as conjoint sessions are useful to enable each spouse to express feelings and to be listened to and understood. Even though there may be cognitive recognition that the marriage is over, opportunity to mourn the loss, to consider one's own and the other's contributions to the breakdown of the marriage, and to let go of the relationship are provided in the treatment process. In this connection it may be useful to wonder why the reluctant spouse is not more dissatisfied. Achieving an understanding of one's own behavior in the marriage and of the responses of the spouse should lead to an acceptance of self and a reasonable degree of toleration of the spouse, enough at least so that they do not continue efforts to fight and destroy each other and so that they do achieve the ability to cooperate on behalf of the children. Each partner should also gain a sense of his or her strengths and individual rights to enable him or her to put in some perspective their feelings of inadequacy and guilt. Hopefully each spouse will be able to acquire a greater sense of separateness and wholeness as a person as a result of these crisis resolution efforts and achievements.

Practical Matters. Resolving practical issues becomes easier as the treatment succeeds in diminishing anger, building self-respect, and achieving mutuality of conviction about the inevitability and advisability of divorce. The spouses, if at this phase one can still call them that, can begin to cooperate better in deciding who is to move and who is to stay, how to divide possessions, what degree of financial self-sufficiency is possible for each, and who will need the support of the other. Decisions about custody of the children and visiting rights should also be easier.

When couples on their own are unable to resolve these issues and seek help for them, the worker's primary task is to elicit facts about what has been, what resources there are, and what the persons involved want to have happen. The information provided can suggest what the range of possibilities might be. While the acquisition of information may be difficult, due to enduring anger and reluctance, an even greater difficulty lies in achieving agreements about all of these matters that are fair to all concerned. Workers need to be as attentive to the possibility that one or another of the participants has been insufficiently assertive in stating expectations or making demands as to the possibility that the other has been overly demanding.

Some therapists have been reluctant to be involved in these matters and feel that their role should be limited to establishing a favorable climate for negotiation so that other mediators can help the couple achieve a settlement (Kressel and Deutsch, 1977). Kelly (1983) distinguishes between treatment and mediation by saying, "The role of the therapist is to encourage exploration of the meanings and levels of dysfunctional psychological reactions. In contrast, the role of the mediator is to manage and contain emotional expression so that the process of reaching a settlement can proceed" (p. 44). Chandler (1985) sees a similar distinction between mediation and social work helping processes. Workers who do not feel comfortable or who lack skills in negotiating practical aspects may profitably refer to mediators for such negotiation. Workers may be encouraged to acquire mediation skills, since they are so closely related to good treatment practices (see Barsky, 1984). It is helpful for therapists, even if they do not handle negotiations themselves, to encourage reasonableness, to suggest what might be equitable, and most of all to discourage vengeance.

Though both therapists and mediators have contended that involvement of lawyers in divorce and custody disputes have often aggravated the difficulty of settlement by single-minded pursuit of individual advantage, they nevertheless affirm the validity and necessity of having lawyers review agreements achieved by counseling or mediation processes to assure that all possible consequences and aspects have been considered and that individual rights have been protected.

Sprenkle and Storm (1983) in a review of the reported research on divorce and custody mediation conclude that mediation and counseling are superior to adversarial approaches in resolving divorce-related issues such as custody of children (to be discussed below) and financial settlements. Agreements are more likely to hold and be less subject to later dispute and court action. Some of the variables related to the success of mediation and counseling are the level of intensity of the conflict, the number of issues involved, and the capacity for reasonableness of the disputants. These suggest that a combination of issue-focused mediation and psychologically focused treatment may both be necessary to successful resolution.

Reestablishing Phase

By this time in the course of events the active steps of dissolution of the marriage have occurred. New households have been established, and the financial picture is fairly clear. The families are settling into a new life and continuing the task of recovery. Reports vary about the length of time involved, but periods of one to five years are mentioned. The ex-spouses have the individual task of developing new lives for themselves and the joint task of co-parenting. We will address the first of these tasks here and defer discussion of the co-parenting tasks to the subsequent section on children.

The absence of rituals of induction into the divorced status has been frequently noted. Ceremonies to solemnize entry to marriage are deemed useful in assuring newlyweds of community consent and support. Such consent and support are markedly lacking for divorcing family members. Some couples, when both are convinced that divorce should occur, have made public announcement of the event in newspapers and even sponsored receptions to honor it. Lewis (1983) reports a variety of rituals that have been used, including religious ones to pronounce the end of a relationship and the commencement of a new life. While rituals may not be necessary or may not do the job, what does seem necessary in this day of dissolving marriages is gaining acceptance, support, encouragement, and direction for the new life ahead.

The emotional issues of the previous stages are still alive, though possibly less intense. Working through positive and negative feelings continues. Self-doubt and guilt, feelings of loss and rejection continue to surface but are put into perspective by increasing acceptance of self and more or less successful adaptation. Emotional release and cognitive restructuring facilitate this process. Coping with loneliness and the absence of another adult are added to the stress of this period.

Questions continue to arise about relationships with the ex-spouse and with one's own and the ex-spouse's family. Management of the children and the effects of the divorce on them are of ongoing concern. Movement to enter new relationships begins and with it new fears and doubts—fears that the new relationship will repeat the old, that rejection may be experienced anew, that unwanted demands may be made. People often feel as if they are adolescents again when it comes to forming new relationships. They have questions about their identity, handling themselves socially, the rules of the dating game, and handling sexual matters.

Development of skills in management of everything that one now has to do is another aspect of the overall adjustment task. Depending on the person and who did what in the marriage, the individual may lack skills in such things as food preparation, caring for the car, or getting/making minor repairs on the house. It is not only a matter of learning to get all these things accomplished, but also a matter of not being overwhelmed by them.

The tasks in this phase are individual ones, and if treatment is sought, it is usually provided on an individual rather than a conjoint basis. Several authors (Granvold and Welch, 1977; Shelton and Nix, 1979; Thiessen, Avery, and Joanning, 1980) report successful work on divorce adjustment through group work. A series of five to seven sessions is offered. Each session begins with a didactic presentation on topics such as problems of communication with the ex-spouse, effects of divorce on children, handling finances, responding to curious family members or friends, unfulfilled sexual needs, effects of divorce on future relationships, and needed supports and social isolation. Group members then share experiences and insights, providing both cognitive grasp and emotional support and working through the various issues. These authors report that the groups have been well received and that members have shown improvement on measures of adjustment and self-esteem.

CHILDREN IN THE DIVORCE PROCESS

As divorce is difficult for the spouses, it is also hard on the children. Their short-term and long-term adjustment is affected by the level of stress and by how their parents handle their relationship to each other and to the children. We have noted earlier that though the marriage ends, the family does not. The parenting relationship continues, and if both parents wish to continue a relationship with the children, they must learn to work together in doing so. To the extent that they can do so the children's adjustment will be bettered. Noble (1983) cautions, however, that while parental cooperation enhances child adjustment, such cooperation may cause the child to wonder why they can't all live together again. It is not unknown for children to try to bring their parents back together, such as the child who insists that the former spouses hug and kiss when one of them picks up or returns the child to the other.

One of the first issues the parents must resolve is custody and domicile for the children. Unfortunately, in early stages of the dissolution, children can become objects for barter. "If you leave, I'll keep the children and you won't get to see them." Or, when anger is strong, "You are not a fit parent, and I will see that you don't get them." Children can get drawn into taking sides. They can also come to feel that they are the cause of their parents' problems with each other and that they are not really wanted.

In the past custody of the children was usually acquired or assigned to one parent or the other. Most generally in recent times this has been the mother, though fathers are increasingly seeking it. Legal custody means that the parent to whom custody is assigned has all rights and responsibilities for the child (Bernstein, 1982) and that the noncustodial parent has none, except for the privilege of visitation and the responsibility of support or whatever else is granted by a custody agreement or court decree. Joint custody means that responsibility is shared and that contact between the parents over many issues (Bernstein lists twenty-three kinds of issues) will need to be frequent. Though it does not differ greatly in outward appearance from single-parent custody with extensive visitation rights for the other parent, it is increasingly sought and agreed to by both parents.

Custody disputes that are not resolved by the parents end with court investigations and decisions about which is the most fit parent. Charnas (1983) notes in this connection, "Although a child may have a qualitatively different relationship with his or her mother and father, it is absurd to posit that after a divorce the courts must change this by designating one parent as more psychologically valuable to the child than the other" (p. 548). Such decisions are often unsatisfactory to one of the parents and frequently result in reopening of the dispute at a later time. Mediation and custody counseling are beginning to show themselves as superior to such adversarial approaches. Joint custody and custody counseling are increasingly advocated. The general goal of custody counseling is to facilitate joint decision making and parental cooperation. Each parent must come to understand and accept the other's approach to the children and allow their separate relationships to flourish and grow. They must be able to negotiate responsibilities and decisions, such as medical care, vacations, and schooling. Since initial decisions come during the worst heat of the divorce process, it is evident that the progress they make in handling other emotional issues will bear upon their ability to cooperate in parenting. Custody counseling is a conjoint effort, and the children may be productively involved at times to allow expression of their observations, feelings, and wishes.

Stress and tensions for children in divorcing families manifest themselves in anxiety, depression, and conduct. They are affected by the same issues as their parents—the possible loss of relationship of a parent and the fear that the other may abandon them as well, possible change of residence, school, and friends, and uncertainty about having their needs met. Acute symptoms tend to subside in a year or year and a half, but "it is strikingly clear that five and ten years after the marital rupture the divorce remains for many children and adolescents the central event of their growing up years and casts a long shadow over these years" (p. 232) (Wallerstein, 1983). Changes in relationship between parent and child occur. The nature of the change depends on the internal reactions of both parent and child, on the age and sex of child, and on the relationship between custodial (in the sense of parent with whom the child lives) and noncustodial parent. Parents in the midst of their own conflicts are at times less attentive and available to the children but may at other times be intensively attached to and dependent upon them.

Wallerstein (1985) has engaged in intensive study of the adaptations made by a clinical population of children of divorce. She groups them into several categories. The common feature is that they are all overburdened with care and responsibility. Children in one group take complete responsibility for themselves and make minimal demands, a manner of role-taking which taxes them beyond their capacity. Another kind of child feels responsible for the parent and serves "as arbiter, protector, advisor, parent, sibling, comrade in arms against the other parent or the world, confidante, lover or concubine" (p. 119). Children in a third group are overburdened by the continuing custody battle that rages around them. While some of the custody conflicts embody genuine concerns about adequate care for the child, others are more reflective of the parent's intense need for the presence and companionship of the child.

Morawetz and Walker (1984) categorize the behaviors of parents that put children into those overburdened roles. They say that single (we are saying, divorced) parents create problems for their children when they see them as an embodiment of the absent parent, when they put the child in the role of spouse, when they see the child as an overwhelming burden, when guilt impedes their own functioning, and when the parent's reentry into the social scene is experienced as a return to adolescence. It is of obvious importance to help the parent with these issues if the child is to make a successful adjustment.

Bonkowski, Bequette, and Boomhower (1984) report that only 25 percent of the children of divorce as compared to as many as 90 percent of the parents receive professional help. Our impression is that many more children could benefit from professional help than actually receive it. Kalter (1984) reports that individual work with adolescent girls from divorced families resulted in frequent dropping out of treatment and that conjoint work with girls and their mothers promoted continuance. The conjoint sessions served to mediate mother-daughter conflicts and opened the way for the girls to address issues of separation, self-esteem, lovability, and femininity. Bonkowski describes a successful group experience for six- to seven-year-old children. The group enabled the children to deal with changes in family structure, the causes of divorce, and their feelings about it. They could also talk about the predivorce family, the losses they experienced, and how they saw themselves in the future.

These treatment group achievements address the tasks that Wallerstein says need to be accomplished by the children of divorce. Children need to acknowledge the reality of the marital rupture, to disengage from the parental conflict, to resume normal pursuits, to resolve their loss, anger, and self-blame, to accept the permanency of the divorce, and to achieve a realistic hope regarding future relationships and to become willing to take a chance on loving and closeness. In Wallerstein's view, children do have their own working through to do and should have the benefit of treatment. They tend not to be referred for help during the divorce process, but only when serious difficulties manifest themselves. Yet, help during the divorce process should be available and could be naturally and beneficially provided when their parents seek help by seeing them at times together with their parents and sometimes referring them to groups of children experiencing the same crisis in their lives.

SUMMARY

Family dissolution is an increasingly common phenomenon. Because it has been considered a deviant form in the family life cycle, there are no firm pathways for the participants to follow to guide and support them through it. But because it is so common, it is important to understand what happens and what is needed for all family members to survive the process and make postdissolution adjustment that is as successful as possible.

The time span between marital dissatisfaction and postdivorce adjustment may be seen in three phases. The predivorce phase focuses on the decision to continue or end the marriage. Treatment may begin with an effort to rescue the marriage and end in this phase with a decision to separate and divorce. A restructuring phase centers on the planning needed to reorganize the family, who is to move or to stay, where the children will go, what the financial situation will be, what each parent's relationship to the children will be like. A resettlement phase completes the work of resolving all the issues raised in the dissolution and the work of developing an ongoing life-style.

Divorce is a crisis for family members and engenders great emotional pain for them. Coping with the crisis is facilitated by enabling family members to handle their emotions and to achieve a cognitive grasp on what is needed to reorganize their lives. Personal and interpersonal issues must be dealt with through all phases of the crisis. Individual goals for the adults are to achieve a constructive dissolution of the marriage in as humane a way as possible and to enable them to regain their self-respect and confidence so that they can build their future lives as stronger and more capable persons. While ending the marriage constructively is necessary, it is also necessary, if there are children, to enable the ex-spouses to develop and continue a constructive co-parenting relationship because the family of parents and children continues to exist. Success in achieving a constructive divorce is crucial for the subsequent adjustment of the ex-spouses. Their ability to be constructive also enables better adjustment of the children.

Substantial numbers of divorcing spouses do seek treatment at some point during the divorce process. Children are brought to treatment less frequently during the divorce process, but from knowledge gained about children from divorcing families who have been brought to treatment, it is clear that the divorce has not been adequately handled in their adjustment. Individual treatment has in the past been seen as the treatment method of choice for the divorce process. We have taken the position that in the predivorce, decision-making phase and in the restructuring phase, conjoint family sessions can serve very usefully. In addition, particularly during the restructuring and resettlement phases, support groups for the adults and for the children have been shown to be helpful in facilitating change.

REFERENCES

Ahrons, C. 1980. "Redefining the Divorced Family: A Conceptual Framework." *Social Work* 25(6):437-41.

Barsky, M. 1984. "Strategies and Techniques of Divorce Mediation." *Social Casework* 65(2):102-8.

Beck, D. 1975. "Research Findings on the Outcome of Marital Counseling." *Social Casework* 56(3):153-81.

Bernstein, B. 1982. "Understanding Joint Custody Issues." *Social Casework* 63(3):179-81.

Bonkowski, S., Bequette, S., and Boomhower, S. 1984. "A Group Design to Help Children Adjust to Parental Divorce." *Social Casework* 65(3):131-37.

Chandler, S. M. 1985. "Mediation: Conjoint Problem Solving." *Social Work* 30(4):346-49.

Charnas, J. 1983. "Joint Custody Counseling—Divorce 1980's Style." *Social Casework* 64(9):546-54.

Cookerly, J. R. 1973. "The Outcome of Six Major Forms of Marriage Counseling Compared: A Pilot Study." *Journal of Marriage and the Family* 35:608-12.

Counts, R., and Sacks, A. 1985. "The Need for Crisis Intervention During Marital Separation." *Social Work* 30(2):146-50.

Elkin, M. 1977. "Post Divorce Counseling in a Conciliation Court." *Journal of Divorce* 1(1):55-66.

Goldman, J., and Coane, J. 1983. "Separation and Divorce." In *Helping Families with Special Problems*, ed. M. Textor. New York: Jason Aronson.

Granvold, D., and Welch, G. 1977. "Intervention in Post Divorce Adjustment Problems: The Treatment Seminar." *Journal of Divorce* 1(1):81-92.

Hunter, J., and Schuman, N. 1980. "Chronic Reconstitution as a Family Style." *Social Work* 25(6):446-51.

Journal of Divorce, 1977. Editorial 1(1).

Kalter, N. 1984. "Conjoint Mother-Daughter Treatment: A Beginning Phase of Psychotherapy with Adolescent Daughters of Divorce." *American Journal of Orthopsychiatry* 54(3):490-97.

Kelly, J. 1983. "Mediation and Psychotherapy: Distinguishing the Differences." *Mediation Quarterly*, 1:33-44, September.

Kessler, S. 1975. *The American Way of Divorce*. Chicago: Nelson-Hall.

Kitson, G., Moir, R., and Mason, P. 1982. "Family Social Support in Crisis: The Special Case of Divorce." *American Journal of Orthopsychiatry* 52(1):161-65.

Kressel, K., and Deutsch, M. 1977. "Divorce Therapy: An In-Depth Survey of Therapists' Views." *Family Process* 16:413-43.

Kressel, K., Jaffee, N., Tuchman, B., Watson, C., and Deutsch, M. 1980. "A Typology of Divorcing Couples: Implications for Mediation and the Divorce Process." *Family Process* 19(2):101-16.

Levinger, G. 1965. "Marital Cohesiveness and Dissolution: An Integrative Review." *Journal of Marriage and the Family* 27(1):19-28.

_____. 1966. "Sources of Marital Dissatisfaction Among Applicants for Divorce." *American Journal of Orthopsychiatry* 36(5):803-7.

Lewis, P. N. 1983. "Innovative Divorce Rituals: Their Psychosocial Function." *Journal of Divorce* 6(3):71-82.

Little, M. 1982. *Family Breakup*. San Francisco: Jossey-Bass.

Lyon, E., Silverman, M., Howe, G., Bishop, G., and Armstrong, B. 1985. "Stages of Divorce: Implications for Service Delivery." *Social Casework* 66(5):259-68.

Morawetz, A., and Walker, G. 1984. *Brief Therapy with Single Parent Families*. New York: Brunner/Mazel.

Noble, D. 1983. "Custody Contest: How to Divide and Reassemble a Child." *Social Casework* 64(7):406-13.

Rice, D. 1977. "Psychotherapeutic Treatment of Narcissistic Injury in Marital Separation and Divorce." *Journal of Divorce* 1(2):119-28.

Shelton, S., and Nix, C. 1979. "Development of a Divorce Adjustment Group Program in a Social Service Agency." *Social Casework* 60(5):309-12.

Spanier, G., and Thompson, L. 1984. *Parting: The Aftermath of Separation and Divorce*. Beverly Hills, Calif.: Sage Publications.

Sprenkle, D., and Cyrus, C. 1983. "Abandonment: The Stress of Sudden Divorce." In *Stress and the Family*, vol. 2, ed. C. Figley and H. McCubbin. New York: Brunner/Mazel.

Sprenkle, D., and Storm, C. 1983. "Divorce Therapy Outcome Research: A Substantive and Methodological Review." *Journal of Marital and Family Therapy* 9(3):239-58.

Storm, C., and Sprenkle, D. 1982. "Individual Treatment in Divorce Therapy: A Critique of an Assumption." *Journal of Divorce* 6(1/2):87-98.

Thiessen, J., Avery, A., and Joanning, H. 1980. "Facilitating Post Divorce Adjustment Among Women: A Communication Skills Training Approach." *Journal of Divorce* 4(2):35-44.

Wallerstein, J. 1983. "Children of Divorce: The Psychological Tasks of the Child." *American Journal of Orthopsychiatry* 53(2):230-43.

————. 1985. "The Over-Burdened Child: Some Long Term Consequences of Divorce." *Social Work* 30(2):116-23.

Weed, J. 1980. *National Estimates of Marriage Dissolution and Survivorship.* Hyattsville, Md: United States Department of Health and Human Services.

Whitaker, C., and Keith, D. 1984. "Counseling the Dissolving Marriage." In *Counseling in Marital and Sexual Problems,* ed. R. Stahmann and W. Hiebert. Lexington, Mass.: Lexington Books.

CHAPTER 11

Remarriage and Family Adjustment

When two people, one or both of whom have been previously married to other spouses, join to form a new family, it sets into motion a system that is structurally and psychologically different from the intact nuclear family that normally results from the first marriage. This suggests to social workers and other professional disciplines encountering this type family the necessity of viewing the structure and functioning of this unit in a different way than they view the family generated by an initial marriage. Many aspects of this new family will have a beginning that is different from the nuclear family of a first marriage and will likewise present a different set of problems.

One of the first things contributing to the confusion that surrounds this new family is the names applied to it. Among the names frequently used is stepfamily, blended family, remarried family, recoupled family, reconstituted family, and re-formed family. Without attempting to justify the use of one name instead of another, we shall hereafter refer to this family form as a "stepfamily." This decision on our part does not settle the obvious disagreement on what to call a family group created by the marriage in which one or both of the principals has been married before. However, understanding the structure of this new family and the manner in which it develops and functions as it struggles to reach a cohesive existence is most important. We agree with Kent (1980) that all families, regardless of how they are constituted, operate as a system and the best understanding of the structure and functioning of stepfamilies is reached by the application of a family systems approach when considering the adjustment problems of this group.

In keeping with this position, the remainder of the chapter will present the stepfamily from a family systems perspective with consideration given to various family patterns, the problems the stepfamily is likely to experience, and the adjustments necessary for appropriate functioning in contemporary society.

FAMILY COMPOSITION

The complexity of the stepfamily is reflected in the many different compositions resulting from the joining of individuals who bring to the new family various preestablished and continuing nuclear and extended family relationships. To consider a few patterns of stepfamily organization, there are divorced men and women who have children from previous marriages all of whom live together in a single household; divorced men without children married to women with children; women without children or previous marriage married to men with children; men without previous marriage and divorced women with children from the previous marriage; stepfamilies composed of widows and widowers both with children who live together part or all of the time; and finally the divorced parents with children from previous marriages and children from the present marriage.

While all stepfamilies go through varying periods of adjustment, a number of situations can be anticipated. For example, the household with children from previous marriages will most likely have to struggle with sibling jealousies centering around attention from the biological parent, resistance to the authority of the stepparent, and turf battles over sharing space and possessions. In the case of the woman without children or previous marriage who marries a divorced man with children the lack of experience in being a mother may well be a handicap, as she does not know what to expect from stepchildren, who are likely to react in a hostile manner to what is perceived as her intrusion into their lives. Visher and Visher (1979) found that a similar handicap also existed with men who entered a stepfather situation without parenting experience. Children who spend time with both a stepparent and a divorced biological parent might experience some difficulty with a perception of divided loyalty, or in most cases, struggle with feelings of resentment toward the stepparents especially in the early phase of stepfamily development.

IMPACT OF PAST EXPERIENCES

Stepfamilies are created out of a past marital experience. Many of these experiences have been unhappy due to incompatibilities between spouses which have ended in divorce, and other unhappy experiences have come as the result of losing a mate by death. In any case, a stepfamily begins under the weight of what might be described as "a long cast of characters." This is to say that a number of people are likely to be involved. Both husband and wife may bring positive or negative relationships from a previous marriage as well as friendships developed in different contexts over time. Children from previous marriages bring to the new family current relationships with grandparents, aunts, uncles, cousins, and other acquaintances. Stuart and Jacobson (1985) refer to beginning a stepfamily under these conditions as not marrying just a mate, but marrying a family, and this can put a strain on relationships in the new stepfamily. This is especially so as there are new sets of grandparents, in-laws, and other relatives with whom to interact, which increases the possibility of conflict around divided loyalties, jealousies, and inappropriate expectations. For example, the biological grandparents may think they have first call on the grandchildren's attention and behave in such a way as to discourage the development of an amicable relationship with the stepparent or step-grandparents. On the other hand, the new "step-relatives" may embrace the new family and expect its members to become a part of their network. This places the children in the uncomfortable position of being expected to maintain loyalty to established relationships while, at the same time, entering freely into new relationships with "step-relatives."

Children are not the only ones affected by previously established relationships. In cases where members of the family of origin enjoyed good relationships with the former spouse, the new spouse may find acceptance difficult. Instead of being accepted by reason of position in the family, by becoming the husband or wife of a family member, the new spouse may be required to earn his or her way into the family, and comparison with the former spouse is likely to make this a very difficult process.

Past experiences may also contribute to the stepfamily in positive ways. If both husband and wife have parenting experience, they will enter this new situation with knowledge of what it is like to be a parent and some understanding of the behavior of children and the strategies they use to gain attention and protect themselves against the hurt of rejection. This should be useful in negotiating some of the conflicts they are likely to encounter.

MYTHS AND OTHER EXPECTATIONS

Perhaps the most prevalent myth associated with the stepfamily is the "wicked stepmother." The belief that stepmothers do not function in the best interest of stepchildren is exemplified in the case of the father who always manages to find a way to interrupt all efforts on the part of the stepmother to discipline his children or have sustained meaningful interaction with them. In this case the belief regarding the "wicked stepmother" has been internalized and will likely remain as part of the husband-wife interaction until change in the husband's belief system is effected. However, it should be noted that most stepmothers do not fit the wicked and cruel model that has been perpetuated nor do they experience serious problems in relating to stepchildren. If the stepmother has sufficient ego strengths and is supported by her husband, a wholesome and satisfying stepmother-stepchild relationship can develop (Schulman, 1972).

Another common myth about stepfamilies is that of "instant love" (Wald, 1981). This is predicated on the belief that stepparents are no different from natural parents and, therefore, feel no differently toward stepchildren than they do toward their own natural children. In other words, when one takes on the role of stepparent, he or she is expected to feel instant love for children with whom there is no shared history or bonding experience, and in return these children will show love and admiration for the new stepparent. This is certainly a myth because it implies an instant relationship between people who are for the most part strangers. Relationships between them will require time to build and grow. To expect anything different from people who suddenly find themselves living together as the result of a marriage is to invite feelings of insecurity, disappointment, and anger (Visher and Visher, 1982). It is well to remember that building new relationships between stepchildren and stepparents will involve adjusting to new rules and new roles as well as adjusting to each other over time. And this process is usually made easier if the stepparent can refrain from forcing himself or herself on the children. Stepchildren must be given the opportunity and time to test out the new situation and move closer to the stepparent at their own pace.

In contrast to the myth of instant love, some stepchildren hold a belief that "step is less" (Wald, 1981). This means that the stepchild cannot be loved in the same way as a natural child can and the child cannot love the stepparent as he or she loves the natural parent.

As in the case of all myths, these allegations about the stepfamily are unverifiable and should not be taken as a logical starting point from which to view this new family. In addition to the unverifiability of myths, to hold on to these beliefs denies the presence of individual strengths and the fact that positive relationships can be developed within the structure of the stepfamily.

STEPFAMILY STRUCTURE

The organization of the stepfamily can be best understood when viewed as a social system in the same manner as the nuclear family. It operates from a set of functional demands that determine and guide the interaction of its members. It adheres to a power hierarchy which gives different levels of authority to parents and children. It is composed of subsystems and protected by boundaries, and it passes through stages of development, all of which is common to the nuclear family formed by the initial joining of two adults for the purpose of procreation. However, the stepfamily frequently encounters difficulty in its development because of a number of circumstances peculiar to its origin. Among the things that interfere with the various developmental tasks is the composition or makeup of the stepfamily, which brings together individuals with different life-styles, different values, and different world views. In spite of the prevalence of stepfamilies in society we have not established a clear set of guidelines that can be applied to this family. This handicaps not only stepfamily members, but also practitioners who seek to help this group negotiate developmental tasks. If we are to be successful in this undertaking we must be informed of the makeup of the subsystems and something of the history of those who participate in them.

Spouse Subsystem

As architects of the stepfamily, the spouse subsystem carries major responsibility for family development. As mentioned earlier, these two people may come together from a variety of statuses to form the new family. For example, the marriage may bring together two people who are divorced from previous marriages; one divorced and the other single; one widowed and one divorced; both widowed; or one widowed and the other single. This is important information for practitioners, as it provides a marital history and some notion of where knowledge and common experiences may or may not exist.

In these marriages each partner may bring children, only one partner may bring children, or neither may bring children to the marriage. In some cases children may become permanent members of the stepfamily or divide time between the stepfamily and the divorced natural parent. This is also useful information for the practitioner, as the husband and wife must accommodate each other and differentiate the spouse subsystem by developing clear boundaries. These tasks may become more difficult when children from previous marriages are brought into the family. The presence of these children may stress the functioning of the spouse subsystem which exists primarily as a work place for husband and wife in negotiating a complementary relationship. Under normal conditions of beginning a nuclear family children would not be present, and the boundary of the spouse subsystem would allow the couple an opportunity to focus on their own interest as it pertains to sharing space, developing mutuality, and establishing individuality within this new relationship. The presence of children from the beginning limits the time the couple can spend together in defining what their relationship will be, as some time must be spent involving the children within the context of the parent/child subsystem. Further, complication is likely in the relations of the stepchild and stepparent around a number of experiences. For example, if both parents bring children from previous marriages, there is the potential for a "we/they" complex with children vying for the attention of their biological parent to the exclusion of the stepparent and his or her children. There is also the problem of how much and in what ways the demands of children affect the perception the spouses have of each other. If one parent perceives the other as caring more for his or her natural children at the expense of neglecting the stepchildren, this will create tension within the spouse subsystem, which will interfere with the normal processes of this subsystem. As a result, each spouse may not only be drawn closer to his or her natural children but see the other spouse as disliking the stepchildren. And, out of a need to protect his or her own, a spouse will allow the children to invade freely the boundaries of the spouse subsystem, thereby preventing the development of an appropriate (permeable) boundary that controls the children's access to this subsystem.

In cases where only one parent brings children to the stepfamily, a satisfactory adjustment may well depend on the experience of the other parent in child rearing and the expectations these parents have of each other and the children. Parents with child-rearing experience are usually better able to understand a child's behavior in adjusting to a new family than one who has no experience with children. This understanding can be quite helpful in negotiating with the child in relation to developing trust and gradually giving up some of the closeness to the natural parent and moving into a relationship with the stepparent. This is not to say parents with child-rearing experience are always successful in effecting an adjustment in a stepfamily situation with children. If the experience causes the parent to assume expert status in dealing with children, leaving no room for error, the stepparent will likely behave in such a way as to demand too much from herself or himself and, in turn, expect too much from the child. In this case the stepparent must be helped to reassess his or her role and allow the child to remain closer to the natural parent while gradually developing trust and comfort in relating to the stepparent.

The stepparent who has no experience in parenting may find the stepparent role very frustrating. The lack of knowledge of how to proceed in fulfilling a role already established with the child who is likely to resent an outsider attempting to take the place of the natural parent can reinforce feelings of inadequacy and cause the stepparent to withdraw or, in some cases, react negatively toward the child. Such experiences often create tension within the spouse subsystem. The natural parent is not likely to understand or accept the stepparent's negative reaction while failure in relating to the child causes the stepparent to feel inadequate and in need of support from his or her partner. However, to ask the natural parent for help would further damage the stepparent's self-esteem, and if support is not volunteered, he or she usually chooses to remain silent and resentful of the spouse's failure to come to the rescue. In this situation, priority should be given to work on improving communication between the parents and helping the stepparent to a better understanding of the parenting role.

Parental Subsystem

This subsystem is composed of the same two people as the spouse subsystem. However, as suggested in Chapter 1, it is child-focused and requires the parents to reach a delicate balance between exercising control and promoting independence among family members. When compared to the parental subsystem of the nuclear family, this subsystem in the stepfamily clearly deals with some of the same problems, but also deals with a set of problems quite different from those experienced in the nuclear family. In the first place the parents in this new family do not have the opportunity to experience the spouse subsystem role and effect a beginning adjustment to each other. Instead, they are faced with the necessity of moving into the spouse and parental subsystem roles at the same time. This is to say that at the same time the couple is undertaking an initial adjustment to each other they must also be concerned with responding to the demands of a sibling subsystem which is composed of individuals without kinship ties or shared experiences. As a result, the parental subsystem is likely to be stressed in carrying out executive responsibility for the stepfamily.

Among the areas of stress are the likely violations of boundary structures. For example, children should experience freedom in moving back and forth across the boundaries of the parental subsystem to receive guidance in developing a self and assimilating into the wider society. However, in the case of stepfamilies, care must be taken to prevent children from seeking and receiving unilateral guidance from the natural parent (except perhaps in cases where unalterable dislike exists between stepparent and stepchildren). In any case, unilateral guidance by the natural parent tends to divide family authority and create tension within the parental subsystem. And with increased tension boundaries between natural parent and child may become blurred and lead to involvement of the child not only in the functioning of the parental subsystem but problems of the spouse subsystem as well. Such involvement may seriously interfere with the carrying out of appropriate parental subsystem tasks.

Adolescence is a time at which balancing control and promoting autonomy is perhaps most difficult for parents of the stepfamily. This is the point at which parents' demands are likely to be in conflict with the children's desire for age-appropriate autonomy (Minuchin, 1974). Parental demands in the stepfamily are not always the result of consensus between the parents. In many cases the marital pair have not discussed their likeness or difference with regard to what represents appropriate behavior or responsibility for the children. Nevertheless, failure to communicate does not mean an absence of firm conviction on the part of each parent about how children should behave and how much autonomy they should be given. In the absence of agreement about what will be expected of the children different messages are likely to be given which will reflect the past experiences of each parent. For example, a parent from a family that tended toward enmeshment would likely be reluctant to allow children to move freely outside family boundaries, which would increase opportunities for developing autonomy. In contrast, the parent from a family that tends to be disengaged would not be comfortable with close family ties, but interested in the development of independence. These opposite views signal the need for increased communication within the parental subsystem, and change efforts should be directed toward open discussion of parenting issues and mutual accommodation between parents on the matters of child rearing, and between parents and children with regard to effecting a healthy balance between autonomy and control.

Sibling Subsystem

In this subsystem within the natural family children are customarily afforded their own turf and the opportunity to develop and experiment with behaviors in learning to relate to peers and adults in the larger contexts of the family and society. This subgroup is normally composed of individuals with kinship ties who share common parentage, rules, and values. The sibling subsystem in the stepfamily may exist in many forms. Children from one marriage may be joined by children from another marriage, only the mother's children or only the father's children may be included in the subsystem, or the children from the new marriage may be born into the family and join children from previous marriages of one or both parents. In each case a complex group is brought into existence, and a crisis may be precipitated by the failure of old roles and old boundaries, defined within the contexts of a previous family structure.

If the stepfamily assumes residence in the home of a spouse with children from a previous marriage, these children may perceive the children of the other parent as intruders into their territory and react by attempting to exclude these new members. From a systems perspective, rejecting the new members is their way of safeguarding the boundaries of the old subsystem by closure which will control the input of new energy from the new group. If this new energy is allowed to enter the system, it may threaten the existence of the old subsystem in which the previous occupants have found comfort and wish to preserve.

Sibling rivalry, common to all sibling subsystems, is likely to be more stressful in the stepfamily as members seek changes in coalitions and alliances generated by losses experienced in the breakup of the nuclear family. Jealousies may be acted out in rather destructive ways as children attempt to hold on to natural parents and reject stepparents and siblings. For example, children with a divorced parent living elsewhere may attempt to move back and forth between this parent and the stepfamily whenever they choose not to abide by the rules established in either household.

The development of the sibling subsystem in the stepfamily is not always characterized by continuing conflict. If the parents of the stepfamily have sufficiently resolved their own adjustment problems and are able to pursue relaxed relationships with the children, their behavior will serve as a role model for the children and help them join together and develop a sibling subsystem that will promote the growth and development of its members. However, when intervention is necessary, attention must be given to what the children bring to this new subgroup experience from past associations. Losses and expectations should be dealt with and assurance offered, where possible, that further losses are not likely to occur as a result of developing new relationships with stepsiblings, and old relationships that are important to children need not be abandoned.

Parent/Child Subsystem

This subsystem is characterized by interaction between parents and children. As suggested in Chapter 1, clarity of boundaries and lines of authority is an important factor in the successful functioning of this subsystem. In the nuclear family the parents have shared with each other in a marital relationship before children are born or adopted into the family. And all children in this case belong to the marital couple, forming a nuclear family that customarily lives together until the children reach the appropriate age for separation. This is not the case with the stepfamily. At least one parent has shared a relationship with the children, who are now a part of the stepfamily, before joining the other in marriage. In many instances both parents have experienced ties with some of the children, but not with others, prior to joining in marriage and forming the stepfamily.

For these reasons the stepparent begins at a different point than the natural parent in interacting with children. The parent who brings children to the stepfamily has close ties with this part of the sibling subsystem but must begin to establish new relationships with everyone else. Such an entry into the family system may cause an imbalance in relationships. One of the difficulties in building relationships is that stepparents are often cautious in attempting to establish a relationship with stepchildren out of concern for how they are perceived in this role by these children as well as other members of the family. At the same time, the parent/child relationship from the previous marriage is in place, and the interaction within this relationship is likely to be viewed by others as closing the boundary around this part of the subsystem and denying entry to others. As a result, tension increases and family homeostasis may be disrupted until an understanding is reached regarding new roles and new ways of relating among stepfamily members.

The perception of the parenting role by stepparents and stepchildren is an important factor in determining how they will interact in forming a viable family relationship. Some adults who remarry after divorce or widowhood expect too much of themselves and other family members. For example, many stepparents try too hard to be exceptionally good parents in order to please their mates and expect in return to gain love and respect from the children. Yet, stepchildren are likely to be hesitant in responding to the overzealous efforts of these "superparents" who want to receive instant love from them and immediately enjoy a happy family. Stepparents must learn to relax and allow positive interaction with stepchildren to occur gradually. Immediate acceptance of a stepparent is difficult for stepchildren who are likely to be grieving the loss of the natural parent through death or divorce. In most cases of children of divorced parents, accepting a stepparent is further complicated by the fact that there is an ongoing relationship with the natural divorced parent. And the thought of replacing this parent with another creates feelings of guilt and disloyalty. In the case of deceased parents, many children experience similar feelings especially in the early stages of the stepparent relationship, as interacting with the stepparent is likely to rekindle painful feelings of this previous loss.

Another problem in the parent/child relationship in stepfamilies may be brought on by the stepparent immediately attempting to assume the authority formerly held by the divorced or deceased natural parent relative to family rules and discipline. In most cases this not only causes anger and rebellion among the children, but also creates tension between the parents. If the stepparent continues to carry the instant authority role, the natural parent and his or her children will likely be drawn together against the stepparent, and professional help is usually needed if the family is to become a viable unit. Change efforts should be directed toward the natural parent taking a more active role in setting rules, disciplining the children, and sharing his or her thoughts and wishes about parenting with the stepparent. At the same time the stepparent should be helped to accept a lesser role in parenting until appropriate rules governing family conduct are established and the role of the hierarchical structure is agreed upon.

TASKS AND ISSUES IN STEPFAMILY DEVELOPMENT

The tasks and issues facing the stepfamily are significantly different from those faced by the natural family as it proceeds toward realization of basic goals. Visher and Visher (1982, p. 343) point up the need for the stepfamily to address previous losses, develop new traditions, preserve important old alliances and form new ones, and achieve integration within the stepfamily.

Recognizing Losses

Members of the stepfamily have experienced a number of losses which may prove devastating in establishing the new family if they are not recognized and dealt with by each individual. The spouse who has been married previously and has lost a mate by divorce or death experiences a sense of loss. In the case of divorce, regardless of how unsatisfactory the relationship may have been, there is a sense of loss over failure to have made the marriage the success that was envisioned at the beginning, and the personal investment in trying to make it succeed cannot be recovered. There are always feelings of sadness and loss associated with the death of a spouse; the good times spent together and many old friends that were a part of that experience will not continue to be a part of the new life being fashioned by remarriage. As for children, the death of a parent is one of the most painful losses possible. And disruption of the parent/child relationship by divorce is also a serious loss, together with the disappearance of familiar surroundings such as friends and extended family members who may no longer be readily available due to relocation.

These losses contribute to feelings of sadness and anger that may be displaced in the stepfamily relationships. In this case, help is usually needed to assist stepfamily members in sorting out feelings, identifying sources of sadness and anger, and looking at the new family as an opportunity to develop and share meaningful relationships, without being disloyal to friends and relatives or desecrating pleasant memories from previous experiences.

Establishing New Traditions

Stepfamilies may come together from very different places, bringing values, goals, and traditions established through previous experiences. Although stepfamily members may have been served well by these structures in the past, it is highly unlikely that they will work effectively to bind the new family together. It is well to remember that family relationships are built around shared experiences, and stepfamilies have usually had few, if any, common experiences. Therefore, it is necessary for stepfamily members to establish new goals and traditions through engaging in activities of interest to the new family and deciding together what the family likes and values and how it will go about realizing desired objectives.

Forming Alliances

We agree with Visher and Visher (1982) who suggest a relaxed and gradual formation of alliances in the stepfamily. Forming a new family from members who bring experiences and traditions from a previous nuclear family always reactivates old memories and often introduces conflict. Efforts to expedite this process by exerting pressure on family members including showing excessive amounts of affection or increasing interaction within the family at the expense of eliminating contacts with friends and relatives outside of the stepfamily will most likely fail. It is appropriate for the parents to spend time together without interference from real or imagined demands of the family. Stepparents also need to spend some time with stepchildren. This should be done without the natural parent being present; however, care must be taken to keep this time between step-members of the family casual and of short duration in the early stage of family development (Visher and Visher, 1982). A useful strategy might begin by complimenting the child on something he or she likes to do such as coloring pictures or working with building blocks and later participating briefly in this activity with the child whenever the opportunity is presented.

It is very important while developing new alliances to allow stepfamily members to continue important old alliances established through previous associations. For example, children should be expected to continue communication with grandparents with whom they share close relationships and with friends whose company they enjoy. Stepparents should also continue to be in touch with relatives and friends whose associations they value. By continuing important old alliances, the pressure to become totally engaged in the immediate development of a new family is lessened. And with this lessening of pressure to become completely involved in stepfamily processes, both stepparents and stepchildren can gradually move toward getting to know each other, which sets the stage for development of a viable stepfamily. When there is total commitment to "instant success" in becoming a new family, the members experience tremendous pressure to interact positively, and this often leads to anger, frustration, and failure.

Integration

Integration within the stepfamily is an important task which is facilitated by knowing what to expect. The primary responsibility for achieving integration rests with the parents, who must create conditions conducive to family organization. Since the parents are the architects of the family, they must clarify what is expected of the family and reach consensus on important family rules before attempting to involve the children in forming a new family (Visher and Visher, 1982). This agreement between the parents should help with involvement of the children and provide some support for the stepparent in dealing with them around the issues of roles and expectations.

In addition to arriving at an understanding between the parents, integrating the stepfamily requires nurturing children and setting limits that will allow them to continue appropriate development while the parents remain in control. This is not an easy task for the natural family and is a very difficult one for the stepfamily. Stepparents inherit a family already in existence where controls are needed without having carried out the nurturing elements of child rearing for the stepchildren. As a result these children are without the experience of having received, at an earlier age, the "giving" aspects of a relationship with the stepparent, but are now faced with accepting the limits this stepparent imposes. This is tantamount to having missed the initial phase of the parent/child relationship in which a basis is established for the child's wish to please the parent. Therefore, stepchildren are likely to resent limits imposed by the stepparent, and this will complicate integration of the stepfamily.

Time is also a factor in achieving integration, as members of the stepfamily must get to know each other before the trusting and sharing needed for the family to function as a cohesive unit can develop. A time period of up to two years is sometimes required before a satisfactory state of integration is reached. And stepparents should not become discouraged by the gradual pace at which relationships are developed.

Complex Issues

The development of the stepfamily involves a number of roles, tasks, and issues related to family relationships that preceded the start of this new family. It begins with the remarriage of the couple, at least one of whom has previous marriage experience. In many cases both have been married before. One of the most important considerations for the previously married couple is how well they have resolved issues related to their previous marriages. It is not uncommon for spouses to enter a second marriage with very strong positive or negative feelings about his or her former mate which may be reflected in a number of ways. Feelings of guilt over the breakup of a marriage may interfere with the sharing of one's self with the other or cause one to invest too much in trying to make up for past mistakes by becoming "the perfect spouse." In some situations unresolved positive feelings may surface as divided loyalty between past and present spouses. On the other hand, unresolved negative feelings may contribute to distrust in relating to the new mate or an overinvestment in trying to make life difficult for the former spouse.

Visher and Visher (1982) speak of the exaggeration of power issues in stepfamilies. For example, if the wife is divorced and successfully carries family responsibility as a single parent prior to remarriage, she may enter the new marriage with confidence in her capability to provide for herself and her children. This self-sufficiency represents power and control of her own life, and sharing these with someone else through remarriage may threaten a return to an unsatisfying pattern of dependency. Divorced men who remarry after experiencing difficult financial settlements with previous spouses may feel they have unjustly lost their power and control and become vulnerable to future attacks on their finances, ergo their power. In such cases they may be unwilling to share information about finances with the new spouse or live in a miserly fashion in order to prevent further erosion of their power and control.

Sager et al. (1983) suggest in-laws and former in-laws sometimes have strong influence on the stepfamily system. If in-laws have played a major role in the life of a spouse, especially between divorce and remarriage when support and assistance in managing with children were crucial, they may seek a decision-making role in helping to establish the stepfamily. This is likely to prove disruptive to forming appropriate relationships in the new family system. Former in-laws who enjoy good relationships with their grandchildren may have difficulty accepting the replacement of their son or daughter by someone else who will assume the role of parent.

When children from previous marriages are brought into the stepfamily, there is a parent/child relationship that precedes the husband/wife relationship. This prior parent/child attachment is likely to create an emotional imbalance in family relationships with the child favoring the natural parent while having only minimal contact with the stepparent. In many cases children brought into the stepfamily also cling to the hope that their natural parents will reunite and reestablish the nuclear family, thereby making it unnecessary for them to adjust to the stepparent. The need to balance old ties with children and new ties with the marital partner is one of the most important issues with which stepparents must deal (Wald, 1981).

Unlike the first-marriage family where the marital couple has time to accommodate to each other before turning their attention to the needs of children, the presence of children in the stepfamily makes it necessary for the couple to assume both marital and parental roles simultaneously. This makes it more difficult to accomplish marital tasks as it limits the time, privacy, and energy available to stepparents (Wald, 1981).

In all families boundaries play a significant role in family development and family homeostasis. In stepfamilies issues around boundaries take on a special significance due to the unique structure of these families. Boundary violations may occur at many levels in stepfamilies as indicated earlier in our discussion of stepfamily subsystems. Children may violate the boundary around the spouse subsystem as a result of the previous close association with the natural parent and the lack of experience in relating to the stepparent. This makes it easy for children to turn to natural parents for support and guidance in the same manner as before the stepfamily was established. If the natural parent is ambivalent about the stepparent's relations with his or her children, a closer relationship is likely to be encouraged by the natural parent's own reactions to this situation. Repeated transactions between these principals while excluding the stepparent will interfere with the performance of normal marital tasks and represent a violation of the boundary that should limit the children's access to the private domain of the parents.

A blurring of boundaries may also occur when children share the homes of both the stepfamily and the other divorced natural parent. This often centers around arrangements for the children visiting and spending time in both households. Each household must recognize and respect the boundary of the other, thus allowing for a clear separation of the households with each unit free to exercise control over what takes place within its domain (Visher and Visher, 1982). In this way boundaries remain clear and children are able to function within the boundaries established by each household.

Another problem facing practitioners who work with stepfamilies is the issue of sexual boundaries. Sager et al. describe a loosening of sexual boundaries in the stepfamily which is related to "the heightened affectionate and sexual atmosphere in the home during the new couple's early romantic bonding period" (1983, p. 293). The inclusion of teenagers of the opposite sex in the new family tends to intensify the sexual climate. This, together with the fact that members of stepfamilies have not shared close emotional ties and are without biological ties, makes possible a complete breakdown of sexual boundaries. The extremes of a breakdown of sexual boundaries in the stepfamily may be reflected in sexual relations between stepsiblings and sexual abuse, usually between stepfathers and stepdaughters. If this point is reached, someone in the stepfamily is likely to ask for help, as the members of this family are less likely than those of the natural family to reinforce a breakdown in sexual boundaries through the conspiracy of silence and unconscious collusion often found in natural families (Wald, 1981).

One of the mistakes frequently made is to assume there is no difference in family functioning between the stepfamily and the natural family. This occurs largely out of a lack of knowledge about the complexity of the stepfamily, its structure, and its functions in carrying out various tasks. The confusion begins with the variety of names used to identify this family unit which we have chosen to refer to as the stepfamily. Neither society, by tradition, nor research efforts have as yet developed a widely accepted set of norms for this family. Many myths, some of which we discussed earlier in this chapter, still exist relative to what should be expected from the members of a family that begins without biological ties. Nevertheless, research and experience in working with this type family have provided some information regarding the processes in which it engages that should be recognized by family members and social workers engaged in helping with family adjustment.

The couple who joins to establish a stepfamily should realize that adjustment among all family members will not automatically occur as a result of bringing family members together. Adolescent children are likely to be resentful of the stepparent and openly demonstrate preference for the natural parent. Efforts to force the development of relationships between step-members of the family will result in frustrations and defeat. In most situations, children will be relating to at least the biological parent outside of the stepfamily, and in many cases extended natural family members as well. This does not mean a problem will develop; however, the potential for family boundary disputes and conflicting loyalties is always present in these interactional processes.

When both parents bring children into the stepfamily they should be aware that a difference in feeling toward biological children and stepchildren may exist and a display of this difference in affection might create tension throughout the family. Disciplining children is another potential area of tension, and unless there has been prior discussion and agreement on how authority will be used in this respect, problems are likely to develop.

Disagreement over the use of money is not uncommon in the stepfamily where alimony and/or child support payments are likely experiences. In many instances the marital couple have never discussed such expenditures, and in such cases misunderstanding regarding old and new responsibilities may occur. And finally, it must be recognized by everyone involved in dealing with stepfamily processes that good family relationships are not an instant accomplishment and must be given an opportunity to develop over time.

SUCCESSFUL STEPFAMILY FUNCTIONING

In spite of the difficulty under which the stepfamily begins, not all these families struggle for identity and adjustment in relationships throughout the family life cycle. Some stepfamilies are able to develop sound relationships between family members early in the new family's existence. There are a number of conditions that contribute to successful development of stepfamily structure and functioning. For example, the ages of children who are brought into the family may have impact on the stepparent/stepchild relationship as well as the functioning of the sibling subsystem. The younger child usually has less difficulty in forming intrafamilial relationships in the new family than the adolescent, who is more likely to have a stronger attachment to the biological family by reason of a longer association and a deeper appreciation of the fabric of this family and his or her role in it. Another factor is the individual life cycle of the adolescent. This stage of development is characterized by the adolescent's struggle with issues of identity and the desire for independence, which are demonstrated by rebellion against authority and disagreement with measures of control. The preferred posture of the adolescent is freedom and autonomy rather than forming a new attachment to a stepparent with whom, in most cases, he or she is totally unfamiliar. This presents not only giving up freedom, but also being placed in the position of being controlled by an unfamiliar adult who is taking the place of the natural parent. This usually contributes to the difficulty in establishing relationships that is experienced in many stepfamilies.

When the stepchildren are adults who do not occupy the stepfamily household, the possibility of establishing acceptable working stepfamily relationships is usually good.

Parenting experience by the marital couple is useful in developing the stepfamily in cases where children from previous marriages are involved. Parents with experience in dealing with children bring to the stepfamily some knowledge of what to expect from children and how to relate to them in a number of circumstances. While this does not guarantee instant adjustment, it adds a positive dimension to the stepfamily process.

In addition to these conditions which have the potential for impacting stepfamily adjustment, Visher and Visher suggest four ingredients necessary for successful stepfamily functioning (Visher and Visher, 1982, p. 350). We concur with their suggestion and will extrapolate from these ingredients in developing a constructive approach to the functioning of stepfamilies.

Good Relationship Between Spouses

As architects of the family the marital couple must maintain a good relationship if they are to guide the development of the family successfully. This takes on added importance in the stepfamily, where bonding between the couple is more difficult to achieve than in the case of the natural family. In order to achieve and maintain a good relationship, the remarried couple must be able to communicate with clear messages that spell out their wishes, expectations, joys, and fears as related to their lives together and the establishment of the new family. There must be agreement on matters pertaining to family functioning and their roles in this process. They will also need to support each other in the performance of their respective parental roles. A good relationship between the spouses, together with mutual support and cooperation, are among the necessary ingredients for successful stepfamily functioning.

Relaxed Atmosphere for Children

Children from previous marriages who enter the stepfamily often resist establishing relationships, especially with stepparents. A major factor in this resistance is their attachment to biological family networks and the difficulty they experience in relating to a stepfamily network at the same time. The greatest conflict is experienced in relating simultaneously to biological and stepparents. This problem can usually be overcome if the stepparent does not insist on instant positive relations with the child and allows the relationship to develop gradually. It is also important that children be given the opportunity to continue relating to both natural parents. In this kind of relaxed atmosphere children usually learn to respond positively in stepfamily relationships which enhances the functioning of the family.

Mature Relationship Between All Parental Figures

Much of the difficulty experienced in stepfamily functioning can be ameliorated if a mature relationship exists between the parental adults. Such a relationship requires abandoning attempts to revenge previous wrongs or competing for the affection of children. For example, no adult should demand total loyalty from children who must divide their time and attention between two sets of parents. Instead, they should be encouraged to relate to both natural parents and stepparents. Children's visits with the natural parent outside of the stepfamily should be made as easy and convenient as possible. If negative feelings still exist between the divorced parents, this should not be a topic for discussion with children nor should family boundaries be interfered with by criticism of rules and expectations of stepparents or natural parents. If these adults can relate in a civil manner, children will enjoy their time with them and the families will more likely function in a satisfactory manner.

TREATMENT CONSIDERATIONS

The practitioner who has worked primarily with the traditional intact nuclear family will need to understand what is different about the stepfamily. We can safely say that a family systems approach is recommended for work with all families regardless of the stage of development or the nature of composition. And while the same therapeutic skills used in treating the nuclear family are also used in work with the stepfamily, the dynamics underlying stepfamily problems are often quite different from the dynamics of nuclear family problems. An understanding of this difference and a few specific guidelines for intervention will add to the likelihood of success when stepfamily maladjustment is the object of change.

Social workers and other professionals who work with stepfamilies should be careful not to approach these families as if they fit neatly into the traditional pattern of the nuclear family. This is a family whose members do not share a common history, and one needs to be aware of what is unique about stepfamily structure and the common feelings and situations its members experience. When the stepfamily seeks professional help with problems related to family functionings, Johnson (1980, p. 307) suggests, "The starting point for assessment and intervention planning should be the exploration of those dynamics inherent in the institution of the stepfamily." For example, it is useful to learn what family members expect from each other, as this is likely to be "a well-kept secret." It is not unusual to find that no one in the family has ever made his or her expectations known, in which case there are no guidelines for a family member's behaving in a manner that is totally satisfactory to other members. Helping family members express what they desire from each other introduces a new way of relating. This is especially true with stepparents, who usually enter into remarriage without having addressed many important issues such as role expectations and disciplining of the children. Stepparents do have ideas about these things, and practitioners should assist them in clarifying and formulating these ideas and expectations, supporting what is realistic and helping them to understand and eliminate that which is related to fallacious beliefs often held by remarried couples. This includes such preconceived notions as believing that all family members will love each other and immediately adjust to each other which will allow the family to go forward with its various tasks without difficulty.

It should be kept in mind that members of the stepfamily often bring different life-styles to the task of developing a new family. These differences may center around such things as dress codes, entertainment preferences, disciplining children, attitudes toward sex or the use of alcohol, rules governing the conduct of family members at home and in interaction with others outside of the family, and so on. These differences may result in conflict between family members and should be evaluated as possible sources of difficulty in family functioning when the stepfamily comes for help.

Contrary to the myth that "instant love" should exist between stepparent and stepchild, in some cases the relationship is characterized by competition or even a strong dislike for each other. When no basis for improving this situation can be found, we concur with Johnson (1980) who suggests accepting the fact that in reality a family does not exist and movement in this direction is not likely to occur in the near future. As a result, the ensuing process is usually one of waiting for the child to grow up and leave the family. In working with this situation we also agree with her strategy and support intervention in the direction of the stepparent and stepchild spending as little time as possible together, with the natural parent assuming the major parenting responsibilities.

Sager and his associates (1983) suggest caution in setting goals for stepfamilies. Many couples remarry after divorce with specific individual goals in mind, including the hope that this marriage will be a positive answer to all of the disappointments experienced in the previous marriage. When failure to realize the unrealistic goals sought in remarriage brings the couple into treatment, they frequently try to achieve the same goals through the treatment process. In such cases it is necessary to clarify the situation and establish realistic goals on which the work might be focused.

It may be useful at times to work separately with different subsystems of the stepfamily in the same manner as practiced by many practitioners when working with the nuclear family. For example, when helping the remarried couple resolve issues around discipline and consolidating parental authority, work with subsystems at some point in this process might offer some advantages. The use of support groups for parents and children has also been found to be a profitable undertaking.

Finally, it is important for social workers and other professionals to be aware of their own attitudes toward the concept of stepfamilies and the impact this unit might have on them and vice versa. There is always the potential for emotional reactions that will prove counterproductive, depending on the practitioner's position relative to a number of factors that surround the institution of a family created by remarriage. Sager and others (1983) refer to value conflicts around divorce and remarriage held by some practitioners as having the potential for interfering with treatment. Others may be concerned that their own husband or wife might behave in a similar manner as one of the remarried partners, or be uncomfortable in exploring specific aspects of a previous marriage or family experience that is viewed as negative by a stepfamily member. This can result in the practitioner's acceptance of the anxiety and denial underlying the client's perception of the experience which will diminish the probability of a successful outcome of the treatment experience. And practitioners who are divorced but have not resolved their own ambivalence about their former marriage partners are likely to find it difficult to allow clients to resolve similar problems in their lives. It is not enough to be knowledgeable about stepfamily dynamics. Those who wish to work successfully with this family unit must be aware of their own attitudes and concerns about the stepfamily as an institution, as well as their own life experiences, and how each is likely to impact on the other.

SUMMARY

Divorce and remarriage which creates a new family is by no means a novelty in contemporary society. However, it is still viewed as a departure form the accepted norm of the nuclear family headed by two adults, wedded only to each other. As a result, society has failed to define norms for the stepfamily or establish guidelines for the appropriate behavior of its members. This has contributed to the confusion surrounding this new family which responds to several different titles.

This family has a number of unique features, most of which do not make for a quick and easy adjustment among family members. The family is frequently seen in treatment as it struggles to stabilize its processes and become an organized unit. It is generally accepted that a family systems approach is most applicable to assessing and treating stepfamily problems. The use of support groups is also effective.

It is helpful for practitioners who engage stepfamilies in treatment to be aware that the dynamics underlying stepfamily problems are not always the same as those associated with the nuclear family. Therefore, the stepfamily cannot be viewed in exactly the same manner as the nuclear family. And practitioners must be aware of their own attitudes as well as their personal experiences as they relate to the stepfamily as a functioning unit.

It is difficult to visualize the future relative to the place of the stepfamily and how it will be viewed as an entity among other groupings in society. Nevertheless, it is a family form that will continue to be with us, and we must strive for the most effective ways of understanding and dealing with these remarried adults and their children.

REFERENCES

Johnson, H. C. 1980. "Working with Stepfamilies: Principles and Practice." *Social Work* 25(4):304-8.

Kent, M. O. 1980. "Remarriage: A Family Systems Perspective." *Social Casework* 61(3):146-53.

Minuchin, S. 1974. *Families and Family Therapy*. Cambridge, Mass.: Harvard University Press.

Sager, C. J., Brown, H. S., Crohn, H., Engel, T., Rodstein, E., and Walker, L. 1983. *Treating the Remarried Family*. New York: Brunner/Mazel.

Schulman, G. L. 1972. "Myths that Intrude on the Adaptation of the Step Family." *Social Casework* 53(3):131-39.

Stuart, R. B., and Jacobson, B. 1985. *Second Marriage*. New York: W. W. Norton and Co.

Visher, E. B., and Visher, J. S. 1979. *Step Families: A Guide to Working with Stepparents and Stepchildren*. New York: Brunner/Mazel.

————. "Step Families and Stepparenting." 1982. In *Normal Family Processes*, ed. F. Walsh. New York: Guilford Press.

Wald, E. 1981. *The Remarried Family*. New York: Family Service Association of America.

Part III

The Social Work Agency

Part I presented theoretical perspectives relative to family functioning, and Part II suggested social work strategies for intervention with selected populations of families with problems. While only these limited populations were addressed, extrapolations can be made to work with a wider variety of families with different backgrounds and problems. The unifying theme of Parts I and II is emphasis on the family as a system, with interactions between the subsystems of the family and between the family and the social worker. It also reflects the interrelatedness of the family's problems and its problem-solving efforts.

An important part of effective family treatment is the context in which the social worker provides the necessary services. Many social workers and practitioners are successfully engaged in family treatment in private practice, but the context we consider here is the social work agency. Part III focuses on the role of the agency and its staff in planning and providing treatment to families.

This section endeavors to bring the social work agency more directly into the treatment process by presenting various aspects of agency operations that impact on service delivery to families as clients. Among the issues addressed are treatment within the interdisciplinary agency;

296

colleagial involvement and responsibility in treatment; the responsibility of agency administration; and implications for training social workers to engage in treating families.

Part III is not intended to be an exhaustive presentation of social work agencies. Nevertheless, we believe it is important to supplement our approach to family treatment with at least a brief look at the context in which the treatment is offered. In this way we hope to increase awareness of the mutual responsibilities of social workers, agency administrators, and other staff members in engaging the family as the unit of treatment.

CHAPTER 12

The Agency and the Worker in Family Treatment

Unless families seek private practitioners for the solution of their problems, agencies provide the setting for their contact with the social worker. In many instances, such as the hospital or school setting, the family could not get the services it needs outside an agency context. Were it not for its need for other services, it might not of its own initiative seek contact with the worker.

A multitude of factors in the relations between family members and workers come into play because of the agency context for family treatment. Of central interest among these many factors is the way the agency conceptualizes the problems of individuals and families that come to its attention. A corollary and closely related factor is the congruence (or lack of it) between agency views and worker views of the client and the family. These views have consequences for the way the agency organizes itself for services to the family, and consequently also to the way the worker engages with the family when they are referred.

These conceptions of agency impact on family treatment have clear implications for the kind of training needed by social workers. They imply that if workers are to "think family," the agency must provide them with support. All staff, not only those in direct contact with the family, need orientation and training in order to "think family." Without such orientation, staff and agency practices may impede or prevent effective work with the family.

THE IMPORTANCE OF THEORETICAL CONCEPTUALIZATION OF FAMILY PROBLEMS

At the core of agency impact is the way in which the problems brought to the agency by individuals are defined. Two basically different conceptualizations are possible. One orientation sees the problems as resident in the individuals. The other, which we have presented, sees them as resident in family relationships and in the family's relation to the external world.

Working from the individual orientation, helping systems have readily understood that physical or mental illness, delinquency or crime, and the loss or gain of a spouse, parent, or child are problems for the individuals who present them. They are the ones who have the problems and need to cope with them. In many instances this problem definition has been used even if the problem has been defined by someone, be it family member or person in the community, other than the individual who supposedly has the problem. Diagnostic procedures are designed to illuminate the problem the individual has, and diagnostic staff are recruited accordingly. Treatment procedures are oriented to work with one individual, and staff with skills in individual treatment are recruited.

This orientation may run into difficulty when the individual who supposedly has the problem does not accept the idea that it is his problem but sees it rather as a problem that others, especially family members, impose on him. Individually oriented agencies have responded to such client positions in two ways. Either the client's view is seen as a distorted perception of others, or the problem is viewed as lying in the way the individual responds to family behavior. Family members are not included in treatment and sometimes are specifically excluded. Workers are not permitted time for contact with family members. The treatment focuses on changing the client's perceptions or ways of coping with the family. The need for change in the family is not recognized. While some of these clients may be able to accept such a redefinition of their problems, others will participate in treatment only to convince the helper of their views. Or they may discontinue treatment.

Agencies oriented to treating individuals, however, sometimes see the need to "do something about the family" of a primary client or patient. The family is seen as having a detrimental effect on the patient, creating anxiety, frustration, or rage in the patient, allowing no relief and providing no support. Frequently, in this view, "family" does not mean the entire family but refers primarily to a parent or spouse. A separate worker is assigned to help that family member with his or her problem, or the same worker might see the other family member at a separate time. The problem created by the family member is not seen as "appropriate" for service in the agency serving the identified primary client and is therefore sent to some other agency or another department or branch of the same agency. These separate workers may see the value of consultation among themselves about what is happening in the family, but their good intentions are often foiled by lack of time or their supervisors' lack of understanding of the need for such consultation. Family members may be divided up between agencies for individual treatment. Treatment is for the patient *and* for the family. Another possible consequence of this view is that it can prompt hostility toward the family by agency staff, who see them as at fault. This can result in a need to defend the patient to the family.

This orientation is not, in our view, a family systems conception of the situation. The "patient *and* the family" view, as contrasted to "the family *as* the patient," attends to the effects of the family on the patient but gives insufficient attention to the effects of patient on family and their continuing efforts to influence each other. It also seems to be a dyadic view which does not account for the participation of third persons and alliances that may arise.

We have taken pains in this book not to define family systems treatment as the use of conjoint family sessions. Nevertheless, it does seem possible that the greater use of individual sessions is associated with the position that the problem resides in the individual or separately in client and family members.

If problems are defined by the agency as problems in family operations, as they have been in this book, very different agency procedures follow. There is insistence that other members of the family participate in the diagnostic process and in some or all of the treatment. Different diagnostic procedures are used. Home visits and whole-family interview sessions for observation of family interactions serve as the basis for assessment. These take the place of a lengthy social history or psychological or psychiatric examinations. Current transactions are more important than historical developments and psychological introjects.

When the problem is presented by the individual or the family as a family problem, family assessment procedures pose no difficulty for the family. The procedures seem ultimately sensible to them. When the individual who presents his own or someone else's problem as a problem of the individual is confronted with the family orientation of the helping system, however, the encounter may be experienced as an affront. This can easily give rise to hostility and uncooperativeness toward the helping system. Consent to participate will come only when the individual is convinced of the relevance of the family's participation and its use to him.

Social workers are prepared to cope with such hostility and resistance when they and the agency have a thorough grounding in family systems theory. They must be able to see readily the ways in which the family system impinges on the problem-solving ability of the person presenting the problem. Several brief examples will illustrate the issues.

> A mother and her 14-year-old daughter were seen on a walk-in basis at a community mental health clinic. The mother complained that her daughter was not investing herself in her school work and was only doing passing work, when she could be doing much better. Also, her daughter neglected her household responsibilities and had to be constantly prodded to do them. Both home and school problems resulted in frequent conflict between mother and daughter. Mother's request was that the clinic find out what was wrong with her daughter and change her.
>
> In this instance the social worker did not agree that the problem presented was the problem of the 14-year-old daughter alone, though her lack of cooperation and apparent stubbornness would in some agencies have been defined that way. In that event efforts would have been made to interest the girl in individual or group treatment and to offer, but not push upon the parents, the "opportunity" to be seen. Instead, the social worker expressed concern about the difficulty that the mother and the father were having in gaining their daughter's cooperation, suggesting that all three needed to be seen in order to understand and solve the problem.
>
> While the mother expressed some awareness of the need for her to be involved, her resistance was expressed in terms of her husband's unwillingness to be involved. She felt that he saw the children as her responsibility. Though this left her feeling unsupported in child-caring responsibilities, she saw no way of gaining his cooperation. At this point she had given up on her efforts to involve her husband. Her agreement to try to bring him for the following appointment was seen as an attempt to reengage him. While the focus remained on the presenting problem, there was also the simultaneous emphasis on changing the family system and its way of coping with the problem.

This brief case description includes only the initial impact on the family. But even in the initial efforts to work on the problem there is a redefinition of family roles, of the images that family members hold of each other, and of the means they use to negotiate and communicate about their problems. The focus on the roles, expectations, and images of family members and their effort to communicate about and change them is also central to the continuing treatment process.

Unintentional consequences may arise in the family system even when all parties concerned—agency, client, and family—initially agree that a given person has the problem. In the following example all three systems defined the problem as resident within the individual. Unfortunate consequences arose because they did not define it as a family problem.

> A middle-aged, married male was admitted for psychiatric hospital treatment on the basis of complaints of severe depression and inability to work. In his conversations with hospital staff, the patient began to air negative feelings about his marriage and to express a wish to proceed for a divorce. The hospital staff had experienced the wife as extremely managerial and dominating and had observed that the patient was upset after his wife's visits, being more depressed and manifesting a great deal of body twitching. Given their view of the problem as one individual coping with a difficult relationship, they accepted as realistic the patient's efforts to distance himself in this relationship. They saw this distancing as crucial and valid treatment in his recovery from depression. They supported him by limiting his wife's visiting and by encouraging consideration of divorce.
>
> The wife's response was to employ their adolescent son to tell both his father and the hospital staff how much the father was needed in the family. The wife also got her minister to talk to the hospital chaplain about how she was being deprived of the opportunity to visit her husband. Finally, she cruised the hospital grounds in a car, waiting for her husband to leave the ward so she could visit him.

While it is evident that the hospital staff saw themselves as helping the individual patient to cope, it is also clear that they did not anticipate the impact on family relationships of a change in the identified patient. They were unrealistic in the amount of or kind of separateness achievable in this instance and in their means for achieving it. The wife clearly had not counted on distancing as a consequence of the help that she wanted the hospital to give her husband. Relieving depression did not mean to her this kind of a change in their relationship. The wife's response was to attempt to change the hospital system rather than permit change in the relationship.

A "family is the patient" response on the part of the staff to this problem would have engaged both husband and wife in solving the problem of the depression, recognizing that some alteration in husband/wife roles and expectation of each other might be necessary to the achievement of that goal. Awareness of the transactional qualities of the relationship would have led the staff to see that the patient's withdrawal behavior was a stimulus for the wife's managerial behavior, and vice versa. The focus would have been on their transactions, and this would have resulted in a different experience for both patient and spouse.

In a case discussed in considerable detail, Hoffman and Long (1969) give a vivid picture of the way in which agency orientation can have a profound effect on family relationships. When family income exceeded allowable levels in the public housing project in which a couple was residing, the housing worker suggested that the husband seek to have himself declared disabled because he had been having alcohol-related employment and health problems. Such a move would reduce family income and allow them to remain in the housing project. However, it would also alter the husband's status with his wife, leaving him feeling even less powerful in the relationship than he already felt and encouraging the wife's unilateral decision-making and control efforts. Efforts on the part of a family worker to reduce the husband's helplessness by getting treatment for his alcoholism revealed the wife's wish to keep her husband numbed and helpless by alcohol and medication. It was just easier for her that way. The family worker engaged the spouses in efforts to solve specific marital relationship problems, which altered the pattern of dominance and submission in the relationship. The authors' report does not indicate how the housing problem was finally resolved, but it does indicate that the husband was able to take initiative in returning to employment after the balance in marital relationships began to change.

Hoffman and Long's example demonstrates the interrelationships among agency practices, problem impact, and family process. The housing worker's suggestion did not take these interrelationships into account and would have left the husband as a nonfunctioning family member. In our view the social worker was family systems oriented in attending to the way in which the family system was organized and went about solving its problems. Systems thinking enabled a ready awareness of the effects of agency policy on family relationships. The individual orientation of various agencies and the confusions between agencies interfered with family problem solving rather than enhancing it. Treatment for the family in this instance was effected by reregulating the behavior of external systems.

CONSEQUENCES OF MIXED THEORETICAL POSITIONS

When individual treatment orientations exist side by side with a family orientation in a given agency, or during a time of changeover from one orientation to the other, cases such as the one just described may become more complicated. A given worker may hold to an individual problem definition in contrast to the agency's family orientation, or vice versa. Staff disagreements may arise over philosophy and procedure. An individual-problem-oriented intake worker may tell client and family of the need for individual treatment, and a family-oriented continuing worker may at a later point have difficulty engaging the family. Staff may be confronted with the same difficulties in solving the problem of how to deal with the client that the family group faces in solving its problems.

Staff therefore need to agree on a common value or theoretical perspective about families. They must find ways of resolving their differences if they are to function and agency service is to be effective. Otherwise client or family contacts with staff will produce different interpretations of the problem, inconsistent treatment, confusion instead of help, and frustration of the family's own efforts at problem solution. These difficulties, and others, have led Haley (1975) to the facetious suggestion that agencies should not shift to a family treatment orientation. Foster (1965), using experience in a medical hospital, makes the more positive suggestion that the social worker has a specific dual role in the midst of such difficulties. The first is to enable the resolution of staff differences. The second, which follows from the first, is to make it possible for agency system and family system to work together. In order to do this in the hospital setting, the problems of the patient in the family and the problems of the family need to be taken into account. Similarly, in a school system situation, Freund and Cardwell (1977) demonstrate that conjoint work with school problem children, parents, and school personnel is useful in resolving adolescent school problems.

There is therefore a need for clarity and consistency in the theoretical perspective in both worker and agency. In an agency that is family systems oriented, procedures, starting at intake, are used to engage the family as a group in the assessment and treatment process. All staff who have contact with any member of the family are sensitive to the way in which family relationships affect work on the family problem and to the way in which a particular staff person's interventions influence family relationships. Time is available to meet with members of the family other than the identified problem person, either separately or as a group with the patient. Solutions to problems that other family members are having are seen as relevant to the solutions of the problems of the person for whom agency contact originated. There will be less likelihood of dividing the family up between agencies or workers.

SPECIAL PROBLEMS OF INTERDISCIPLINARY AGENCIES

Social workers are not always the ones that determine agency policies, and thus they are not totally in control of the decision about whether or how to engage the family in treatment. This is true in psychiatric, medical, school, and residential settings. The family-oriented worker, therefore, not wishing to stand alone or to leave families unassisted, may have to take a position of advocacy for the family and for a family systems view. The worker's primary approach in this regard is to orient other staff members or disciplines to the needs of the family and to the way in which agency procedures interfere with or support the family's own efforts at problem solving.

This orientation is likely achieved initially on a case-by-case basis (see Foster, 1965), but it may require more systematic training. Beyond this, it may entail considerable effort to change agency procedures and budget to allow more time for work with family members and to minimize the referral of family members to other agencies. And it may entail considerable worker effort to moderate staff reactions to family members or to lessen differences among staff members about how to intervene in the transactions between client and family members.

SPECIAL PROBLEMS OF MULTIPLE-PROBLEM FAMILIES

A variety of forms of intervention is needed for multiple-problem families (for example, child abuse, problem poverty, and alcoholism families) due to their relatively closed nature and their isolation from the larger community. A one-worker-to-family relationship which emphasizes talking appears to be insufficient for their needs and provides only limited support and access to the larger community. More contact hours per family and the possibility of home visits need to be made part of the agency repertoire. Doing with, being with, going with in relation to everyday activities and specific needs of the families are important aspects of worker activity. The simultaneous provision of information, ideas, and access are all conditions of contact which enable family members to relate to the worker, the agency, and other available services in the community, and to each other in a new and meaningful way.

Agency willingness and capacity to relate to such family systems on these terms is predicated on the kind of understanding about modes of operation that has been put forth in this book. Where agencies persist in seeing such families as unmotivated, additional services and different modes of engaging the families will not be available, and the families will continue to be viewed as hopeless and hard to reach. A change in agency thinking and operations is required before change in the families will be possible. Such a change in the agency may not guarantee success with the family, but it will make it possible or more likely.

Where agencies have continued to define problems as problems of individuals rather than of families, the tendency to divide families up among agencies has persisted. The adult with problems is seen at one agency, the children at another, and workers from still other agencies providing special services are also involved. Each worker in each separate agency sees only part of the problem and gets only an individual member's report of what is happening. Decisions are made with or about the family member that do not take into account the reactions of, or consequences for, other family members.

At a minimum, all workers involved with the family should confer enough to come to a common understanding of the family's structure and process. This understanding should reveal the effects the family has on individual capacity and performance, the effects of individual performance and capacity on family operations, and the changes required in the family's process and structure if performance is to change. One worker must be enough of a case manager to be in regular contact with all the workers involved and keep them abreast of needs and changes. Additionally, case conferences involving all workers are imperative. Joint meetings between family members and their various workers serve to promote the exchange of information, improve communication, and facilitate decision making in the family. Multiple-service agencies that can provide services to all family members are better able to promote such interaction than single-service agencies serving only one family member. The crucial factor, however, is not where the service is provided but whether case analysis is done on a family systems basis.

ISSUES OF CONFIDENTIALITY

The difference between an individual and a family orientation in an agency is also revealed in the way in which confidentiality in the client-worker relationship is handled. Initial assurances of confidentiality between family members are less likely to be given by the family-oriented worker and may indeed be moot in the worker's way of structuring the initial contact. In a situation which is seen as a problem for the family system and in which all members are affected in one way or another, whether as leaders, opposers, followers, bystanders, perpetrators, or victims, and in which change between persons rather than within persons is an objective, workers structure the situation to increase the exchange of information and feelings between family members. The worker frames the situation as one in which significant others need to be involved in the problem solving process right from the beginning by providing information needed to understand the problematic situation.

By contrast, where the individual is seen as the primary client, worker assurances are given that client communications to the worker will not be revealed to others, including family members, without client consent. This is seen as necessary to enable clients to deal more directly and openly with thoughts and feelings of anger, anxiety, or guilt, to experience some relief from ventilating those feelings in a nonthreatening relationship, and to reorient their thinking and feelings in a more realistic way.

The feelings and reactions revealed in individual treatment often arise in transactions with significant others. The fact that they have not been resolved with those significant others suggests an impediment in the communication and relationship between the individuals involved. It is not only a problem of having the thoughts and feelings, but of how these might be expressed to another and how they might be received by another. What is discussed between worker and client in individual treatment must eventually be surfaced and resolved in intrafamily relationships. In that sense it is not subject matter that can be held in confidence between worker and client if the worker is to be at all helpful. Adherence to usual rules of confidentiality would limit the worker's ability to be helpful.

Treatment for child's behavior problem was initially structured to provide separate workers and individual treatment for the child and the
mother, who was divorced from the child's father. Both child and mother
were given assurances of confidentiality. The child's worker received a
phone call from the father in which he said that the child was complaining to him of maltreatment by his mother, but he did not want the mother
to know that he had called. It seemed to the worker that he may have
been exaggerating to make a case for himself as a better parent because
he also said he was suing for custody. Hemmed in by rules of confidentiality, the workers in this situation had difficulty in obtaining needed
facts to assess the validity of the father's complaint.

A family-oriented worker would likely have viewed the child's problems as
a function of his life situation and sought participation of both parents at
the beginning of contact. Conjoint sessions with all family members would
have implied open exchange of information and thus minimized the problems of confidentiality that appeared here. If parents had not agreed to
conjoint sessions, the worker could still structure in the necessity of sharing
information among all family members.

When confidentiality is offered at the time of initial contact, the worker
leaves him- or herself vulnerable to becoming a keeper of secrets between
family members. When separate sessions are sought by a family member,
they are often sought for the purpose of enlisting the worker's understanding of the member's particular view of a situation, which is biased against
another member. This not only puts the worker in an uncomfortable position, but also creates a collusion or an alliance between the worker and that
particular family member that may foster other family members' suspicion
and distrust in the worker and prevent their constructive involvement in the
treatment effort. They may see the worker as siding with the other family
members against them and become resistant to participation.

It is sometimes useful to accede to requests for separate interviews to
enable the family member to open up subject matter they would otherwise
hesitate to deal with directly with others in the family. However, the worker
in acceding to separate sessions frames them as sessions in which the family
member will not be encouraged to bring up anything that they would not
subsequently want to have surfaced with relevant other family members,
and in which they would be helped to find ways of doing so.

This is not to say that everything needs to be privileged to all family
members. Some matters, for example, may concern only members of the

parental generation. Our purpose here is not to offer detailed guidelines about confidentiality, but to stress that in a family systems view of problematic situations, in which the family is seen as the client, information pertaining to the system is not appropriately secreted between one member of the system and the worker. The inability to communicate openly and directly may in itself be the core of the family's difficulties.

IMPLICATIONS FOR TRAINING WORKERS

A family-oriented way of conceptualizing presenting problems in agencies has implications for training and staff development. Social workers need to have knowledge of the way family systems work and of the ways in which problems and external systems affect the workings of the family and the individuals in it. Based on this theoretical understanding, they need to have skills which will guide family members in more constructive approaches to problem solving and which will involve them jointly in the problem-solving effort. These needs clearly should influence the training of the worker who meets the family.

Where there is unanimity between the agency and the worker about this way of viewing the problems of individuals and families, the worker and the agency support each other in the provision of services. Where other staff members are at odds with the worker, some effort must be made to orient or train other staff members, including those who are not in direct contact with client and family. Liddle and Halpin (1978) note that various amounts of attention have been invested in this aspect of training. Their comprehensive review of training for and supervision of family treatment discusses theories and modes which can be applied in these efforts.

A family systems approach is not merely the addition of a treatment technique such as conjoint family interviewing (though that technique may be used) to another conceptual base and set of skills. It is a different way of thinking about presenting problems. Knowledge about intrapsychic dynamics and skills in individual treatment is, therefore, not always a prerequisite for engaging families. Workers who have no knowledge of individual dynamics often learn just as easily about the way families work, and they need not face the problem of having to dispense with previous learning. Workers who shift from thinking about individual dynamics to the family orientation sometimes have just as much to learn about family dynamics as those who have no knowledge of individual treatment.

The individual-treatment orientation of many social work students and staff members accounts in part for the persistent lack of family contact in agencies. Levande (1976) notes,

> Many social work students are hesitant about becoming involved with the family as a whole as the designated client. Part of this reluctance may stem from having a theoretical frame of reference which provides understanding of the individual as the unit of treatment, but having only a limited knowledge when confronted with the possibility of conceptualizing the family system or any of its sub-systems as the unit of intervention. (p. 295)

The view of Beck and Jones (1973) that the family service field in general does not use a truly family-centered approach to family problems fits these observations.

This brief discussion of training for social workers has not considered means, modes, or content. Rather, it has emphasized the need for training to develop a different conceptual approach, centered on the family system. Such an approach is a prerequisite to the worker's willingness to attempt to engage whole families, as well as a requirement for the successful engagement of families. Sager, Masters, Ronall, and Normand (1968) report that after workers received training in family systems theory, the rate of engagement of families in treatment increased markedly.

Schools of social work are increasingly offering classroom training in the understanding and treatment of family systems. Skilled supervision in the field is often unavailable, however, because supervisors themselves lack the necessary conceptual base and experience. For the time being, therefore, continuing education courses and in-service training are needed for workers who wish to move in this direction. Both of these forms of training are open to workers, regardless of the kind or level of previous training. Thus, paraprofessionals, persons with bachelor's, master's, and doctoral degrees, and persons with training in psychiatry, nursing, psychology, guidance, and social work all can acquire family treatment skills.

In some instances, as Haley (1975) has noted, this has resulted in a blurring of the distinctions between professional backgrounds and levels of education. Since prior training often is less relevant in the family systems approach, the emphasis on family treatment puts staff members in a different relationship to each other. This creates or at least opens the possibility of staff rivalries and conflicts equaling those of the family, particularly between those of different disciplines but also between workers and supervisors. In such circumstances the awareness and training of persons at supervisory and administrative levels are as important in the implementation of family treatment efforts as are those of the workers who have direct contact with the family.

REFERENCES

Beck, D., and Jones, M. 1973. "Progress on Family Problems." New York: Family Service Association of America.

Foster, Z. P. 1965. "How Social Work Can Influence Hospital Management of Fatal Illness." *Social Work* 10:30-45.

Freund, J. C., and Cardwell, G. F. 1977. "A Multifaceted Response to an Adolescent's School Failure." *Journal of Marriage and Family Counseling* 3:59-66.

Haley, J. 1975. "Why a Mental Health Center Should Avoid Family Therapy." *Journal of Marriage and Family Counseling* 1:1-14.

Hoffman, L., and Long, L. 1969. "A Systems Dilemma." *Family Process* 8:211-34.

Levande, D. I. 1976. "Family Theory as a Necessary Component of Family Therapy." *Social Casework* 57:291-95.

Liddle, H., and Halpin, R. 1978. "Family Therapy Training and Supervision: A Comparative Review." *Journal of Marriage and Family Counseling* 4:77-98.

Sager, C., Masters, Y., Ronall, R., and Normand, W. 1968. "Selection and Engagement of Patients in Family Therapy." *American Journal of Orthopsychiatry* 38:715-23.

Index